Tony
Soprano's
America

Tony Soprano's America

The Criminal Side of the American Dream

DAVID R. SIMON

with Tamar Love

A Member of the Perseus Books Group

Westview Press books are available at special discounts for bulk purchases in the United States by corporations, institutions, and other organizations. For more information, please contact the Special Markets Department at the Perseus Books Group, 11 Cambridge Center, Cambridge MA 02142, or call (617) 252-5298, (800)255-1514 or email j.mccrary@perseusbooks.com.

Published in 2002 in the United States of America by Westview Press, 5500 Central Avenue, Boulder, Colorado 80301–2877, and in the United Kingdom by Westview Press, 12 Hid's Copse Road, Cumnor Hill, Oxford OX2 9JJ

Find us on the World Wide Web at www.westviewpress.com
A Cataloging-in-Publication data record for this book is available from the Library of Congress.

ISBN 0-8133-4036-5

Cover image © Joshua Sheldon, 2002.

The author thanks the following for permission to reprint:
Dr. David C. Korten and Yes for permission to quote from "The Postcorporate" in the Spring 1999 issue of Yes; and Harcourt Brace for permission to reprint sections from my *Private Troubles and Public Issues: Social Problems in the Postmodern Era* (written with Joel Henderson).

Text design by Jeff Williams
Set in 11.5-point Fairfield Light by The Perseus Books Group

The paper used in this publication meets the requirements of the American National Standard for Permanence of Paper for Printed Library Materials Z39.48–1984.

10   9   8   7   6   5   4   3   2   1 – 05   04   03   02

Contents

Preface   *vii*

Acknowledgments   *xi*

1 The Contradictory Sopranos and Us   *1*

2 Tony Soprano and the American Dream   *13*

3 The Sopranos and the Higher Immorality   *35*

4 Tony and the World: The Global Economy, Organized-Crime Syndicates, and Narco-Terrorism   *59*

5 Lies, Entertainment, and Alienation, Soprano Style   *79*

6 Tony Soprano and the Crimeogenic Department Store   *109*

7 The Sopranos' Family Life. . . and Ours   *145*

8 Everyday Life in Tony Soprano's America   *177*

9 Solutions to the Crises of Tony Soprano's America: The Real Meaning of Tony Soprano   *207*

Selected Bibliography   *231*

Notes   *245*

Index   *261*

Preface

With its fourth season approaching, HBO's *The Sopranos* remains a national cultural phenomenon, equally captivating to average viewers as well as psychologists and sociologists, all of whom have a vested interest in the show's depiction of contemporary society. Because the show's hero, Tony Soprano, is a gangster, there is a temptation to center any analysis of *The Sopranos* merely on organized crime and its current state. This, I believe, is a mistake; the show is not a snapshot of gangster life but a panoramic view of modern American culture. Specifically, *The Sopranos* is a microcosm of America's social problems, and it needs analysis as such.

This book argues that *The Sopranos* is in numerous ways a metaphor for the ills of contemporary American life. The show is not merely about a crime family: it is about the different ways crime has shaped our modern society, bending the rules until they break. It mirrors the state of the nation: we are disillusioned, alienated, and alone. But *The Sopranos* is also a reflection of a dysfunctional family, wherein children don't know what their father does for a living, a wife is never sure of her husband's fidelity, a mother plots her son's murder, and family members treat each other with little, if any, genuine warmth or kindness. It is also about a gangster who, driven by panic attacks, seeks enlightenment through a controversial therapeutic relationship.

Movies and TV shows about the Mafia typically depict frenzied criminal activity and illicit behavior, with little emphasis on the outside world. *The Sopranos* portrays a multigenerational family's criminal behavior played out against the backdrop of daily life. We see the characters interact within the context of their family and community—a doctor's office, school, and church. The show humanizes the Soprano family, promoting a sense of strong personal identification and prompting critics to say things like, *"The Sopranos* are us." They certainly *seem* like us, like "regular" people—some of whom just happen to use violence to solve their problems. Viewers can identify with the characters in the series as human beings, and thus the vicarious criminal lives of Tony and his crew may seem seductive compared to the audience's more ordinary daily lives.

When we think about *The Sopranos,* we need to remember one important fact: while the stressors Tony Soprano suffers from overlap those of many Americans, they are at the same time extreme and often exceptional. Tony worries about his marriage, his children, his career, and his mental health, as do many of us. Most of us, however, don't have to fear being arrested by the FBI, getting "whacked" by rival gangs, disgruntled friends, and irate family members, or being betrayed by an informant. In some important ways, therefore, *The Sopranos* are *not* us.

As much as we would like to pretend otherwise, Americans cannot be divided neatly into two camps: the criminal and the law-abiding, the Sopranos and us. Respectable members of society also regularly engage in criminal activity, usually of the white-collar variety. We condemn those who break the Ten Commandments, yet many of us dishonor our parents, lie, cheat on our spouses, and steal. The characters in *The Sopranos,* fascinating as they are to their upright, upper-middle-class viewers, are the symbolic embodiment of the criminal heart of America. Each of their very human contradictions is at the core of this book.

Tony Soprano's America examines *The Sopranos* as a symbol of our national pathologies.

Dr. David R. Simon

Acknowledgments

A number of wonderful friends and colleagues found the idea for this book intriguing and stimulating, and provided positive encouragement for its completion. Jack Levin's role was a great source of inspiration. Some long-time friends and scholars distinguished in the field of white-collar crime, with whom I sit on the U.S. Department of Justice White-Collar Crime Research Center's Scholar's Consortium, found this project an excellent idea, including Henry Pontel of the University of California, Irvine, David Frederichs of the University of Scranton, and Frank Hagan of Mercyhurst College.

I must acknowledge the brilliant creator of *The Sopranos*, David Chase, and his inspired cast, especially Edie Falco, Lorraine Bracco, the late Nancy Marchand, and, of course, James Gandolfini.

My heartfelt thanks to Fred Francis and Norman MacAfee for their tremendous work.

Finally, Tamar Love has been a constant source of ideas, excellent editing skills, and cooperation throughout. All of the errors herein are, of course, mine.

To My Family

To my daughter Molly, and sons Danny and Joshua,
to Ken, my daughter-in-law Marianne, grandson Andrew,
and granddaughter Hali Ember

My Love to You All

The Contradictory Sopranos and Us

TONY SOPRANO AND HIS WIFE Carmela live next door to Bruce and Jean Cusemano, a well-to-do Italian-American couple who earned their way into their rich, suburban New Jersey neighborhood through Bruce's lucrative medical practice. At a dinner party, the Cusemanos' equally wealthy friends ask about the Sopranos. Do they know them? What are they like? What have the Cusemanos seen? Bruce indulges his guests by telling them about the box of Cuban cigars Tony gave him recently, about the way having a gangster as a neighbor can keep down neighborhood crime and raise property values. Tony Soprano may be a criminal, but he's also a celebrity. He fascinates the Cusemanos and their guests. They may not want to associate with him, but they want to know everything about him.

Just like the Cusemanos, many of us watch *The Sopranos* every week. We're fascinated by them, involved with their convoluted lives, addicted to their unethical behavior. We love to watch them hang themselves with their own rope. The show is a fluke, a dream, a runaway hit—even its stars thought no one would ever watch it. But here we are, four years later, and *The Sopranos* has millions of regular viewers.

The Sopranos is much more than a television show about a Mafia capo whose incapacitating panic attacks drive him to a psychiatrist's couch; it is a psychological cauldron of incongruities, paradoxes, and borderline self-destructive behavior. The contradictions faced by its characters are representative of the American disposition and culture at this early moment in the twenty-first century—their issues are the issues with which our entire society is grappling. In many ways, *The Sopranos* represents our Jungian dark side, the accumulating clog in our collective septic tank that will ultimately stink up our lives both personally and as a civilization unless we confront it head on.

In one sense the lives of the typical *Sopranos* viewers are all very deceiving. With a bright economic outlook, life remains comfortable in our mostly upper-middle-class neighborhoods. We, like the Cusemanos, remain content to enjoy our luxuries and to speculate idly about crime and corruption that we imagine as part of other people's lives, not our own. Underneath, however, in the world Tony Soprano's basement represents, there lurks a murky swamp of conflicts built into the very structure of our personal and professional lives, conflicts so profound they compel us to ask some big questions:

- What has become of morality in American life?
- Who are our heroes? Do any still exist?
- Does work have any meaning for us beyond a paycheck?
- Why do our business and political institutions seem so corrupt?
- Why are so many American families dysfunctional?
- Why do Americans seem so preoccupied with sex, yet so troubled with sexual dysfunction?
- Why do we remain such a violent culture?

We can find some answers to these questions by examining the characters in *The Sopranos* and their interactions within the cultural context that constitutes their moral foundations.

The complicated characteristics the Soprano family members exhibit are the essence of conflict and contradiction, the spice of the show. Tony, the patriarch of the family, is a walking contradiction, a man who is never at home anywhere but who never leaves work, even when he is at home. However, he can't conduct business as would anyone else working at home; his fear of being spied on by the federal government compels him to conduct business in the basement, the only location in his house where he feels he has complete privacy. Otherwise, he takes business where it belongs—to his backyard, to the waterfront, to his strip club Bada Bing, to Artie Bucco's restaurant—none of which are "traditional" business venues. But in many respects Tony is a very traditional guy: he believes in strong family values and the importance of respecting his elders, adhering to the old-school Mafia rules, behaving with honor and governing his employees with a soft touch and an iron fist. At the same time, he also believes in punishing dishonor with death, in responding with swift and immediate vengeance to anyone who defies his business practices, and in collecting on his debts immediately—no matter what the situation. Tony is a liar, a cheat, a racist, and a bigot, but we like him nonetheless. He adheres to his own moral code.

Tony's wife, Carmela, is the classic unfulfilled suburban housewife, circa 1950s, craving both physical and emotional intimacy from Tony, longing for him to be closer to her and to his children. She tries fulfilling her unmet needs with ultimately unrequited affairs—with a priest, then a contractor. As the show has progressed, Carmela has taken strides to assert her independence and achieve her own sense of happiness. She attends sessions with Tony and his psychiatrist then begins to see a therapist on her own, who advises her to leave her Mob husband. Instead, she begins to stand up to Tony, forcing him to examine his behavior and taking more ownership of decisions that affect her and her family, decisions traditionally made by Tony. Of all the characters in *The Sopranos*, Carmela has undergone the most significant emotional transformation, from docile and unhappy to frustrated and assertive. It seems unlikely that she will complete the transformation by leaving Tony—Mafia wives just don't do that—but when you recall that *The Sopranos* began by teaming a Mafia capo with a female psychiatrist, who knows what will happen?

Tony's children also embody the same kind of contradictions. His daughter, Meadow, is an overprotected suburban child of innocence and entitlement, yet she continually comes face to face with the effects and implications of her father's criminal activities. She discovers information on the Internet linking her father to organized crime, and, in another episode, actually sees him being taken away in handcuffs. Meadow loves Tony, but faced with troubling aspects of his nature—as when he forbids her to continue seeing her college boyfriend, who happens to be African American—she has trouble reconciling her love for him with his flaws.

Tony's son, Anthony Junior, A.J., is an overweight, alienated adolescent whom Tony wishes would become a "real man." However, in Tony's world, being a real man means having the ability to break open someone's head, an act the gentle A.J. is unlikely ever to perform. Tony is forever wondering if his son could, would, or should be up to the task of running the family business. In an effort to teach A.J. some responsibility, he threatens to send him to military school, an effort that falls apart when A.J. begs his father not to send him to "that place" and begins having anxiety-driven fainting spells much like his father's. Perhaps as his son grows up, Tony will begin to realize that what A.J. really needs, the factor that he has been missing most in his life, is his father's acceptance. However, even though Tony knows from personal experience the ill effects of having a parent who is disappointed in his or her child, he finds it difficult to see past his own psyche and treat his son differently than he himself was treated.

Impossible to please, Tony's widowed and now-deceased mother, Livia, was a demon-possessed matriarch. Her enormous, lifelong resentment of her son was exacerbated when he moved her from her home, which she was no longer able to care for, to an upscale retirement facility. She felt so angry toward Tony that she put out a contract on him. Likewise, Tony's rage toward his mother has been palpable since the first episode; yet, he kept trying to please her, one of the factors that led him to experience panic attacks and seek psychiatric help. Ironically, Livia erroneously believed Tony spent psychiatric sessions denouncing her to his therapist—an approach that probably would have helped him make a true therapeutic breakthrough but which he has so far been unable to do to any significant degree.

Tony's sister Janice is only slightly less nightmarish than his mother. Her earthy sensuality and big mouth represent yet another contradiction, one aggravated when she takes up with a psychopath, Richie Aprile, a "made" member of Tony's crew just released from prison. When Richie punches her in the face, she shoots and kills him, then calls Tony. As her big brother methodically disposes of Richie's body, we begin to see how Tony has emotionally cleaned up after Janice his entire life.

Tony's Uncle Junior, a longtime mobster and sometime rival to his nephew, is just as believably insane as his sister-in-law, Livia. When Uncle Junior's loyal longtime girlfriend boasts about his prowess in performing oral sex, the news gets back to Tony, who ribs Uncle Junior about a bedroom activity that Tony and his macho cronies scorn as unmanly. Uncle Junior's humiliation and fury seriously deepen the potentially murderous breach between the dysfunctional relatives, and he, too, orders a hit on Tony.

Like his family, Tony's crew is made up of walking contradictions. Tony's young nephew, Christopher Moltisanti, an apprentice member of the gang, is also an aspiring screenwriter, a profession no real Mafioso could consider, given the importance of secrecy in organized crime. Yet when he is "made" in the third season, we see Christopher back off from his screenwriting aspirations and take up a mantle Tony has long held for him.

Another of Tony's crew, Pussy Bompensiero, represented perhaps the strongest link to the friends of Tony's youth, but when Pussy

the FBI, Tony had him killed. Silvio Dante manages
〉all day—hiring and firing young women who often
......es—yet appears to have the most stable family life of
any member of the crew. Then there is Paulie Walnuts, a murderer
with a savage temper, who shows great warmth and tenderness
toward his girlfriend and her children.

Dr. Jennifer Melfi, Tony's psychiatrist, has her own contradictions. She is attracted to and repelled by Tony. She possesses a profound sense of ethics, yet comes dangerously close to asking Tony to
murder the man who raped her. Critics and psychologists have
praised the relationship between Tony and Melfi, whatever its proce-
dural flaws or dramatic license, as the most realistic portrayal of the
therapeutic model in the history of television. And the centrality of
their relationship reflects the real significance of *The Sopranos*.

American culture has long made heroes out of outlaws, gangsters,
and mobsters, and Dr. Melfi's reactions to Tony parallel that troubling
fascination. What is it within the American character that leads us to
engage in such unhealthy hero worship? It isn't Tony Soprano who
needs a psychiatrist—it's us! Back in the 1920s, reporters often asked
Al Capone his opinion about the morals of America's youth, as if
Capone were a qualified expert on moral decline. The popularity of
The Sopranos indicates that not much has changed.

The Sopranos and the Sociological Imagination

Tony Soprano has his hands in all manner of financial scams, not all
of which lead directly to someone being beaten or killed. Yet Tony's
activities have far-reaching consequences and countless victims, even
when they remain unseen. He sets up a junk stock to telemarket to
elderly retirees but feels a genuine respect for the World War II generation being defrauded by his scam. He works closely with men who
push drugs for a living yet despairs at the urban blight he sees around
him. Many of the ills Tony Soprano sees around him are linked to his
own actions, but he never draws the parallels.

Many Americans are confused about how to think about social problems. Indeed, American culture is biased toward individual personalities, individual cases, and individual rights, causing people to lose sight of society as a whole. The confusion Americans sometimes feel about the social ills of our era is shown in *Twilight of the Golds,* an off-Broadway play by Jonathan Tolins, later made into a movie.[1] Every Sunday, Mrs. Gold tells us, she sits down with the week's issues of the *New York Times* and spends all day reading them. When she finishes, she feels overwhelmed by all the information she has absorbed; she has no way to sort out what it all means.

The sociologist C. Wright Mills described the nature of Mrs. Gold's confusion decades before the play was written, remarking that ours is an era of uneasiness and indifference, a time when people experience their personal lives as a series of traps.[2] In the 1950s and 1960s, Mills warned against the dangers inherent in celebrity worship, mass-media addiction, militarism, criminal and unethical behavior among the nation's leaders, conformity, status-seeking behavior, bureaucracy, and alienation. That prophetic list reads like a description of America today.

Mills believed that ordinary people, including those in the media who often interpret the world for us, lack a sociological imagination— the ability to see the interrelationship of their own lives with the historical period and society in which they live. A mode of critical thinking that helps us understand how social problems affect us personally, the sociological imagination allows us to conceive of the relationship between seemingly private, individual troubles and larger social problems, to understand that responsibility belongs not only to individuals but also to communities, religious organizations, media outlets, advertisers, corporations, and government entities.

Personal Troubles and Social Issues

Tony Soprano is a man beset with problems, not all of which can be solved in therapy. His disastrous relationship with his late mother, for instance, might be worked out with Dr. Melfi's help. However, his tendency to take violent shortcuts to achieve his goals may not be resolved by taking Prozac and confronting his feelings. C. Wright Mills argued that our personal troubles, our feelings of being trapped and manipulated, our marital and career fortunes, our goals and our tools for achieving those goals, are sociological in origin and consequence. This is what Tony does not understand. To use the sociological imagination, we must learn to interrelate the structural causes of social problems, major trends, private troubles, and public issues that occupy our everyday existence.

According to Mills, personal troubles "occur within the character of the individual and within the range of . . . immediate relations with others; they have to do with [the] self and with those limited areas of social life of which [one] is directly and personally aware."[3] Personal troubles lie within our immediate environment, our family, workplace, school, religious organization, or neighborhood; our perceptions of personal troubles and our solutions for resolving them also lie in this environment. For example, if two college roommates quarrel and decide they no longer wish to room together, each can resolve the problem by finding a more compatible partner; most college campuses have a place to post "seeking roommate" notices. Thus, the problem can be resolved within the immediate environment of the college campus. Social problems, on the other hand, are of a dramatically different nature.

Consider unemployment. If, in a society of over 100 million workers, the only people who are unemployed are those who refuse to work, that is a personal trouble. The cause lies within the character of individuals who have chosen their unemployed status. If, however, that society suffers massive layoffs as businesses downsize and move factories overseas in search of cheap labor and of other financial advantages, sociological forces take over. No amount of counseling or punishment of errant workers will resolve a crisis of permanent recession cycles. No amount of headlines lauding the 94-percent employment rate will soothe the 6 percent out of work.

Consider education. If a few hundred high school students of various backgrounds drop out annually, we can point to various personal deficiencies that inhibit learning. However, when almost 12 percent of the nation's secondary students withdraw before graduation, and another 700,000 graduate despite their inability to read and write, then clearly some institutional factors are at work.[4] Insufficient educational achievement causes great financial harm, because high school and college graduate earnings greatly exceed those of high school dropouts. As more people fail to graduate even high school, not to mention college, our national educational level drops, placing us even further behind other nations in the intelligence race.

Consider marriage and family. If only a few thousand divorces and cases of abuse were reported annually, we could conclude that a few dysfunctional personalities needed therapy. However, when half of first-time marriages end in divorce and 4,000 spouses and significant others murder each other every year, something is clearly wrong with the way we are building the institutions of marriage and family.

Consider violent street crime. If only a hundred or so murders took place annually, the problem might be attributable only to a few violence-prone individuals. Unfortunately, the homicide rate in the United States is ten times higher than that in Europe, Canada, and Japan combined. Clearly, such numbers suggest the presence of societal-patterned violence.

Consider corruption. If a few ward politicians in a few cities were on the take, their corruption could be blamed on a deficiency in personal integrity. But when prosecutors indict five public officials every day, and the nation regularly experiences scandal after scandal, what does that say about our societal integrity?

Finally, consider the seemingly most individualistic of problems, mental illness. If a minute portion of the population exhibited neurotic symptoms or psychotic episodes, then hormonal imbalances or childhood traumas would be the relevant issues. But when one in five persons needs professional help, as evidenced by soaring therapy rates and pharmacological substance dependence, societal stresses and cultural strains merit critical examination.

Social Harms

Social problems are objectively harmful conditions. In other words, the harms involved can be measured or counted. These measurable harms are of three types. These include:[5]

1. Physical harms: physical injury, illness, or death.
2. Financial harms: robbery, fraud, and various scams not legally defined as fraud but that nevertheless deprive consumers and investors of their funds without receiving the goods or services for which they contracted.
3. Moral harms: deviant behaviors exhibited by elites (people who head governmental and corporate institutions) that encourage distrust, cynicism, or alienation among the rest of the population. Before Richard Nixon resigned from the presidency in 1974, for example, his administration had been involved in a broad range of deviant acts: burglarizing the headquarters of the Democratic National Committee, lying to Congress and the American people about the secret and illegal bombing of Cambodia, committing bribery, and evading taxes.[6] After the Watergate scandal and Nixon's resignation, American confidence in its government plummeted and has never fully rebounded.

Not all schools of thought agree that social problems are measurably harmful conditions. The idea that social problems are value-relative social constructions is popular among contemporary liberal intellectuals. In this view, social problems are "real" only if they are publicly recognized as problems.[7] The problem with this approach is that harm often exists whether a problem is acknowledged or not.

Consider poverty. Before John F. Kennedy was elected president in 1960, poverty was not publicly defined as a social problem, but many poor people were hidden in America's rural areas and urban ghettos. Once Kennedy drew attention to the issue, Congress held hearings and passed legislation as part of the War on Poverty. By 1980, however, concern over poverty and the expectation that government could solve the problem had drastically waned. Yet there were more poor people in the United States in the 1980s than there had been in the 1960s. The problem, very real, had not gone away, even though it was no longer as publicly recognized as it had been.

It is important, therefore, to view social problems as harms that exist *regardless* of public recognition. Social problems have "careers," over the course of which public concern about them and the resources devoted to their resolution wax and wane.[8] If left unresolved, the problems merely reappear later, and when they do, they tend to be worse.

What then is a social problem? A social problem is a socially patterned condition involving widespread physical, financial, and/or moral harm caused by contradictions stemming from the institutional arrangements of a given society. Such harms exist whether or not they have gained the attention of the mass media or politicians. If harms are suffered at high rates with regularity by groups of people with certain characteristics and in specific historical circumstances, they may be said to be socially patterned. If harms are socially patterned, it follows that they must be caused by social conditions. Recognizing such conditions is a key element to developing a sociological imagination.

The Sopranos parades a microcosm of American social problems before the nation each week. What follows is a sociological analysis of *The Sopranos* through the eyes of the sociological imagination.

In the chapters that follow, we explore the great contradictions and social problems plaguing American life. Chapters 2 and 3 examine the structure of wealth and power and the great immoralities following from both. The role of organized criminal syndicates, like those presented on *The Sopranos,* in the service of legitimate elites receives special attention.

Chapter 4 explores the role of organized crime in the context of the ever-expanding global crime syndicate, as evidenced by the link between the thriving drug-trafficking industry and terrorism.

Chapter 5 looks at the causes and consequences of contemporary forms of structural alienation, which emanates from the mass media in the form of advertising, government propaganda, and corporate public-service announcements. It examines the problematic ramifications of society's permeation by these bombardments, in part using *The Sopranos* as a case study.

Chapter 6 locates *The Sopranos'* place in the overall structure of the American crime problem. Organized criminal syndicates represent the great bridge between the "upper-world" crime of white-collar executives and corrupt political elites, on the one hand, and the violent crime underworld inhabited by drug-peddling street gangs and drug-addicted street criminals, on the other.

In Chapters 7 and 8, analysis focuses on "micro-social" problems, issues of marriage, family, and the crises of everyday life. Chapter 7 notes that in *The Sopranos,* marriage and family life seem to thrive on dysfunction, making the show a symbolic representation of what goes on in the American family today: divorce, adultery, spousal abuse, elder abuse, child abuse and neglect, and murder. Chapter 8 explores those harms inflicted by the workplace and religious and educational institutions in America.

Finally, Chapter 9 offers some solutions to the great contradictions of American life. It provides a blueprint for what a just society would resemble and makes recommendations concerning what it would take to rid ourselves of our Tony Sopranos.

Tony Soprano and the American Dream

TONY'S NEIGHBOR BRUCE CUSEMANO invites him out to the local country club to play a round of golf with his rich friends. They are delighted to have him there, even suggesting that they might sponsor Tony for membership at the posh club. The men barrage Tony with questions about the way the Mob works and whether he thinks *The Godfather* was an accurate portrayal of organized crime. Their enthusiasm so annoys Tony that he finally shuts up the wide-eyed group with a ridiculous story about real-life mobster John Gotti outbidding him for an ice cream truck.

Tony Soprano is the latest object of affection in America's long love affair with gangsters, outlaws, and villains. America has a habit of making heroes out of these nefarious characters. Famed outlaw Frank James charged visitors 50 cents to see his home after his brother Jesse was killed. During the Depression, bank robbers were likened to Robin Hood. Humorist Damon Runyon gave gangsters cute nicknames and endearing linguistic qualities, then put them on Broadway in *Guys and Dolls*. Then came U.S. intelligence agencies, which for decades hired gangsters for covert operations, giving them, once their secret exploits were revealed, a perverted legitimacy in the public's eye.

This false legitimization of organized crime has produced a collective schizophrenia toward the Mafia: we abhor their tactics, based on violence, corruption, adultery, intimidation, lying, and stealing. Yet we also admire their efficiency. Unlike most bureaucracies, organized crime is not hampered by red tape, paperwork, and protracted internal investigations. Most crime syndicates have family structures, and their members feel a sense of belonging to something larger than themselves, which is one of the most basic human needs.

But we admire gangsters for an even more fundamental reason: the Mob is an American success story. There is a myth about the Mafia that views it as an alien conspiracy, an un-American phenomenon. Nothing could be further from the truth. Organized crime is merely another route of social mobility taken by people who have found a short cut to the American Dream.

Crime and the American Dream

The Mob, in a cultural sense, symbolizes a national contradiction that is rarely explored and explained: America is the first nation in the history of the world whose founding creed involves the unalienable right to pursue happiness. Tony broaches this subject with Dr. Melfi after hearing that fact on the History Channel, and he demands to know where his happiness is. Yet in the view of many of his contemporaries, Tony has achieved happiness as they define it. Financial success has been widely accepted by most Americans as the definition of happiness. So important has the accumulation of wealth become that profit in America is frequently realized without the restraints placed on capitalist economies in other nations. In the United States, attempts to regulate the excesses of business have been criticized as government interference or even "socialism." Moreover, noneconomic forms of success have been devalued. Thus, as criminologists Steven Messner and Richard Rosenfeld point out, in America teachers, mothers, child-care workers, and nurses are paid very little,[1] and bartenders make more money than do people who work with children. Few profits stand to be made from raising good children. Profits come largely from products and services that people are willing to pay a lot of money for.

In the pursuit of Americans' dream of wealth, their institutions have accommodated to the needs of business. Terms like "the bottom line" and "cash flow" have become part of everyday language. The United States remains the only advanced industrial democracy without paid family leave, without national health care, and without an extended family vacation policy. Only with the Clinton administration was a family and medical leave bill enacted. It is all but impossible to support a family in America unless both parents are employed, and so we have had to rethink our traditional patterns of child rearing, having children later in life, placing them in day care instead of raising them at home, and squeezing the duties of parenthood in between work, meetings, and other obligations.

After the family, our educational system is the next-largest casualty of the scramble for money. America has the reputation as the most anti-intellectual nation in the Western world, precisely because its primary definition of success involves making money, not educating its citizens. Thus, most people go to college not because they have a love of learning, but because college leads to a middle-class occupation afterward. That's certainly why Tony and Carmela want their own kids to pursue a higher education. It comes as a surprise to them when Meadow explains that A.J.'s existential crisis about his confirmation is the product of education not of disobedience. To them, education is simply the ticket to a bigger paycheck.

Government, too, in America has historically and increasingly served the needs of business. The primary responsibility of modern government is not to provide for the needs of the citizenry but to ensure economic growth. Certainly the manager of Tony's legitimate business front, a waste management company, easily dodges government oversight regarding health hazards or other infractions. The odds are stacked in his favor. Much of American foreign and defense policy seeks to protect the holdings of multinational corporations, not to ensure human rights and democracy in other nations. This is one reason why the federal government has spent over $4 trillion on defense since 1947, most of it on budget-busting, often useless weapons systems. Moreover, American government at all levels grants generous subsidies, tax breaks, loans, loan guarantees, and government contracts to American business in the hope of stimulating economic growth, although much of the money ends up lining the pockets of corporate CEOs. This is, after all, Tony Soprano's America.

Many politicians believe the way to solve the problems of government is to run government like a business. Thus, when H. Ross Perot ran for president in 1992, he promised to bring the principles that made him a billionaire businessman to bear on governmental problems. Moreover, many individuals from the private sector are appointed to cabinet-level positions under the assumption that if they know how to run a business, they know how to run a country. Some might even suggest that Tony Soprano himself might make a very able leader. After all, he knows how to get things done.

Again, all this is part of a central contradiction in American life: American culture places so much emphasis on the goal of success, of achieving the American Dream, that it tacitly endorses unethical means to that end. The resulting lack of morals motivates many people and organizations to emphasize winning by any means. We measure success by accumulation of wealth, but our social structure fails to provide the equality of opportunity necessary for all to achieve this goal. Instead, American society has managed to create a structural form of amorality, a lack of norms concerning the means to success. This contributes to our admiration of the Tony Sopranos of this world, those who take short cuts to the American Dream.

Messner and Rosenfeld define the American Dream as a "broad cultural ethos that entails a commitment to the goal of material success, to be pursued by everyone in society, under conditions of open individual competition."[2] Unfortunately, they argue, the values and behaviors that make it possible for us to pursue the American

Dream—universalism, achievement orientation, the fetishism of money, and individualism—cause some of our worst social problems.

Elements of the American Dream
Universalism

The American Dream is open to all, regardless of race, age, gender, class, or level of education. Equally open are the chances of success or failure. Fear of failure, intense in America, increases pressure on individuals to abandon conformity to rules governing proper conduct in favor of expedience. Many people—average Americans as well as America's Tony Sopranos—come to view the rule of law as an unnecessary barrier to achieving their own success.

Achievement Orientation

An orientation toward achievement creates pressures to "make something" of oneself, to set and achieve goals—often, but not always, material success. Although this is a shaky basis for self-esteem, many Americans nevertheless view their personal worth much like a stock, which rises or falls according to how much money they make or whether or not they make it to the top of their profession. This amounts to an endless striving, workaholism, and, not infrequently, stress-related diseases. Tony's vicious and greedy lieutenant Richie Aprile succumbed to just such thinking. It drove him to plot against Tony when he felt economically slighted one too many times.

The Fetishism of Money

Money has attained an almost sacred quality in American life. Accumulation of wealth provides our scorecard in the game of success: whoever dies with the most money wins. As the distinguished criminologist Elliott Currie has noted, the pursuit of private gain has become the organizing principle for all of social life.[3] As sociologist Charles Derber has argued, during the Reagan-Bush era, increasing inequality in the distribution of wealth, combined with an ethic of "greed is good," gave the American character an element of narcissism, a personality disorder characterized by distorted self-love and selfishness, coupled with a lack of guilt.[4] Large numbers of upperworld crooks began to engage in a quest for power, status, and attention in the Reagan-Bush "money culture." The result was an unrestrained quest for personal gain—mirrored by Tony Soprano, his rivals, and his crew in every episode of *The Sopranos*.

Individualism

The notion that Americans possess not only autonomy but basic individual rights is inherent to the American Dream. Unlike the cultures of other nations, Americans make individualistic decisions about every aspect of their lives, including marriage, career, religion, and political outlook. Whereas the quality of individualism has many positive facets, when combined with the drive to succeed, the love for money, and the universal possibility of achieving our dreams, our rugged American individualism often yields amoral choices. Fellow citizens become rivals, competing for rewards and status. Intense personal competition increases the pressure to succeed. People learn to disregard restrictions on their own means to success when those restrictions threaten to interfere with personal goals. Many of the gangsters in *The Sopranos* choose personal gain over the good of their comrades, even though such infighting goes against their cherished codes and weakens their organization.

Tony Soprano is the fictional embodiment of this amorality. He seduces a fellow patient of Dr. Melfi's and then lies to Melfi about it. Tony operates an endless number of schemes involving both force and fraud to make his money: bribes, fixed poker games, scams, prostitution, murder, strong-arm collection tactics, all in the name of business.

"Good American Values"

As much as we would like to believe that our county is crime ridden because it was invaded by immigrant criminals, the reverse is true. Social critic James Adams, who coined the term "the American Dream," remarked, in his 1929 book *Our Business Civilization,* that many people coming to America's shores were relatively law abiding before they arrived here; they "were made lawless by America, rather than America being made lawless by them."[5] America's wide open spaces, promise of success despite circumstances, and fixation on achievement, individualism, universalism, and the fetishism of money have made us—and the Sopranos—what we are.

So why isn't all this amoral selfishness obvious to everyone? Alongside those contributing values that constitute the American Dream exists an equally embraced opposite set of values, what I term the "Good American values." These more positive values are characterized by such non-individualistic and non-instrumental notions as love, family, patriotism, charity, justice, democracy, and God, and they are just as irrational and impractical as those values associated with the American Dream. Tony Soprano himself espouses many of these values as important to him and his family, even citing the preservation of "honor, family, and loyalty" as reasons for "poor Italians" getting involved in organized crime in the first place. We, like Tony, use this set of values to make us feel good about ourselves, to neutralize any guilt we feel when our leaders blunder into Vietnam, Watergate, Iran-Contra, or countless corporate scandals. These good American values allow us to enjoy one of the most "have your cake and eat it too" ideologies in the history of the human race, namely the way we, as a society, condone breaking the rules in the pursuit of this ubiquitous Dream.

This ideology applies to all matters, foreign and domestic, but most of all, perhaps, it applies to crime and deviant behavior. Put these two sets of values together, those comprising the instrumental American Dream and those constituting the irrational "Good America," and they produce a sense of entitlement, imperviousness, and impunity that allows Americans to commit all sorts of deviance and still feel that they are a good and God-fearing people. Even Tony Soprano feels he is a good and God-fearing man—despite the fact he is a murderer, a flesh peddler, an overseer of dope dealers, and a thief—enjoying the luxury of having his neighbors' admiration. He is, in short, a symbolic embodiment of one of the central contradictions of American life, that good and evil can coexist in one entity, that having a perverse code of morality is acceptable, as long as you are a success at pursuing the American Dream.

Suckers and Wiseguys

In a diatribe about the plight of the "poor Italians" whom a rapidly industrializing America used to build its vast infrastructure, Tony Soprano notes that "some of us wanted a piece of the action," citing the Carnegies, the Rockefellers, and J. P. Morgan as opportunists themselves and likening the Italian Americans involved in the Mafia to the robber barons. "It was all business," he declares. Industrialists and mobsters alike sought only to succeed in a land that promised so much. Over a half century ago, sociologist Robert Merton pointed out that one great contradiction of American culture is its stress on winning and success but the lack of opportunity it provides to achieve such success.[6] This contradiction arises due partly to what the French sociologist Emile Durkheim (1858–1917) called anomie, a social situation in which norms are unclear.[7] Success in America has no official limits; the private accumulation of wealth is without "a final stopping point."[8] No matter what their income level, many Americans always want 50 percent more money—which, of course, becomes 50 percent more once achieved, then 50 percent more, and so on.

Robert Merton has noted that crime "is a very common phenomenon" among all social classes in the United States.[9] Polls indicate that 90 percent of Americans admit to committing serious crimes for which they could be imprisoned for at least a year.[10] A 1991 survey by advertising executives James Patterson and Peter Kim also showed a high percentage of Americans engaging in criminal behavior.[11] The characters on *The Sopranos,* even those not in the Mafia, engage in crime both directly and tacitly. Tony's lawyer helps his client skirt the edges of the law. Uncle Junior's doctor allows his office to be used as a clandestine meeting place for discussions of Mob business. Artie Bucco withholds information about Tony's involvement with the arson at Artie's restaurant rather than risk losing his insurance money. Yet one of our persistent myths about crime is that America is divided into two populations: one law abiding, the other criminal.

American elites serve as role models to the rest of society. For generations, Americans have held members of elite society in high regard: the Rockefellers, the Kennedys, the Vanderbilts, and the Morgans have all proven the American Dream can be realized. When these members of elite society exhibit deviant behavior, bending and twisting the rules to achieve success, "ordinary" people see an excuse to engage in crime without feeling guilty. Elite deviance sends the message that it is stupid not to commit crime if one has the opportunity and can get away with it. Many a drug dealer and street gang member has remarked that they are just doing what the Rockefellers, Carnegies, and other robber barons did in the nineteenth century—establishing monopolies. *The Sopranos* merely embodies a long tradition of crimeogenic role models for the American public, so it should come as no surprise that Tony's "straight" suburban neighbors often seem to admire him. His neighbors the Cusemanos know his route to the exclusive neighborhood they share came through violence and crime, yet they often seem to relish his being among them.

The same ideology exists among organized-crime figures. When political scientist Peter Lupsha investigated their life stories, he found that none of them had embarked on criminal careers because there were no legitimate jobs to be had—or "blocked opportunities," as some theorists of organized crime supposed. American gangsters,

Lupsha discovered, tend to divide the world into "suckers" and "Wiseguys."[12] Suckers are working-class people who toil at legal jobs and struggle to make ends meet. In *The Sopranos,* Tony's friend Artie, urged by his wife Charmaine, struggles to remain honest, or, in Wiseguy terms, stay a sucker. Wiseguys are gangsters who do what they want and have plenty of money to show for it. With the working world divided into these two possible futures, who in their right mind would elect to be a sucker? Certainly not a Wiseguy, someone who knows how to work the system.

American culture is disturbingly tolerant of certain forms of deviant behavior that stem from the American values of success and making money. Even as much as he tries to stay away from Tony's activities, Artie Bucco still rationalizes his involvement with him. When Charmaine complains about their restaurant becoming a hangout for gangsters, he tells her that "a certain amount of that element creates a buzz."

Our emphasis on the goal of accumulating wealth and ignoring the means to achieve that goal hits hardest those groups that have the least opportunity to accumulate wealth. This is one reason why the poor commit violent street crime. When other opportunities to make money are lacking, turning to crime becomes a viable choice for people who feel they have nothing to lose. Yet the poor don't have a monopoly on deviant behavior, and most of the poor are not criminals. All class levels in American society commit crimes and cause other harms that in turn cause social problems. Yet Americans have a tendency to turn a blind eye to matters of social class, with most Americans considering themselves middle class regardless of which social class they actually belong to. In reality, class inequality and its attendant characteristics lead to some of the nation's worst social problems.

In this case, more looms, something deeper, uglier, as the mysterious Mr. X remarked in Oliver Stone's 1991 film *JFK.* America's national upper class does not exist as a relatively unorganized mass but contains within it an elite of power. This elite comprises a mere one ten-thousandth of 1 percent of the American population,[13] yet it regularly makes crucial policy decisions regarding war and peace, economic prosperity versus decline, racial progress versus increasing tension, and other big decisions in both American and global life. Moreover, within this elite exists a more or less institutionalized set of deviant behaviors that have produced and continue to create corporate and governmental scandal after scandal at an alarming pace since 1947.

The Political Economy and the Power Elite

In 1956, the great sociologist C. Wright Mills warned the American people of a growing centralization and coordination of wealth and power in the United States. He wrote:

> The economy . . . has become dominated by two or three hundred giant corporations [which are also very politically influential], and together hold the keys to economic decisions. The political [system] has become a centralized, executive establishment which has taken unto itself many powers previously scattered, and now enters into each and every cranny of the social structure. The military . . . has become the largest and most expensive feature of government, and, although well versed in smiling public relations, now has all the grim and clumsy efficiency of a sprawling [bureaucracy]. . . . There is no longer, on the one hand, an economy, and, on the other hand, a political order containing a military establishment unimportant to politics and to money making. There is a political order linked, in a thousand ways, with military institutions and decisions. . . . If there is government intervention in the corporate economy, so there is corporate intervention in the governmental process.[14]

For Mills, the distribution of power in America differs from that described in political science textbooks, a fiction that holds that America's power structure is pluralistic, distributed among competing interest groups that clash in the political realm over conflicting issues. These interests allegedly ally with competing political parties as well: business with the Republicans and labor with the Democrats. This myth is indeed what passes for education in this country, which is exactly why one researcher has defined education as the "lies they are currently telling to children." The real story of power in America and throughout the new globalized capitalist world is actually much more interesting.

Six years after Mills first warned the nation about the power elite, President Dwight D. Eisenhower called it the "military-industrial complex" in his Farewell Address. These two terms are now frequently used interchangeably.

The power elite is not a conspiracy. Rather, it is a series of interests and institutions that evolved out of World War II. What was established between 1941 and 1945 were the roots of a permanent warfare state and military-industrial complex. A confluence of munitions makers, intelligence-gathering agencies, military personnel associations, and members of congressional committees all learned of their common interests during the Cold War. The result was continued high levels of military spending and endless undeclared wars, from Latin America to Asia, which continue to this day.

Within this combination of corporations, government agencies, and political interest groups lies the power elite itself. Based on their successes and failures in the business and political worlds, different individuals and entities evolve into it and out of one of four sectors: the Corporate, the Military, the Political, and the Research and Policy-Formulating. The members of each of these sectors, like any member of Tony Soprano's crew, seek by any means they deem necessary to gain and keep power and control. It is why C. Wright Mills accused the power elite of turning America into "a network of rackets."[15]

The Corporate Sector

The power elite's corporate component illustrates the "network of rackets" structure beautifully. It consists of the largest industrial corporations in the nation and the insurance companies, banks, and other financial entities that own stock in them. The 100 largest industrial corporations dominate the entire corporate sector of the U.S. economy, controlling 60 percent of industrial assets—with the remaining 199,900 or so companies fighting over the rest. The five largest industrial corporations—General Motors, Exxon, Ford Motor Company, IBM, and General Electric—control 15 percent of the nation's industrial assets.[16]

The Clayton Antitrust Act of 1914 forbids any company to own stock in another company in the same industry. Thus General Motors, for example, cannot own stock in Ford. However, if a large bank buys a 5-percent interest in GM and a 5-percent interest in Ford, the bank can sit on both boards of directors. This practice, known as an "interlocking directorate," is the story of much corporate ownership. Over 250 directors of the top 500 American corporations hold seats on the boards of competing firms; one study of the 250 largest American corporations found that all but seventeen of them had at least one chief executive sitting on the board of another corporation. The fifty largest banks, which control 66 percent of all banking assets, hold seats on the boards of America's 500 largest firms. The Rockefeller–owned Chase Manhattan Bank is interlocked with the nation's 100 largest corporations. Additionally, big banks and financial institutions also own blocks of one another's stock. Citibank and Chase Manhattan, for instance, are the largest owners of Morgan Guaranty Trust.[17]

What all this means is that the 200 or so largest corporations and some fifty financial institutions control about two thirds of all business income and half of all bank deposits. These firms are interlocked by directorships controlled by less than one one-thousandth of 1 percent of the nation's population.[18] This intense concentration of corporate ownership and the immense political influence that corporations exercise have enabled corporate America to escape effective regulation by government and to take control of that regulation themselves. This all seems the very apotheosis of Mills's "network of rackets."

The Military Sector

The military component of the military-industrial complex consists of the major branches of the military services—army, navy, air force, and marines—as well as the nation's intelligence community: the National Security Council, the Central Intelligence Agency, the Defense Intelligence Agency, and the intelligence arms of the various branches of the military. Involved as well are the Veterans Administration and organizations representing the nation's veterans such as the Veterans of Foreign Wars and the American Legion. The secrecy of the intelligence apparatus and its web of affiliations with the military services have created something of a secret government.[19] Since 1945, the actions of this secret government have had immense consequences for the nation's foreign and defense policies.

Many Americans wonder if there is still a military-industrial complex in the post–Cold War world. The answer is that it is as big and as bloated as ever. The Department of Defense usually awards the largest 100 corporate firms about 75 percent of the contracts for major weapons systems, which accounts for about 30 percent of the nation's military budget. Defense contractors have hired over 4,500 high-ranking retired military officers and 350 retired civilian Pentagon employees and employ almost 16 percent of the civilian work force, including nearly 20 percent of all U.S. corporate managers and administrators.[20] Although the Pentagon's budget was cut somewhat during the 1990s and before September 11, 2001, weapons are still being produced in significant numbers and varieties. And of course, since 9/11, defense has become the government's top priority, with increased budgets and new initiatives. Even while domestic orders for weapons were declining, the U.S. defense budget was still larger than most national economies. Moreover, as of the early 1990s, most weapons purchased by foreign nations were produced by U.S. corporations, many of the sales being paid for by U.S. taxpayers as part of foreign aid. In 1994, for example, Israel received $1.8 billion in foreign aid to buy military aircraft. The export arm of the defense industry is thriving. The 2002 defense budget is $400 billion, about 20 percent of the entire federal budget, but the total is much more than $400 billion if you add Veterans Affairs and interest on the debt due to military spending. This is truly a network of rackets.

The Political Sector

The political sector of the power elite includes defense-contracting lobbies, members of Congress who sit on the appropriations committees, the Joint Chiefs of Staff, and the civilian administrators—the secretaries of defense and of the various armed services—who oversee the nation's military establishment. Two thirds of all the nation's congressional districts either contain or border on military installations or defense plants.[21]

The Research and Policy-Formulating Sector

The lion's share of Pentagon-funded research goes to twelve elite universities (mostly from the Ivy League) and to think tanks—private research firms, such as the Rand Corporation and the Stanford Research Institute—that do research, much of it highly classified. Through private foundations, the nation's largest corporations have also set up a series of policy-formulating associations that publish journals and issue white papers on various policy questions. The think tanks typically receive money from corporate and government sources. Rand and Stanford Research are annually awarded about 5 percent of the Pentagon's research and development budget.

The Power Elite

The power elite itself is dominated by a group of people who compose a segment of America's national upper class, as defined by a few characteristic indicators. Their names and addresses appear in the *Social Register*, a volume of socially influential people published in major

U.S. cities. About 138,000 Americans are listed in the various editions of the *Social Register*. They invariably attended private preparatory schools and elite universities.[22] They belong to exclusive social clubs like the Knickerbocker Club and visit upper-class vacation retreats, such as Bohemian Grove and Pacific Union. They sit on the boards of directors of the nation's largest corporations. Their annual income is usually in the millions of dollars, and their wealth typically totals tens of millions of dollars; this one half of 1 percent of Americans—some 1.5 million plutocrats within a population of nearly 300 million Americans—possess 25 to 30 percent of all privately held wealth.

Among the members of the power elite, we find much interlocking of the Corporate, Military, Political, and Research and Policy-Formulating Sectors.

According to the Center for Responsive Politics,

President George W. Bush, of course, is a Texas oilman, although not a very successful one. His company, Arbusto, merged with Spectrum 7 in 1984 as it was on the verge of bankruptcy. Spectrum was bought out by Harken Energy in 1986, giving Bush a seat on Harken's board, some stock options, and a $120,000 consulting contract. As the first president to have an MBA, Bush has surrounded himself with people with similar (and more successful) corporate backgrounds. Vice President Dick Cheney was, until last year, the CEO of Halliburton, the world's largest oil field services company. Halliburton, through its European subsidiaries, sold spare parts to Iraq's oil industry, despite U.N. sanctions. The Bush administration is already considering whether or not it should alter the sanctions policy against Iraq, hinting that it might allow for more normalized trade with the country.[23]

- Ann Veneman serves as George W. Bush's secretary of agriculture and is former head of California's Department of Food and Agriculture. She sat on the board of directors for Calgene Inc. In 1994, Calgene became the first company to bring genetically engineered food, the Flavr Savr tomato, to super-market shelves. Calgene was bought out by Monsanto, the nation's leading biotech company, in 1997. Monsanto, in turn, became part of the pharmaceutical company Pharmacia in 2000. Monsanto, which donated more than $12,000 to George Bush's presidential bid, wants two things this year: no mandatory labeling of biotech foods and better access to inter-national markets. Veneman also served on the International Policy Council on Agriculture, Food and Trade, a group funded by Cargill, Nestlé, Kraft, and Archer Daniels Midland.

- George W. Bush's treasury secretary, Paul O'Neill, was CEO and chairman of Alcoa, the world's largest aluminum manu-facturer. O'Neill decided to dissolve his company's political action committee (PAC) in 1996. "What's going on with cam-paign financing has reached well beyond a reasonable limit," he told *Fortune* magazine. "Some people said we'd have a problem with access [to elected officials]. That hasn't been the case."[24] That's probably because Alcoa relies on Vinson and Elkins, a Texas-based law firm, to lobby the government on its behalf. While Bush was still governor of Texas, Vinson and Elkins engineered a loophole in the state's environmental reg-ulations that will allow Alcoa to continue emitting 60,000 tons of sulfur dioxide annually into the air, solidifying Alcoa's posi-tion as one of Texas's top polluters. Vinson and Elkins was Bush's third largest campaign contributor, giving him more than $200,000. Before joining Alcoa, O'Neill was the presi-dent of International Paper. He has also served on the boards of Lucent Technologies and Eastman Kodak.

- Defense Secretary Donald Rumsfeld joined the private sector as the CEO of G. D. Searle, a pharmaceutical company that is now a subsidiary of Pharmacia, in 1977 after being Presi-dent Ford's defense secretary. He was also the CEO of General Instrument, a telecommunications parts supplier that was eventually bought out by Motorola. Lately, though, Rumsfeld has spent his time serving on the boards of several companies: Gilead Sciences, a fledgling biotech company; newspaper giant Tribune Company, which owns the *Los Angeles Times* and the *Chicago Tribune*; Amylin Pharmaceuticals; Swiss firm Asea Brown Boveri; and such Fortune 500 behemoths as Kellogg, Sears, and Allstate. As a director for Gulfstream Aerospace, his stock in the company reportedly was valued at $11 million when the company was acquired by defense contractor General Dynamics in 1999.[25]

Most of the people who run the government have corporate backgrounds and share remarkably similar educational and cultural experiences and affiliations.

Numerous additional studies support the finding that the upper class not only is overrepresented in governmental circles but also runs corporate America:

- Fifty-four percent of members of boards of directors of the twenty largest American corporations are from the upper class.
- Sixty-two percent of members of the boards of directors of the nation's fifteen largest banks are from the upper class.
- Forty-four percent of members of boards of directors of the nation's fifteen largest insurance companies are from the upper class.
- Fifty-three percent of members of boards of directors of the nation's fifteen largest transportation companies are from the upper class.[26]

The power elite makes sure its wishes are given every consideration in Washington and in other governmental circles by exerting an influence on the policy-making process.[27] The corporate rich exert their political influence by donating billions to political candidates;

occasionally running for office; holding posts in the executive branch of the federal government; establishing private foundations and elite associations and sponsoring university research; and spending billions in "institutional" advertising and "charitable" ventures to create a favorable public image and socialize the public in the ideology of free enterprise.

Major corporations are not the only institutional players in the policy-making process. A mere fifty foundations (out of over 1,200) control 40 percent of all foundation assets, and twenty-five elite universities and colleges annually garner half of all educational endowment funds, with some 656 corporate elites sitting on their boards of trustees. Elite civic associations, such as the Council on Foreign Relations, bring together national and international elites from the corporate, educational, legal, and governmental worlds. Membership in them is often a prerequisite for a high-ranking cabinet post: twenty of the last twenty-one secretaries of state, for example, have been members of the Council on Foreign Relations.[28] Twenty-eight large law firms do much of the legal work for corporations and the upper class. Ninety percent of all the legal work in the United States is done for a mere 10 percent of the population. These law firms are heavily involved in the lobbying process in Washington, and many of their partners are former members of the various presidents' cabinets, as we have seen.

The mass media are central to the policy-making process because they set limits on the breadth of ideological views that enter the policy-making debate in the United States. The media choose which stories to emphasize and which to ignore: thus, the major media almost completely ignored the savings and loan scandal until the industry's losses became so overwhelming that Congress had to vote billions of dollars to bail it out. Finally, the media are run by a group of corporations owned by other corporations and financial institutions. Controlling shares in the three major television networks are owned by five large New York banks (Citibank, Chase, Morgan Guaranty, Bank of New York, and Banker's Trust). The 500 largest American corporations account for 90 percent of all prime-time television network advertising revenues.[29]

Numerous studies have confirmed the power of elite networks in America and other modern democracies.[30] No one has described the current policy-making process better than the journalist William Greider,[31] who notes a fundamental contradiction in American political and economic life: the public has great contempt for its politicians, and the feeling is mutual. The two groups remain locked in a state of mutual distrust, cynicism, and alienation. Most congressional politicians know that it is not "the people" who are their constituents but the elites who finance elections. Democracy has become a ritual dance in which politicians profess to care about the common people and their needs (jobs, health care, and homelessness), but behind the scenes the interests of organized money groups call the tune.

What has emerged in Washington is a shadow government, and not just the one George W. Bush planned to rule the nation in case of an emergency caused by terrorists. The real shadow government is made up of public relations firms, think tanks, and polling organizations, all funded by corporate interests. The results are staggering:

- One hundred forty-six members of the House of Representatives are either founders or officers of tax-exempt organizations—such as the American Enterprise Institute, the Heritage Foundation, and the Olin Foundation—that produce either research statistics or corporate propaganda for lobbying purposes.[32]
- In 1960, fewer than 400 lobbyists were registered with the U.S. Congress; by 1992, 40,000 were so registered,[33] and many of them represent U.S. and foreign corporations.
- In the 1970s, new think tanks were established and richly endowed by corporate money. The right-wing Heritage Foundation was started with a $250,000 donation from the Colorado beer tycoon Joseph Coors. The patrons of the conservative American Enterprise Institute include AT&T, Chase

Manhattan Bank, Exxon, General Electric, General Motors, and Procter and Gamble. The "institute" quickly became a "primary source of Washington opinion," shaping the policy positions of Washington politicians and the mass media.[34]

Elite rule has made the United States less democratic by converting not only American democracy into what Greider terms "a busy commerce in deal making,"[35] but also much of American society into Mills's "network of rackets."[36]

The Sopranos and the
Higher Immorality

IN THE FIRST EPISODE OF SEASON two of *The Sopranos,* Tony stumbles down his driveway in his bathrobe to pick up the morning paper. We can just imagine our fictional gangster protagonist, scanning the headlines, learning his daily lessons from the power elite. Watergate. Iran-Contra. Enron. Halliburton. Arthur Andersen. WorldCom. Headlines like these may have inspired Tony to set up his cold-calling operation pushing the junk stock for Webistics.

A central contradiction among the power elite is that it has no compunction about violating the laws it is sworn to uphold. The power elite operates by the rules of the "higher immorality."[1] It is a system of violations that occur largely because of the way corporate, political, and military intelligence institutions are structured. As bureaucracies, they have structures intended to regularize crime and deviance.

Bureaucratic organizations are goal oriented; they exist to make money, to expand their power, or to achieve some other organizational goal. Because they recognize goals above moral constraints, businesses most often become amoral entities. From time to time, most organizations want to achieve goals they cannot pursue within the limits imposed by existing rules, laws, or ethical codes. When this happens, organizations of all kinds secretly engage in illegal or unethical behaviors. These behaviors include secret alliances and arrangements with the underworld inhabited by the likes of Tony Soprano.

Power in bureaucracies is concentrated at the top. The people who head the organizations remain shielded from their workers and from the public by layers of secretaries, public relations departments, and lawyers. The hierarchical structure makes secrecy a central characteristic of bureaucratic life. The combination of goal orientation and secrecy makes scandal a frequent occurrence.

In the 1970s, for example, the Ford Motor Company rushed its Pinto automobile into production, even though it contained an unprotected gas tank that exploded if the car was hit from the rear at speeds as low as five miles an hour. Ford executives wrote a secret memo, subsequently leaked to the press, comparing the estimated amount of money the company would have to pay out in wrongful death claims with the estimated amount it would have to pay to fix the gas tanks in all the vehicles. The memo clearly demonstrated that it would be more profitable to let people die or be seriously injured than to insert an $11 rubber bladder inside the gas tank. The result: Ford let the unsafe Pinto roll off the assembly line and hundreds of people were killed or maimed

Or take the Iran-Contra affair. After the right-wing Nicaraguan Contras, conspiring to overthrow the leftist Sandinista government, mined the harbor at Managua in 1982, the U.S. Congress voted to cut off all military aid to them. The Reagan administration, determined to continue helping the Contras, set up a secret operation, selling arms to Iran and funneling part of the profits to the Contras. Organized-crime syndicates played an important role in this scandal, paying bribes to the Contras in order to be able to transport Colombian cocaine across Contra territory, and helping the CIA spread crack-cocaine in America's ghettos in the 1980s. As a result of the Iran-Contra scandal, several members of the Reagan administration resigned from office or were sent to prison.

The Ford Pinto and Iran Contra are not the only instances of the higher immorality in action. Socially patterned deviant and criminal acts among the power elite take many forms. At times, it seems there is little difference between legitimate organizations and organized criminal syndicates. With such examples from the ruling elite, the popularity of the Tony Sopranos of the world makes sense. The higher immorality, then, consists of institutionalized deviant behaviors among the nation's power elite, including the following.

Violations of Antitrust, Advertising, and Pollution Laws

Corporate crime in the form of violation of antitrust, advertising, and pollution laws costs American consumers $200 billion a year, forty times more than losses from street crime.[2] Only 2 percent of corporate crime cases result in imprisonment. One study, conducted in the 1970s, showed that employees of 60 percent of the 582 largest American corporations had committed at least one serious crime in a twenty-four-month period.[3] Nearly half the crimes occurred in just three industries—automotive, petroleum, and pharmaceuticals—which contain some of the nation's largest and most politically active companies. Of those firms charged with at least one crime, the average number of crimes was 4.2 per firm—a rate approaching habitual criminality. Sociologist Amitai Etzioni[4] found that between 1975 and 1984, almost two thirds of Fortune 500 companies had committed one or more incidents of corrupt behavior, such as bribery, price-fixing, tax fraud, or violations of environmental regulations. A study of the twenty-five largest Fortune 500 corporations found that all were either found guilty of criminal behavior or fined for civil violations between 1977 and 1990.[5]

The Scandalization of America

Revelations about government conspiracies and cover-ups also contribute to the belief by the Tony Sopranos of the world that even cherished institutions operate with no regard for law or morality. Between 1860 and 1920, the United States suffered only two major crises involving corruption on the federal level, the Crédit Mobilier scandal of the 1860s and the Teapot Dome scandal of the 1920s, amounting to just one scandal every thirty years. However, beginning in 1963 with the cover-up/investigation of the assassination of President John F. Kennedy, the federal government has experienced repeated scandals, which themselves pose serious social problems, causing all manner of social harm.

On November 22, 1963, in Dallas, riding in a motorcade, in an open limousine with his wife and the governor of Texas and his wife, President Kennedy was assassinated. The question of who killed Kennedy has been passionately debated ever since. A week after the president's death, JFK's successor, Lyndon B. Johnson, set up a blue-ribbon, bipartisan commission (including, ominously, the director of the CIA) headed by Supreme Court Chief Justice Earl Warren, a liberal Republican, to investigate the assassination.

Issued in September 1964, the Warren Report concluded that there was no conspiracy, that Lee Harvey Oswald had acted alone in shooting the president, and that Jack Ruby had acted alone in shooting Oswald. There was even an impossible explanation—the so-called single-bullet theory—about how one bullet struck the president, coursed through his body, and emerged to wound the governor of Texas, who was sitting in front of him.

Since the Warren Report, hundreds of books and thousands of articles have taken issue with its findings. The dominant view of most of these works is that Kennedy was assassinated because of a conspiracy. But who did it? And why? Was it because JFK was going to withdraw from Vietnam after the 1964 election? "In the end," he had said to Walter Cronkite on the CBS evening news two months before his death, "it is their war." So, according to this view, those behind his assassination would be the permanent-war forces, within the government and the defense industry, that have controlled American foreign policy since 1947.

Another view is that the Mafia—listen up, *Sopranos* fans!—in cahoots with Fidel Castro killed the president. The Mafia, the story goes, had helped JFK win his narrow victory in 1960 with some dodgy activity in West Virginia and Chicago, but when JFK's younger brother, Robert, became attorney general, he declared war on the Mafia. When RFK was chief counsel to the Senate Select Committee investigating labor racketeering in 1957, he had made a name for himself prosecuting crooked union leaders like James Hoffa. Fearful of more harassment and feeling double-crossed, the Mob put out a hit on the president.

Are either of these theories correct? Are they any less ludicrous than the single-bullet theory? America has existed for four decades with a central event in its history, the assassination of a president, unsolved and subject to wide theorizing and wild speculation—government conspiracy or Mafia hits or both or more!

Subsequent investigations into the crime by the House Special Committee on Assassinations found numerous inconsistencies in the case. The HSCA concluded that President Kennedy "was probably assassinated as a result of a conspiracy," and likely suspects included members of organized crime.[6] The HSCA speculated that Mafia bosses in New Orleans and Florida had the "means, motive, and opportunity" to assassinate the president and/or that anti-Castro activists may have been involved.

The precise nature of the conspiracy was never determined, and theories abound. Between 1966 and 2002, over 600 books and 2,000 articles were written about the Kennedy assassination. The JFK assassination investigation/cover-up marks not only the first major postwar scandal but also the beginning of a drastic decline in public confidence in government agencies and politicians.

After Kennedy's death, the Johnson administration escalated U.S. presence in Vietnam, propping up its corrupt South Vietnamese ally with free-fire zones, defoliation, and napalm, and dividing public opinion and contributing to more distrust of government. Vietnam was followed by the Watergate scandal, which caused public trust to decline even further.

The Watergate scandal, which brought down the administration of Richard Nixon, was the mother of all political scandals—the name itself spawning subsequent other-gate scandals, such as Irangate,

Travelgate, and Zippergate. Watergate was the higher immorality enacted by the power elite, but the dramatis personae were right out of *The Sopranos*. Burglars, paid by the Committee to Reelect the President (affectionately shortened to CREEP), broke into the headquarters of the Democratic National Committee in the Watergate complex in Washington and planted eavesdropping devices. The burglars, former CIA agents (some of them associated with the 1961 Bay of Pigs fiasco, the CIA's aborted attempt to overthrow Fidel Castro), had received promises of executive clemency and hush money from the White House.

The administration, acting less like the power elite and more like a certain Jersey gang, also broke into the office of a psychiatrist treating Daniel Ellsberg, a longtime civilian Pentagon employee who had grown increasingly critical of American involvement in Vietnam. Ellsberg had finally leaked a top-secret history of the Vietnam War, the so-called Pentagon Papers, to *The New York Times,* which published it. Ellsberg was now standing trial. While the trial was in progress, the judge announced that the Nixon administration had offered him the directorship of the FBI. He declared a mistrial.

During his time as president, Nixon bugged his own office and those of his top aides; the resulting tapes depict high government officials acting like the gang at the Bada Bing. Nixon's vice president, Spiro Agnew, confessed to accepting kickbacks on government contracts and resigned from office as part of a plea bargain. A White House secret intelligence unit, called the Plumbers because they were intended to stop leaks to the press, engaged in a host of dirty tricks aimed at smearing potential Democratic presidential candidates.

Nixon's administration also generated an "enemies list" of its critics and illegally misused the Internal Revenue Service by requesting tax audits of those critics. It manipulated the FBI and CIA into cutting short the investigation into Watergate, and the head of the FBI even destroyed evidence in the case by burning files along with Christmas wrapping paper. Nixon lied repeatedly to Congress about both his involvement in the case and his possession of evidence that would reveal his involvement. Nixon offered his two top aides, John Ehrlichman and H. R. Haldeman, money in exchange for their silence. He had his personal attorney solicit illegal campaign contributions in exchange for promises of ambassadorships. Money from these contributions was illegally laundered to conceal the donors' identities.

Nixon's Attorney General John Mitchell, the nation's chief law-enforcement officer, helped plan the bugging of the Democratic National Committee. Mitchell and numerous other Nixon administration officials were convicted of perjury, conspiracy, and obstruction of justice and sent to prison. Following Watergate in 1975, investigations into the postwar activities of the CIA and the FBI revealed that both agencies had engaged in systematic violations of the civil liberties of thousands of American citizens. Such violations by the intelligence agencies continue to this day.

Since 1947, the FBI has committed over 1,500 illegal break-ins of headquarters of American organizations and foreign embassies. From 1947 to 1975, the CIA illegally experimented, without their knowledge or consent, on a variety of U.S. citizens, scientists from the Army Chemical Corps, and even its own agents, giving them knockout drops, incapacitating chemicals, and the hallucinogen LSD. During the Reagan administration (1981–1989), the FBI spied on citizens and groups opposed to administration policy in Central America, including the United Auto Workers, the Maryknoll Sisters, and the Southern Christian Leadership Conference.[7]

Abroad, the CIA has been involved in various assassinations of foreign heads of state, including Congolese Prime Minister Patrice Lumumba, President Rafael Trujillo (Dominican Republic), President Ngo Dinh Diem (South Vietnam), and President Salvador Allende (Chile). In 1985, CIA Director William Casey secretly arranged for the murder of Shiite Muslim leader Sayyed Fadlallah in a deal with Saudi intelligence.[8]

In 1987, news broke concerning the most damaging scandal of the Reagan administration, the Iran-Contra affair, involving the diversion of funds from profits on missiles sold to the Iranian government, to the Nicaraguan Contras, a counterrevolutionary force practically created by the CIA.[9] At first, the entire episode was blamed on a marine, Lieutenant Colonel Oliver North, with virtually all high-ranking officials of the Reagan administration claiming they had been "out of the loop." Subsequent investigations and trial testimony, however, pointed to a massive cover-up by White House aides and others.

North's 1989 trial revealed that a 1984 national security group meeting, attended by Vice President George Bush, the Joint Chiefs of Staff, several cabinet officers, and President Reagan discussed Contra aid, based on solicitation of "third" parties (foreign governments). They adopted this strategy as a way of getting around the Boland Amendment, passed by Congress, which had made further military aid to the Contras illegal. President Reagan personally solicited the largest contributions for Contra aid from foreign nations, and a number of Latin American governments cooperated by falsifying arms sales transactions so knowledge that the weapons were intended for the Contras could be hidden. Those nations agreeing to falsify such documents were promised increased U.S. foreign aid. The illegal arms sales and solicitation of funds were orchestrated by a secret group, the Enterprise, set up apart from the CIA and other governmental agencies to assure secrecy. The Enterprise's members included retired military and intelligence personnel, arms dealers, and drug smugglers.

In the 1980s, the State Department dubbed the Iran operation "Operation Polecat," because department members thought it stank so much. Vice President Bush lied, claiming he had been "out of the loop" and unaware of Iran-Contra activities. Even though Bush had headed a Vice President's Task Force on Terrorism, which concluded that it was futile to make deals with Iranian hostage-takers, he later admitted that he was aware of the hostage deal but did not admit to knowledge of diversion of funds to the Contras.

The entire cover-up, the lying to Congress, and the hiding of evidence had been intended to protect Ronald Reagan from impeachment. In June 1992, Special Prosecutor Lawrence Walsh indicted former Secretary of Defense Caspar Weinberger in order to attempt to prove a conspiracy to cover up Reagan's involvement. The charges, based on entries in Weinberger's diary, claimed that he had lied to Congress and obstructed justice.

Finally came the 1992 "Christmas Eve Massacre," in which lame-duck President George Bush pardoned most of those convicted or under investigation, claiming that they "did not profit or seek to profit from the conduct," that they were acting in what they believed to have been the national interest, and that the Iran-Contra investigation represented an unnecessary "criminalization of policy differences." The pardons left Walsh little choice but to close down the probe. The message George Bush sent in issuing the pardons was that government officials may freely violate the Constitution.

In March 1993, the United Nations Commission on the Truth about crimes committed against civilians in El Salvador's twelve-year civil war released its official report. It concluded among other things that the majority of the political murders in that nation's civil war occurred with the encouragement and financial support of the Reagan and Bush administrations. Over 80,000 people, one in seventy Salvadorans and most of them unarmed civilians, were murdered in the war. After the release of the report in March 1993, the Clinton administration—and more specifically, Secretary of State Warren Christopher—appointed a panel to investigate charges that members of the State Department misled Congress about the atrocities in El Salvador throughout the 1980s. The CIA's own report concluded that one major beneficiary of secret aid under Reagan and Bush, Roberto d'Aubuisson, who headed a right-wing death squad, trafficked in illegal drugs and arms and plotted the assassination of San Salvador's Archbishop Oscar Romero. In 2001, it was learned that the U.S. military has a hidden arms dumping ground off the Salvadoran coast.[10]

The scandals listed above share common characteristics:

- They were the result of secret actions of government agencies, especially the FBI, CIA, and executive office of the president, that were illegal or unethical and caused severe physical, financial, and moral harm to the nation.
- All have taken place since the passage of the National Security Act of 1947, which institutionalized the most secret aspects of what President Eisenhower termed the military-industrial complex and C. Wright Mills called the power elite and the higher immorality.
- Organizations with immense resources, not merely corrupt individuals, were involved in criminal acts and their cover-ups.
- All the episodes discussed became the subject of official government hearings or investigations—the Watergate and Iran-Contra hearings being nationally televised.
- Despite official investigations, the original causes of most of these episodes remain unknown.
- The official investigation of modern scandal tends to become part of the scandal itself, leaving unanswered questions concerning the causes of and mysterious events surrounding scandals to linger.
- Recent political scandals, especially the Iran-Contra and the savings and loan episodes of the 1980s, relate not only to each other but to other types of crime and deviance as well.

The pro-business Reagan and Bush administrations from 1981 to 1993 made greed seem moral and corruption an everyday fact of political life and caused a wave of corporate, political, and military scandals unique in American history. This is significant in part because sociologists usually consider deviant behavior as abnormal, characterizing a minority of people, whereas American scandal seems endemic. In such an environment, it can seem naïve to rely on hard work and ethical behavior to get ahead. With so many examples of people in power being on the take, Tony Soprano might very well see himself as no more than a small player in a global game.

Physical Harm

Defending his way of life to Dr. Melfi, Tony once declared that everyone involved in his business knows the stakes. They're all "soldiers," in Tony's view, and they go into the life accepting the possibility that they might die for their cause. Yet his view ignores entirely those who don't get to choose whether or not they want to be a part of Tony Soprano's world. The small-business owners his men shake down, the citizens who suffer the effects of the drug trade around them, the truck drivers beaten or killed for the goods they're hauling—none of these people enlisted in the war that Tony imagines he and his men are fighting. Nor does Tony consider his crimes' ripple effects, which reach far beyond his New Jersey hangouts and fall disproportionately on the more powerless segments of society.

Similarly and to a greater degree, the power elite ignores the effects of its machinations. In addition to the vast moral harm it causes, the power elite also directly inflicts physical harm on the powerless. For instance, the war that began secretly with the CIA's training of the South Vietnamese police resulted in the deaths of 2 million Vietnamese and 58,000 Americans and cost the United States nearly $160 billion (about $700 billion in today's dollars) to fight. Many people who served in Vietnam thought the war was immoral and did not want to serve but were forced to do so. Money needed to alleviate poverty and rebuild infrastructure at home went instead to conduct the war. More than 40,000 Vietnamese civilians were murdered in the covert, CIA-sponsored Phoenix program aimed at eliminating civilian enemy agents, most of them without trial. More than 5 million acres of South Vietnam were sprayed with defoliating chemicals, including Agent Orange, which caused high incidences of cancer, birth defects, and other diseases in American service personnel. Yet the government withheld information on

Agent Orange's dangers until 1993, when President Bill Clinton released it to the public.

Physical harm caused by the power elite extends beyond that caused by military activities. The National Commission on Product Safety estimates that dangerous products injure 20 million Americans each year in home accidents, resulting in 10,000 permanent disabilities and 30,000 deaths. Approximately 100,000 American workers die each year from diseases attributable to exposure to dangerous chemicals at work. An additional 3.3 million workers suffer work-related injuries that require medical treatment, and 400,000 workers suffer occupational diseases. Such figures would never bother Tony Soprano, who thinks more of efficacy than safety. When an organic pesticide fails to work as well as he'd like, he tries to cajole a garden store clerk into selling him DDT, despite the fact that the chemical has been banned. As far as Tony is concerned, the regulations are a mere nuisance.

Tony's not so forgiving about the food industry, at least when it inconveniences him personally. When he thinks he may have gotten food poisoning from Artie Bucco's restaurant, Tony is quick to make accusations about the safety standards in the kitchen. Artie tries to pin the blame on an Indian restaurant where Tony had also eaten. Yet both men care only about how they are personally affected by the incident at hand, and neither of them sees the real dangers the food industry poses to the public, nor the immense scale of the industry's influence and potential for harm.

The food industry is the largest in America, with fifty of 20,000 firms making 60 percent of all the profits. Much of the industry consists of fast-food restaurants, which currently serve about half the restaurant meals in the United States. Much fast food contains high levels of saturated fat, sodium, and sugar, which are associated with the most common causes of death in America: heart disease, cancer, and high blood pressure. After Americans got hooked on fast food in the 1950s, consumption of saturated fats in the United States went from 45.1 pounds per person per year in 1960, to 60.7 pounds in

1989. (One need look no further than the stout frames and immense stomachs of many of the male characters on *The Sopranos* to see the prevalence of this trend.) Today, in the United States well over half the adult population and 11 percent of children are considered obese. The percent of obese children and teens has nearly doubled since 1980.[11]

Another serious form of physical harm is industrial pollution. Deserved or not, Tony's home of New Jersey has long had a reputation as a blighted, polluted state. Shortly before one of his panic attacks, Tony observes with dismay a tableau of barren factories, soot-blackened smokestacks, and graffiti-covered walls. The United States, with a mere 5 percent of the world's population, is responsible for 50 percent of the world's industrial pollutants. In 1993 the Environmental Protection Agency (EPA) and the Harvard School of Public Health estimated that particle pollution from factories causes 50,000 to 60,000 deaths each year. Most vulnerable are children with respiratory diseases, asthmatics of all ages, and elderly people with such ailments as bronchitis. Since the poor and the working class tend to live close to chemical factories, they suffer the highest rates of pollution-caused cancer. Indoor pollution from cigarette smoke and radon gas causes 5,000 or more cases of cancer annually.[12]

Financial Harm

Some harms caused by the power elite are less physical, but no less far-reaching. The same is true for organized crime's various operations, including prostitution, fraud, and other nonviolent crimes. In Tony Soprano's world, such crimes provide an important revenue stream. Tony's investment firm pushes stock in a company with an ineffective miracle cure, his men defraud phone companies by selling cut-rate phone cards for long-distance minutes never paid for, and he and his cronies recover debts by pushing a business owner into planned bankruptcy.

The financial harms of the power elite are, of course, infinitely more varied and far-reaching than Tony's. Price-fixing, a criminal act in which two or more firms conspire to rig prices, costs American consumers about $60 billion a year. Price gouging, which is legal in non-emergency situations, is especially common in the prescription drug industry. For example, 100 tablets of Abbot's brand of the antibiotic erythromycin wholesale for $15.50, but the generic tablets wholesale for $6.20.[13] Fraud, the crime of inducing people to part with valuables or money by lies, deception, and misrepresentation, represents the most common nonviolent crime in the United States. It costs American consumers tens of billions of dollars every year. Repair fraud alone costs consumers $20 billion annually. Perhaps the largest fraud in American history was the savings and loan scandal of the mid-1980s. Investigators estimate that 60 percent of the $500 billion to $1 trillion lost in the scandal was due to fraud. Since the late 1990s, the FBI has been investigating some 7,000 of these cases, 100 of which were selected for priority prosecution. The scandal could cost each American taxpaying family about $5,000 over a twenty-year period.

In the summer of 2001, a massive financial scandal that was threatening to cripple the Bush administration was about to go public. The four planes of 9/11 changed all that, but amazingly, the collapse of Enron—a Texas energy conglomerate with close links to Bush—a month later managed to make huge headlines, even as Americans tried to awaken from the 9/11 nightmare.

The details of the fall of Enron can be mind-numbing. But the essential story is fairly simple: Enron's top executives knew the company was collapsing and refused to let its thousands of employees sell the Enron stock they had when it was still worth something, while a handful of the top executives with their insider knowledge secretly sold high. When the company declared bankruptcy in December 2001, the employees lost their life savings and their jobs. The executives are still billionaires.

Enron was a house of cards, which spent tens of millions to pass legislation that protected its secret practices. Its best friends in Washington were the new Bush administration, and President Bush, who gives everyone a nickname, happily called Enron founder and CEO Kenneth Lay "Kenny Boy."

Vice President Dick Cheney, who headed Halliburton, the world's largest oil field services company from 1995 to 2000, recruited Lay and other oil moguls to serve on a secret commission to draft the new administration's national energy policy in early 2001. The mind boggles at so blatant a "network of rackets." But 9/11 has slowed down investigations of Bush administration corruption and its collusion with Enron and Halliburton. When the investigations start heating up, the administration issues another terror alert and everyone runs for cover.

But the dots are there, and people are connecting them. Here are some of those dots.

The Bush White House was deeply penetrated by a company that became the nation's seventh-biggest corporation—not by making energy, but by making deals. Bush economic counselor Lawrence Lindsey had been a paid adviser to Enron, Bush political strategist Karl Rove a big investor in Enron, Republican national chairman Marc Racicot a paid lobbyist for Enron.

The scandal itself occurred because Enron became a sort of giant middleman in strange deals wherein it contracted with both sellers and buyers, profiting from the difference between selling and buying prices. It also kept its books shut, making it the only entity that knew both prices. Enron's contracts became more complex and increasingly risky, and its stock price rocketed. Partnerships were created that allowed the firm secretly to transfer debt off its books.

Enron and its accounting firm, Arthur Andersen, had warnings that such debt might have to be paid in exchange for stock in early 2001. By October 2001, Enron was forced to admit a $638 million loss, and in November it admitted it had overstated its earnings for the previous four years by $586 million and was responsible for some $3 billion in debts in its various partnerships. Lenders downgraded the corporation's credit rating to junk bond status. The company had kept financial losses off its balance sheet, but many of those losses were incurred through dealings with private partnerships run by Enron executives. The collapse angered rank-and-file employees, who were blocked from selling company shares in their own retirement portfolios, even as the price nose-dived from a high of $90 to its June 2002 value of less than a dollar.

Ten separate congressional investigations were begun, as was a Justice Department investigation to determine if Enron defrauded investors. The Securities and Exchange Commission (SEC) began looking into Arthur Andersen's role in the scandal, including its shredding of documents and its accounting practices. After a lengthy trial, Andersen was found guilty on one count of obstruction of justice in June 2002.[14] Enron's rapid descent into bankruptcy became the subject of investigations by the Bush Department of Justice, the Securities and Exchange Commission, and the House Energy and Commerce Committee. The Senate committee began investigations into whether executives or board members broke the law, whether accounting rules should be tightened, and whether the SEC should have done a better job of spotting trouble at the company.

Enron has long been tied to George W. Bush and powerful members of Congress from Texas like Senator Phil Gramm, whose wife, Wendy, was an Enron director, House Majority Whip Tom DeLay, and House Majority Leader Dick Armey. Enron was the strongest proponent of deregulation of the electric utility industry, and its CEO, "Kenny Boy" Lay, apparently played an important role in the development of the Bush energy plan. Enron's campaign contributions and aggressive lobbying tactics were familiar to those on Capitol Hill, and the company had usually gotten its way on crucial votes.

According to a Center for Public Integrity analysis of SEC records,[15] the Bush presidential campaign received $74,200 in contributions made by the two dozen top current and former executives and board members in the 2000 election cycle. This included $40,000 from Lay to the 1999 State Victory Fund set up to benefit the winner of the 2000 Republican presidential primary. Employees and directors of Enron have given $623,000 to Bush over the course of his political career (which only began in 1994), including $220,700 from the executives and board members named in the suit, who directed another $110,100 to other political candidates and $97,500 in hard money to party committees. They also gave $135,487 to the Enron political action committee (PAC). The balance, $381,910, went to Republican and Democratic Party committees in "soft money" contributions, the controversial, unregulated, and unlimited donations made to political parties.

Among the executives, "Kenny Boy" Lay and his wife, Linda, gave the most money to federal campaigns, totaling $87,850 since January 1999. Half of that money went to George W. Bush's campaign for president. Lay also gave $282,910 in soft money to the Republican National Committee and $25,000 to a leadership committee headed by then-Senator and now Attorney General John Ashcroft. Lay, a one-time energy policy maker for Richard Nixon, was one of the 214 Bush "Pioneers," supporters who raised at least $100,000 for the candidate. He also chipped in for Bush's Florida recount battle after the 2000 presidential election. In addition, Lou L. Pai, chairman and CEO of the Enron Accelerator division, former Enron CEO Jeffrey Skilling, and former Enron Vice Chairman Joseph Sutton gave a combined $59,000 in soft money to the Republican National Committee prior to the 2000 election. The $135,487 given to the Enron PAC went to both national parties equally and to the president's campaign. The PAC also kicked in $4,999 to Ashcroft's campaign committee for his failed Senate bid in the 2000 election.

The support from Enron's top brass extends back beyond the presidential campaign. Not included in the above totals is $146,500 Bush received from Enron executives during his two races for Texas governor. Of that amount, Lay gave $122,500. After the 2000 election, Lay, Skilling, and the corporation itself each contributed the maximum $100,000 to the Bush inaugural festivities. But by far, the biggest contributions made to political activity by Enron came from the corporation itself. Federal election laws outlaw contributions from corporations but allow unlimited donations to national political parties for "party building" activities. The corporation gave $1,895,964 from 1999 to 2001 in soft money contributions, usually to the Republican and Democratic national parties, according to the Center for Responsive Politics. Contributions to the GOP, of course, outdistanced those to the Democratic Party three to one. Enron Corporation also gave $25,000 in soft money to Ashcroft's leadership committee.

Campaign funding tells only part of the story of Enron's clout inside the Bush White House and on Capitol Hill. Once the nation's largest buyer and seller of natural gas, with power plant and pipeline projects that spanned the globe, Enron had an expansive lobbying operation, pushing a wide range of legislative and regulatory issues, from utility deregulation to tax breaks, trade and telecommunications.[16] It did well at recruiting political heavyweights as they left public office: after Bill Clinton's victory in the 1992 presidential election, Bush Secretary of State James A. Baker III was out of a job, and Enron hired him as a consultant.

Enron's lobbying expenses in 2001 exceeded $2 million and included a stable of high-profile lobbyists and consultants, including former Christian Coalition head Ralph Reed, one-time Energy Regulatory Commission chairwoman Elizabeth Moler, Marc F. Racicot, the new Republican National Committee chairman, and even a Democrat, Jack Quinn, former White House counsel to President Clinton.

Perhaps the company's most effective advocate in Washington was Kenneth Lay himself. He met privately with Vice President Dick Cheney in 2001 when Cheney led the National Energy Policy Development Group—made up of Cheney and various department and agency chiefs—that drafted the Bush national energy policy. Bush created the task force in January 2001 to gather information and make recommendations about a "production and distribution of energy" strategy. The task force's May 2001 report became the basis for the administration's energy legislative package. When the White

House refused requests from the congressional General Accounting Office for records of Cheney's energy policy meetings, the GAO, whose head is a *Reagan* appointee, filed a civil suit to force the administration to open its records. At this writing, the suit is still being litigated due to Cheney's adamant refusal to release the very limited information requested by the GAO.

Enron's lobbying influence extends to Capitol Hill. In 2000 it secured an exemption in a bill that could have spelled trouble for the company's questionable accounting practices—the Commodity Futures Modernization Act, which have brought Enron's trading operations under greater regulatory scrutiny. Enron lobbied successfully to exempt certain types of derivative trading, in which it was heavily engaged, from provisions of the bill. At the time that lobbying on the bill got underway, Enron's soft money contributions and direct giving to certain members of Congress skyrocketed. The bill was introduced June 8, and by the end of the month, Republican and Democratic national parties had taken in $220,000 in soft-money contributions from Enron's political action committee.

While Enron executives made hundreds of thousands of dollars in campaign contributions, they collected millions on insider stock trades. Lawyers representing Enron shareholders recently filed a class action suit claiming that, between October 19, 1998, and November 27, 2001, twenty-nine current and former company officials traded 17 million shares of Enron stock worth $1.1 billion. The suit names the twenty-nine, as well as the company's accounting firm, Arthur Andersen. The company's annual reports for 1998, 1999, and 2000 indicate that the twenty-nine comprise nearly every board member and senior executive who worked at the company during that period. The suit accuses Enron of perpetrating "one of the most serious securities frauds in history." Lawyers allege that Enron executives had information that would have "disintegrated Enron upon disclosure" when the execs traded their stock during that three-year period.

Among those identified as selling large amounts of stock is Lay, who got rid of more than $100 million worth, or 27 percent of his holdings. Jeffrey Skilling, who stepped down as chief executive officer in August 2001, sold 39 percent of his holdings, or $67 million. Like many of the other insiders, Lay and Skilling spread much of their sales out over those three years.

As the courts sort out the class action suit against the Enron insiders, the Securities and Exchange Commission has come under increasing pressure from Congress to improve accounting standards to protect American investors. Those demands come after Arthur Andersen told a congressional committee that Enron officials may have illegally withheld information about its accounting practices. But even efforts by the SEC to examine the circumstances surrounding Enron's Chapter 11 filing face potential conflicts of interest. The Bush-appointed SEC Chairman Harvey Pitt—a securities lawyer who was a partner in the law firm of Fried, Frank, Harris, Shriver, and Jacobson until his appointment—had represented Arthur Andersen in recent years.

Moral Harm

Of all the harms Tony Soprano and his "business" cause, the ones he least regards are the moral ones. When his nephew Christopher is shot and has near-death glimpses of himself and his fellow Mob members going to Hell, the subject of Tony's amorality comes into sharp focus for him. Yet when Dr. Melfi asks Tony who deserves to go to Hell, Tony declares that only the very worst people deserve it— bloodthirsty dictators and child murderers, for example. Tony and the others all follow codes governing their behavior; morality is a nonissue. Tony knows from watching those in power that business is business. He unknowingly imparts these same attitudes to those who look up to him, including his son, A.J., who begins engaging in a series of petty crimes, much to Tony's surprise and consternation.

Another contradictory aspect of American society is that wrongdoing by the powerful serves as a model of behavior for the powerless. This moral harm causes citizens at all levels of society to become distrustful of their political and corporate leaders. This attitude makes it more likely that people will cheat on their taxes, especially if they believe the government wastes their money or spends it only to benefit the wealthy and powerful. (Ironically, of course, Tony is a scrupulous taxpayer . . . at least on that part of his income he can legally declare.) People who work for corporations are more likely to steal from them if they do not trust them. The homicide rate generally increases after an execution has been publicized, thereby forming a link between the actions of political elites, who promote capital punishment, and those non-elites who commit capital crimes.[17]

Many aspects of the higher immorality, especially subsidies, tax breaks for the wealthy, and excessive corporate salaries, have only worsened inequality in the United States, and a great degree of inequality makes many micro-social problems into larger, macro problems. During the 1980s, the poorest 40 percent of Americans saw a decline of $256 billion in their wealth. The wealth of African Americans declined from 24 to 19 percent of the wealth held by white Americans.[18] From 1973 to 1993, the number of young people living in poverty increased by 51 percent. Between 1983 and 1993, crime among youth increased 50 percent.[19]

Great inequalities of wealth and income also worsen social problems of relative deprivation. That is, people who may not need to steal for food or rent may instead steal to obtain consumer goods they cannot afford. In the 1980s, gold jewelry, $100 sneakers, and Mercedes-Benzes became status symbols of the "lifestyles of the rich and famous." The more the rich and powerful parade their possessions, the more the less powerful try to copy. This is one of the leading contradictions of inequality in America: the more the well-off and the powerful emphasize the American dream of material success, the more crime the powerless commit, because the poor emulate the elite and strive for affluence by any means. Thus by displaying wealth and material goods, especially through advertising and movies, the powerful intensify the social problems suffered and inflicted by the powerless.

Material wealth and status pervade the world of *The Sopranos*, with all of the major characters grasping for the best clothes, the latest gadgets, the fanciest cars, and all the other visible trappings of success. Even relative bottom-feeders like Christopher's crew members Matt and Sean (who later shoot Christopher when they think they're not advancing quickly enough) emulate those above them, dressing in top-of-the-line clothing and outfitting their spare apartment with a massive high-definition television.

The behavior of the powerful not only influences that of the powerless but is also influenced by it; the social problems caused by the powerless also influence the social problems caused by the powerful. According to sociologist Alex Thio, the problems of the powerless "help to deflect, weaken or nullify the social control over the powerful, thus freeing the powerful to engage in their own deviant pursuits."[20] Thus, the power elite defines lower- and working-class street crime as "the crime problem." The vast majority of the resources of the criminal justice system are devoted to apprehending, prosecuting, and incarcerating street criminals. The powerful define the "real" criminals as muggers and burglars, not the corporate executives who fix prices or the politicians who lie to the public, take graft, or rig elections. Thus the powerful judge the acts of the powerless as morally wrong and rationalize their own wrongdoing.

When the powerful are caught, their punishment pales in comparison to that meted out to the powerless. Between 1987 and 1992, for example, during the Reagan and Bush years, 75 percent of the cases of criminal fraud referred by federal regulators to the Justice Department in connection with the savings and loan scandals were dropped. In those cases that were prosecuted, the average prison sentence was 2.4 years. The average prison sentence for bank robbery in the United States is 7.8 years.[21] The powerful thus have little incentive to avoid wrongdoing. They stand a good chance of getting away with it. If apprehended, their punishment often consists of a fine or a brief stint in a federal minimum-security facility, complete with golf course and tennis courts.

Most victims of street crimes are poor people; acts of victimization reflect the culture and social institutions in which they occur. The likely victims are not merely people who happen to be in the wrong place at the wrong time. They are, tragically, members of victimization-prone groups whose life chances are adversely affected by their social statuses—their lower-class positions and their minority racial and gender makeup. For example, women represent over 90 percent of rape victims, but minority women are three times more likely than white women to be raped. People at the bottom of the class structure in the United States—and nearly everywhere else—are "more frequently the victims (and perpetrators) of violent crime, less likely to be in good health and more likely to feel lonely. Those at the top [of the class structure] are healthier, safer and more likely to send their children to college."[22]

Indeed, people at the bottom of the class system even have a greater risk of being victims of "natural disasters that presumably threaten all alike." When moviegoers thrilled to the scenes of the Oscar-wining blockbuster *Titanic* a few years ago, they may not have known they were witnessing an important sociological principle at work. Almost everyone knows that the ocean liner *Titanic* sank on its first crossing of the Atlantic in 1912. The real story the movie depicts, however, is one of elitism and life chances at work. Among the ship's female passengers, who were expected to be given priority in the few lifeboats available, only 3 percent of first-class passengers drowned, in comparison with 16 percent of the second-class and 45 percent of the third-class passengers. Sadly, these differential rates of victimization were no accident. The third-class passengers were ordered to stay below decks, some at gunpoint, as the movie accurately related, and passengers with lower than first-class status were kept away from the lifeboats.[23]

All of the life-enhancing opportunities in a society may be viewed as lifeboats. When opportunities to enter society's lifeboats are perceived as unequal and in fact are unequal, social problems occur. Victimization by elites, street criminals, and Sopranos-like organized-crime syndicates reinforces inequality by keeping the poor poor (or making them poorer), thus diminishing their life chances. Although in some ways Tony Soprano symbolizes the achievement of the American Dream of self-determined power and success, he does it only at the expense of those least able to protect themselves against his taking what he wants.

Tony and the World: The Global Economy, Organized-Crime Syndicates, and Narco-Terrorism

As HE CONSOLIDATES THE VARIOUS ENTERPRISES taken from Uncle Junior after the older man's arrest at the end of season one, Tony Soprano travels to Italy to negotiate with Mafia associates about the terms of a stolen-vehicle racket. Locally, men working for Tony steal high-end cars from the streets of New Jersey, but the market for those cars is overseas, where the great demand for luxury autos allows the Italian end of the racket to sell them for several times their standard price. Although he may eschew narcotics trafficking, a more common and lucrative international business for those in organized crime, Tony is still a player in the global economy.

Tony Soprano's world stretches far beyond not only New Jersey but also the shores of the United States. The world's societies—including the organized criminal syndicates within them—are interdependent economically, politically, culturally, and environmentally. Conflict anywhere on the globe affects conditions in other nations. A fundamentalist religious terrorist organization can, with careful planning, send planes crashing into the World Trade Center and the Pentagon. Unseen global connections link these terrorists to global crime syndicates through the world heroin trade.

The real power blocs of globalization gain their strength more from economic prowess than from traditional military might. These blocs, relics of the Cold War, are composed of three groups of nations, traditionally known as the First, Second, and Third Worlds.[1]

The First World

There is now essentially one international capitalist economy from which all national economies derive. Economically, politically, and culturally, this world system is dominated by the First World, which includes the advanced capitalist democracies of North America, Western Europe, and Japan.

The European Union

The European Union (EU) consists of fifteen member states—Austria, Belgium, Denmark, Finland, France, Germany, Greece, Ireland, Italy, Luxembourg, the Netherlands, Portugal, Spain, Sweden, and the United Kingdom. Thirteen more nations are in line to become members over the next few years. The EU's principal objectives are to:

- Establish European citizenship (Fundamental rights; Freedom of movement; Civil and political rights);
- Ensure freedom, security, and justice (Cooperation in the field of Justice and Home Affairs);
- Promote economic and social progress (Single market; Euro, the common currency; Job creation; Regional development; Environmental protection);
- Assert Europe's role in the world (Common foreign and security; The European Union in the world).[2]

Introduction of a single European currency, the Euro, supplanting the pound, mark, franc, lira, etc., began in 2002. Within the

European Union alone there are half a billion potential consumers, and with the anticipated accession of thirteen nations from Eastern and Southern Europe, the figure will double.

The Asian Pacific Bloc

A second bloc of advanced capitalist powers is found among the rapidly developing nations of the Pacific. Popularly known as "the flying geese," they are Japan, South Korea, Singapore, Thailand, Taiwan, and Malaysia. These nations have achieved huge trade surpluses since 1980. During each year from 1984 to 1993, the United States imported goods worth over $100 billion more than those it exported, and most of these imports came from Japan. The Asian "geese" nations trade with one another and have developed a considerable number of joint ventures. They are also economically active with the People's Republic of China, the world's fastest-growing economy.

The Americas

A free-trade agreement signed by the United States and Canada in 1988 created a potential $6 trillion consumer and manufacturing zone. Mexico joined the North American Free Trade Agreement in 1993. The potential of this alliance rivals that of the EU and the Asian Pacific nations.

Together, the First World nations generate almost four fifths of all economic activity.[3] Although First World nations often come into conflict—witness Japan's "invasion" of the American automobile market—they also cooperate.

Inequalities of wealth and power within and between the three groups of nations cause numerous social problems.

The Second World

The Second World nations include the former communist nations of Eastern Europe and the old Soviet Union. Russia is now scandal-ridden and in continual economic and political turmoil. The only way many Russians survive economically is by engaging in crime. The Eastern European nations are also struggling, but most of them will soon be members of the EU.

The Third World

The Third World is composed of the poorest nations of Asia, Africa, and Latin America. In these nations, 20,000 people die of starvation each day, and 1.5 billion people lack basic medical care.[4] The average annual per-capita income ranges from less than $700 in Ethiopia and Kenya, to under $1,600 in the forty-eight least developed nations, compared to $22,000 among industrial nations.[5] Life in some Third World nations is improving: China, Indonesia, Thailand, and Malaysia have already achieved limited degrees of industrialization, and massive famines no longer happen in China. Eight additional nations—including Brazil, Mexico, Argentina, and India—still poor in many ways, have become global manufacturers of many consumer products. Technologically, all of these nations remain dependent on the technology of First World corporations.

Another dozen nations, members of the Organization of Petroleum Exporting Countries (OPEC), play a unique role in the global economy. Dominated by autocratic desert kingdoms in the Middle East, these nations are able to import entire factories and any products their affluent populations require. What they lack are the engineering and scientific skills to develop their own industrial bases. What manual labor they require is imported from poor nations, and First World corporations continue to provide technological expertise in these rich, but non-industrial monarchies.[6]

In some forty other Third World nations, however, between 1 and 3 percent of the population owns 60 to 90 percent of all private wealth, and military dictatorships attempt to keep the poor masses from creating revolutions that might bring a better life. These dictatorships hold onto power in large part through military and other aid from advanced capitalist nations, especially the United States. Collectively, Third World nations owe First World governments and banks over $2.17 trillion,[7] a debt that makes Third World nations vulnerable to First World demands regarding wage levels, trade practices, and a host of other policies. Meanwhile, multinational corporations make substantial returns on investments in Third World nations but do not reinvest their profits in these poor lands. Instead, profits tend to be paid to CEOs or stockholders or invested in other overseas ventures in First and Second World nations. As a result, the Third World remains plagued by myriad social problems, many with global consequences: overpopulation, illegal emigration to the First World, pollution, wars, famine, and violations of human rights.

Human Rights Violations in the Global Economy

Just as Tony Soprano's actions to realize greater profits and maintain his power ripple through the lives of others in his world, both those close to him and unknown strangers throughout his community, so the power elite's actions profoundly influence the lives of people near and far. While in Italy, Tony and Paulie are dismayed to witness their Italian associates viciously beat a local boy for creating a disturbance with firecrackers. Back home, they would have considered the stunt a harmless prank, but the political climate and the Mob's stranglehold on the local populace dictate more aggressive tactics. These are the people with whom Tony does business, and no matter how much it may unsettle him, he tacitly supports their methods.

The principle is the same for both the mobster and the power elite. Only the scales of the offenses and of their effects are different. Whenever it suits its purposes, the American power elite supports Third World governments that grossly violate human rights as defined in two treaties signed by the United States: the United Nations Declaration of Human Rights of 1948 and the Helsinki Agreement of 1975. Among these rights are freedom from arrest without probable cause, freedom from kidnapping and torture, and freedom of speech and of the press.

Guatemala

A U.S. corporation formed in 1899 to grow and export bananas from Central America, the United Fruit Company soon became notorious for exploiting the land and the workers, making the nations of the region into what became known as "banana republics," more companies than countries. In Guatemala in 1954, the government of Jacobo Arbenz, implementing land reform, was planning to require United Fruit to sell any land not under cultivation at the low valuation it had long claimed for tax purposes. Without any basis in fact, the Eisenhower administration branded Arbenz a communist and, using the CIA, overthrew his government and replaced it with a U.S. Army–trained officer, Carlos Castillo Armas. Castillo Armas immediately issued a decree giving himself all executive and legislative functions, halted the land-reform program, canceled the registration of more than 500 labor unions, and required all unions to be certified free of communist influence by a government committee. Castillo Armas was assassinated in 1957, but his policies lived on. Between 1963 and 1993, his U.S.-backed successors kidnapped, tortured, or killed 200,000 of their own citizens. Between 1982 and 1991, the government forcibly relocated a million Indians, and the Reagan and first Bush administrations gave Guatemala $77 million in aid during this period.

By 1990, Guatemala's human rights record was so horrendous that, under pressure from a Democratic Congress, the Bush administration was forced to suspend aid.[8] Still, the next year, Bush claimed that the Guatemalan human rights record was improving, despite ample evidence to the contrary. Human rights groups documented 730 assassinations and 100 disappearances in the first nine months of 1991. In 1992 a Guatemalan Indian woman, Rigoberta Menchu, won the Nobel Peace Prize for her efforts to stop the government from relocating and killing her people.

Chile

In 1973, the CIA supported a coup that ousted the democratically elected government of Marxist President Salvador Allende Gossens, who was murdered in the overthrow and replaced by a brutal dictator, General Augusto Pinochet. A reign of terror followed. People were routinely held for twenty days or more without notification to their families. A wide range of torture methods were used: rape, electric shock, sleep deprivation, mock execution, submersion in water, and live rats being shoved into victims' mouths. Pinochet finally left office in 1989, after losing a plebiscite. In 1998, on a visit to London he was arrested on a Spanish warrant on charges of gross violations of human rights. After 503 days in detention, he was finally freed and returned to Chile, where he was declared mentally unfit to stand trial.

El Salvador

Between 1978 and 1993, more than 40,000 people were killed in El Salvador by government-supported right-wing death squads, and 800,000 people (20 percent of the population) became refugees. Between 1979 and 1984, the Reagan administration gave El Salvador six times more aid than it had received in the previous thirty years. In 1980, the government's death squads raped and murdered four American nuns. Amnesty International declared the death squads' activities a gross abuse of human rights. Human rights abuses in El Salvador continued into the 1990s: a United Nations observer mission reported 105 assassinations, fifteen kidnappings, and 281 illegal captures by security forces in 1992 alone.

Cooperation Between Organized Crime, Corporations, and Governments

Crime syndicates often cooperate happily with corporations and governments, and collude, knowingly or not, with terrorists. In August

1999, the largest money-laundering investigation in American history began. While the scandal's full dimensions may well never be known, it appears that the tentacles of those involved reach from the most powerful New York banks to the Kremlin. In the middle are several layers of Russian organized crime and nearly $8 billion in laundered cash. The scandal provides an important metaphor for the way corruption works in the new global economy.

On February 16, 2000, Bank of New York (BONY) Vice President Lucy Edwards and her husband, Peter Berlin, a Russian-born businessman, pleaded guilty to laundering money through a series of Russian specialty banks from 1996 to 1999. Berlin moved $7 billion for the Russians through a number of his front companies: Benex, BECS, and Loland. The monies were laundered through the BONY accounts to evade Russian taxes on legitimate business transactions, avoid Russian custom's duties, and launder profits made in Russian criminal enterprises through banks, including $300,000 collected as ransom in the kidnapping of a Russian businessman.

Edwards and Berlin received $1.8 million to launder the funds and laundered their payoff to an offshore account to avoid paying U.S. taxes.

The specialty banks are owned by Russian businessmen, politicians, and organized-crime figures. Two Russian banks, Flamingo and DKB, are offshoots of two other banks, MDM and Sobinbank, both of which had the backing of the Kremlin. Berlin's front company, Benex, had a BONY account, but was staffed by employees from DKB. Edwards even had a BONY computer installed in the Forest Hills, New York, office of Benex. In 1998, DKB acquired control of the Flamingo Bank and asked Berlin to create another front company, Lowlands, to launder money for Flamingo.

Russian organized crime funneled untold millions through BONY from legal businesses, extortion rackets, and tax fraud schemes (especially in Italy). Some $5.5 million went from Benex to the Italian bank account of Russian gangster Boris Rizner. For its part, BONY has been content to fire the employees involved and let them make plea bargains with prosecutors, but the blame extends further. The fact is that banks routinely establish accounts for phony companies without effective due diligence to check out their customers. Law-enforcement agents are hamstrung by state corporation recording procedures that make it hard to ferret out bogus companies set up by crooks. Once money moves through secret offshore havens like the Cayman Islands, it's generally impossible to locate or recover monies, because those jurisdictions won't open bank records to law enforcers.

Global crime syndicates can only launder money through corporate banks as long as bank and corporate secrecy allows gangsters and corrupt politicians to hide behind secret foreign accounts and front companies. Major American international banks have offshore subsidiaries where they gladly help clients evade the laws of their own nations. Numerous New York banks, including Chemical Bank, BONY, and Citibank, have all been involved in money laundering in recent years.[9] In fact, it is now estimated that $500 billion to $1 trillion in laundered money flows through European and American banks each year. Citigroup, for example, has repeatedly broken many of its own rules in handling the cash of dictators from around the world. These New York banks have 40,000 clients with assets of over $3 million each, some of whom are dictators, corrupt politicians, and organized-crime members. The BONY case is merely one instance of the alliance between legitimate corporate and governmental elites and global crime syndicates. What's even more appalling, these alliances extend to nations that sponsor terrorism.

Terrorism, Drug Trafficking, and Organized Crime

On September 11, 2001, America got a first-hand view of its real crime problem. It learned that what it sees every week on *The Sopranos* is really the tip of a very dangerous iceberg. Too often, the nation's fascination with serial killers and other lone wolves of the violent crime underworld blinds it to the forest of evil that comprises the overall global reality of contemporary narco-terrorism. With its obsessive "if it bleeds, it leads" ideology, the news media has done its best to convince us that the crime problem in America is only about lower-class, violent "street" crime, as reported in the FBI's Uniform Crime Reports statistics—data that are both largely invalid in their definition and unreliable in their measurement.

What surfaced on September 11 was a nasty Afghan-American specter left over from America's Cold War past, one that had come home to roost in the most painful manner imaginable. The insanity that destroyed the World Trade Center towers and sent a plane crashing into the Pentagon began many years before.

In 1979, after a period of violence and assassinations in Afghanistan, the Soviet army invaded its southern neighbor to prop up the new Marxist regime there. The CIA began supplying arms to anti-Soviet factions of Afghans under Afghani General Hekmatyar and his Mujahidin, or holy war fighters. Hekmatyar and his army promptly went into the heroin business, and by 1988 they had 100 to 200 heroin refineries just across the border in Pakistan. By the late 1980s, heroin from these Southwest Asian nations accounted for half of the European and American heroin supplies;[10] by 2000, it accounted for 75 percent of the world's heroin supplies. Today, in 2002, Pakistan has a $1 billion underground heroin economy, and neighboring[11] Tajikistan is a shipping point where one wing of the Russian Mafia buys heroin for sale to Western Europe.[12]

Some of the opium poppies that grow in South Asia—about $100 million worth from Afghanistan—are refined into heroin that finds its way into the arms of New York City's smack addicts with the cooperation of global organized-crime syndicates.[13] Because the American Mafia has been dealing there since the late 1940s, New York City is home to one in four of the nation's heroin junkies. The Mafia end of the heroin-trafficking business imports its product with the aid of the Italian Mafia, which, in turn, cooperates with terrorists like the ones responsible for the September 11 attacks on America.

As Neal Pollard of the Terrorism Research Center has noted,[14] since the end of the Cold War, the U.S. national security community has been particularly concerned about four issues—proliferation of weapons of mass destruction (WMD), terrorism, transnational organized crime, and international narcotics trafficking. The decade of the 1990s saw profound geopolitical, economic, social, and technological changes, and the national security community fears that the four security issue areas are now widespread and unchecked enough, with sufficient technological and economic power, to pose a strategic threat to the interests of the United States.

Terrorist groups are currently working with transnational organized-crime syndicates, especially narcotics cartels. The Peruvian Shining Path and Colombian FARC (Revolutionary Armed Forces of Colombia) guerrillas have provided mercenary security support for narcotics production and trafficking lines in South America. According to the Global Organized Crime Project, experts estimate that over half of FARC's funding comes from drug cultivation and trafficking, with the rest coming from kidnapping, extortion, and other criminal activities.[15] It is estimated that FARC makes $700 million annually from the drug trade. Cuba had been a major contributor to the FARC cause, providing funding, training, and refuge for FARC soldiers, but along with the end of the Cold War came a significant reduction in Cuban support. The successful campaigns to eradicate coca crops from Bolivia and Peru pushed the trade to areas controlled by FARC in southern Colombia.

An alarming trend has been the increasing cooperation between FARC and elements of the Russian Mafia. The Colombian drug cartels have cultivated a relationship with the Russian Mafia since the early 1990s, but with the decline of the cartels and the rise of guerrilla armies in the drug-trafficking business, new relationships developed. Never ones to shy away from opportunities with new customers, the Russian syndicates increased their business deals with FARC. The Russians built an arms pipeline to Colombia, bringing in thousands of weapons and tons of other supplies to help FARC fight its war against the Colombian government. Weapons included assault rifles, military helicopters, and shoulder-launched surface-to-air missiles.

Evidence has surfaced regarding an arms-for-drugs deal between Russian organized-crime groups and FARC: Russian cargo planes loaded with small arms, antiaircraft missiles, and ammunition took off from airstrips in Russia and Ukraine and flew to Colombia, where the weapons and ammunition were sold to FARC rebels. Then the planes were loaded with up to 40,000 kilograms of cocaine and returned to Russia, where Russian organized crime distributed the drugs for profit. At the time the story broke, the operation had been ongoing for two years.

FARC is also extending its cooperation to the borders of the United States. The recent arrest of a FARC figure in Mexico has convinced Mexican and American authorities of a Colombian link to the Arellano-Felix-run Tijuana cartel. The State Department believes that FARC supplied cocaine to the Tijuana cartel in return for cash and weapons.

A defeat of FARC would not spell an end to drug trafficking out of South America. History has shown that as soon as one area has successfully been eradicated of drug crops, new areas of cultivation spring up across borders. If FARC is defeated, groups like the ELN (National Liberation Army) and paramilitary groups will likely fill the vacuum. This "balloon effect" may further spread the drug trade and the associated violence into states bordering Colombia, such as Venezuela, Ecuador, and Brazil.

There is strong evidence that the Palestinian PFLP-GC (Popular Front for the Liberation of Palestine—General Command) has been using the available infrastructure in Lebanon to support drug trafficking. In return, these terrorist groups receive enormous amounts of money, more so than in "traditional" fund-raising operations such as kidnapping and bank robbery, which are far riskier than supporting narcotics trafficking. Furthermore, this interaction offers smuggling routes long established and tested by crime syndicates for drug and arms running, potentially providing terrorists with logistical infrastructure to clandestinely move people, arms, and materiel.

Turkey is strategically located between the lush poppy fields of Central Asia and the vast market of Europe. The Kurdistan Workers Party (PKK) has taken advantage of this fact and financed its separatist movement by "taxing" narcotic traffickers and engaging in the trade themselves. The PKK is heavily involved in the European drug trade, especially in Germany and France; French law enforcement estimates that 80 percent of the heroin in Paris is smuggled there by the PKK.

During the NATO campaign against the former Yugoslavia in the spring of 1999, the Allies looked to the Kosovo Liberation Army (KLA) to assist in efforts to eject the Serbian army from Kosovo. What was largely hidden from the public was that the KLA raised some of their funds from selling drugs. Albania and Kosovo lie at the heart of the Balkan Route that links the Golden Crescent of Afghanistan and Pakistan to the drug markets of Europe. This route traffics an estimated $400 billion worth of drugs a year and handles 80 percent of heroin destined for Europe.

The Bekaa Valley continues to be a base of operations for the Hezbolah to export narcotics. Despite efforts from the Lebanese authorities to shut down cultivation in the valley, production of drugs continues. With funding from Iran seen to be dwindling, the Hezbolah may well increase its drug trafficking to fill the void. There is evidence of cooperation with the PKK to export narcotics into Europe. It is clear that Russian organized crime is using Israel and Cyprus as twin bases for its operations in Western Europe and the United States.

The proximity of the Golden Crescent of Pakistan and Afghanistan make Tajikistan, Uzbekistan, Kazakhstan, Turkmenistan, and Kyrgyzstan the crossroads of the opiate trade to Russia, where narcotics consumption is increasing, and Europe. Spurred by radical Islamic fundamentalists such as Osama bin Laden, new cells of terrorists have spawned in the Central Asian Republics. One such group, the Islamic Movement of Uzbekistan

(IMU), using Tajikistan as a staging area, has made incursions into Kyrgyzstan on hostage-taking missions. In the radical Islamist attempt to foment jihad in Chechnya, guerrillas have also used Azerbaijan, Georgia, and Tajikistan as logistical hubs for their attacks on the Russian military.

Maoist insurgent groups in Nepal have turned to drug trafficking for funding. Nepal serves as a hub for hashish trafficking in Asia. The insurgency has grown since its war with the Nepalese government began in 1996. The war began in three provinces in western Nepal but has now spread to sixty-eight of Nepal's seventy-five districts.

In their fight against the Sri Lankan government, the Liberation Tigers of Tamil Eelam (LTTE) rely on the funding generated by expatriates in the United States and Canada. Under the guise of collecting humanitarian relief for victims of the civil war, the LTTE have used the funds to launch hundreds of terrorist attacks, including suicide bombings and political assassinations. The Tamil Tigers have also turned to the narcotics industry. Founded in 1976, the LTTE is the most powerful Tamil group in Sri Lanka and uses overt and illegal methods to raise funds, acquire weapons, and publicize its cause of establishing an independent Tamil state. The LTTE began its armed conflict with the Sri Lankan government in 1983 and relies on a guerrilla strategy that includes the use of terrorist tactics. The group's elite Black Tiger squad conducts suicide bombings against important targets, and all rank-and-file members carry a cyanide capsule to kill themselves rather than allow themselves to be caught. The LTTE is very insular and highly organized with its own intelligence service, naval element (the Sea Tigers), and women's political and military wings.

The Tigers control most of the northern and eastern coastal areas of Sri Lanka but have conducted operations throughout the island. Headquartered in the Wanni region, LTTE leader Velupillai Prabhakaran has established an extensive network of checkpoints and informants to keep track of any outsiders who enter the group's area of control.[16] Sri Lanka lies at an important narcotics transit point, and the Tamil Tigers take full advantage of this. There is evidence of a close relationship with military leaders in Myanmar. In the past, the Myanmar military has provided training and weapons in return for LTTE members acting as couriers of heroin into India and Europe. Whether or not the relationship continues is unknown. Evidence has also surfaced of cooperation between the LTTE and Indian organized crime. Indian traffickers supply drugs and weapons to the LTTE, which in turn sells the drugs. The profit from the drugs goes to repay the Indians for the weapons.

The Abu Sayyaf Group (ASG) in the Philippines has made head-lines recently with the kidnapping of foreigners. According to the State Department, "The ASG is the smallest and most radical of the Islamic separatist groups operating in the southern Philippines. Some ASG members have studied or worked in the Middle East and devel-oped ties to Mujahidin while fighting and training in Afghanistan."[17] The ASG uses bombings, assassinations, kidnappings, and extortion to achieve its goal of an independent Islamic state in western Min-danao and the Sulu Archipelago, areas heavily populated by Muslims in the southern Philippines. Abu Sayyaf has also used marijuana plan-tations in the Philippines to grow crops for profit. The ASG is a good example of an ideologically driven group that has transformed into a criminal enterprise.

Despite publicized efforts by the former Taliban rulers to combat drug cultivation and trafficking, Afghanistan remains the world's largest producer of opium, and production is growing. The routing of the Taliban after 9/11 is unlikely to change the situation. According to the U.S. Government's Counter-Narcotics and Crime Center, opium cultivation grew from 41,720 hectares in 1998, to 51,500 in 1999, and 64,510 in 2000, an increase of over 54 percent in two years. In some districts, as much as 60 percent of the land is used to grow poppies. Poppy cultivation is expanding territorially in Afghanistan as well, increasing into provinces not previously used for that purpose. In 1998 Afghanistan became the world's leading pro-ducer of opium and now produces more than three times as much as

Myanmar, the previous leader—even though Afghanistan has only 58 percent of Myanmar's area of cultivation.

Until it was ousted in 2001, the radical Islamic Taliban regime got funding from taxing all aspects of the drug trade. Opium harvests were taxed at around 12 percent. The heroin-manufacturing labs were taxed at $70 per kilogram of heroin. In the final stage, the Taliban gave transporters a permit for $250 per kilo of heroin to carry for presentation to Taliban checkpoints throughout the country. The Paris-based nongovernmental organization Observatoire Géopolitique des Drogues (now the TMI Drugs and Democracy) estimated that this added up to $75 million a year in taxes for the Taliban. Members of the Northern Alliance, America's anti-Taliban allies, are also heavily involved in the heroin trade.

Unlike Latin America or Europe, where organized crime attempts to penetrate the state, the government of North Korea is penetrating organized crime. With the economy in shambles, the North Korean regime has turned to drug trafficking and organized crime for funding. North Korea is trafficking in methamphetamine, opium, and heroin, and members of the armed forces, the diplomatic corps, and the intelligence service actually engage in drug trafficking.

Western intelligence agencies have confirmed the presence of large-scale opium production facilities in North Korea. But the North Koreans are not limited to drug production facilities. There is also evidence of printing plants used to produce high-quality counterfeit currency. And Japan grows increasingly nervous as members of its local Korean population with ties to the North become involved more deeply in this underground trade.

What America Must Do

Although Tony Soprano disapproves of selling drugs and—based on the way he reacted so angrily to Meadow's admission of having used speed when overburdened at school—taking them, many of his associates have no such concerns. Uncle Junior, Christopher, and several members of the Aprile family have all dealt in and/or taken narcotics. Despite Tony's wishes, drugs still form a significant portion of the family business, just as it does for many in organized crime. The unprecedented cooperation among drug traffickers, organized-crime groups, and terrorists has exacerbated the threat of all three to the United States. The nature of the drug war has changed, and the U.S. reaction needs to change as well. It is a top national-security problem.

Afghanistan and Colombia are the clearest examples of the new threat caused by the convergence of drugs and terrorism to U.S. national security. Although similar, Afghanistan and Colombia pose diverse threats to the United States. Although drug production in Afghanistan is of significant interest to the United States, the main concern is that Afghanistan serves as a haven for Islamic insurgent guerrillas and terrorists. As for Colombia, the destabilization of a country in America's backyard is the major concern. Colombia provides two thirds of the world's production of coca, Afghanistan generates three fourths of the world's opiates, and the trend lines for both are going up. Afghanistan and Colombia command the market share of the opiate and cocaine production in the world. They are the blue chips of the narcotics industry.

The term "war on drugs" has caused us to consider the problem in an unconstructive manner. This challenge cannot be won or lost. The major tactical shift needed to combat organized crime and terrorism is a move to a "campaign" strategy. As with any campaign, this one requires an articulation of objectives, interests, and goals. All aspects of the effort need to be coordinated with these points in mind. A prime example of this is that long-term intelligence-gathering operations are necessary to track and ultimately penetrate these organizations to a level that the subsequent series of arrests have lasting effect. The present focus on individual busts means that low-level participants jam our prisons, with a negligible effect on the industry itself. We need to consider pursuing a "string-them-along" approach (see Chapter 6), rather than simply a "string-them-up" approach. This requires increased interagency cooperation, as well as changes in the law-enforcement culture itself.

Part of the solution consists of strengthening the domestic legal institutions and social organizations in the afflicted countries. The United States cannot solve the problem itself. It must provide these countries with the tools to help themselves and bolster their legitimate institutions. In order to promote trust among the indigenous population, institution building must be transparent to the public. Without strong judicial systems, fostering effective law enforcement and prosecution of criminals and terrorists is impossible. Without strong social organizations that promote democracy and combat corruption, effective change is impossible. Therefore the United States must not only fund military efforts to fight narco-terrorists but also look to fund domestic reforms intended to buttress legal systems and promote democracy.

Too often the debate on the drug problem is cast in demand-side versus supply-side terms—with legalization increasingly polarized against the war-on-drugs approach. We should recall that solutions require initiatives from a variety of seemingly mutually exclusive sources: public health, schools, state and local community organizations, the military, local, state, and national law enforcement, and the intelligence community. The idea that one strategy, reducing drug supplies, for example, will work has proven very short-sighted. The notions that all drug users can kick their addiction and that one type of drug treatment program will work for many kinds of addicts have all been brought into serious question. We examine these issues in greater depth in Chapter 6. Meanwhile, we suggest that American policy makers initiate new visions of what the drug war actually encompasses: addiction, violent crime, global crime syndicates, and global terrorism (some of it sponsored by nation-states and perpetrated by their hired agents).

What Is Needed

Tony Soprano and his organized-crime family represent the tip of a transnational crime iceberg. The convergence of organized crime, drug trafficking, and terrorism demands a new paradigm in strategic thinking. The end of the Cold War and the globalization of the world economy have provided the right conditions for criminal organizations to work together. The dark side of globalization is that whereas it has benefited legitimate people and organizations, it has also assisted criminal groups. The world's governments have not responded coherently. The threat is transnational and so must be the response. To confront the issue, nations must organize as effectively as the drug traffickers and terrorists have.

The lines connecting organized crime, drug trafficking, and terrorism cannot be seen clearly through a lens of diplomacy, military, law enforcement, drug enforcement, or intelligence alone but rather through a prism that reflects all of these and offers a comprehensive and coordinated approach. The United States cannot afford to view the world according to the bureaucratic agendas of its agencies and their organizational charts. The United States must stock its quiver with all the necessary arrows to deal with this new and challenging national-security threat. Seven multi-agency and multi-disciplined task forces on information warfare and information assurance, terrorism, Russian organized crime, Asian organized crime, the narcotics industry, financial crimes, and the nuclear African-American market comprise over 175 senior officials and experts from the academic, defense, diplomatic, intelligence, law enforcement, and corporate communities. Yet will these groups be any more efficient at sharing information with one another than were the FBI and the CIA before, and even after, September 11?

In the future there may well arise a vast partnership between terrorist groups and transnational organized-crime syndicates. Organized-crime syndicates frequently have access to and influence with political leaders, making such syndicates beneficial to terrorist groups that would seek to influence and intimidate, rather than destroy, a government. In return, organized-crime syndicates can exploit terrorist campaigns, capitalizing on the power vacuum present in regional instability, serving as a paramilitary wing of the syndicate, or further coercing a weak government to "look the other way." As offshore banks and inner-city Laundromats once served as notorious Mob fronts, so may terrorist campaigns become operational fronts for organized crime. Such a trend would find a welcome home in many former Soviet republics, whose governments and devastated economies provide fertile grounds for corruption and organized crime. These regimes, which once depended upon the backing of the military for legitimacy and political survival, may find themselves relying on warlords and crime lords for the same. Indeed, we may see the rise of superficial terrorist campaigns serving as "fronts" for regional organized-crime syndicates, campaigns that seek no political objective save that of creating a climate of anarchy and fear in which it becomes impossible for local law enforcement to prosecute or even hinder organized-crime operations.

As prevalent as drugs are both in the United States and around the globe, will the writers of *The Sopranos* eventually have Tony branch out into drug trafficking? As current and accurate as the show attempts to be, such a development seems likely, but with any such development will necessarily come a whole host of implied evils. Will terrorism and its natural complement, counterterrorism, enter the dysfunctional suburban Soprano family? In this family, as viewers well know, anything is possible.

Lies, Entertainment, and Alienation, Soprano Style

TONY SOPRANO lies chronically. His business, after all, is based on deceit and dishonesty. But the need for secrecy spills over to all areas of his life: to his marriage, his children, his psychiatrist, and his friends. In a sense, the lies represent another one of his rackets. In fact, at the very heart of some of Tony's scams is the lie. It isn't just about fraud, though—Tony lies to everybody. For a long time he lied to his children about his career in the Mafia. He lied to Dr. Melfi about his affair with a fellow patient. He lies to his wife about almost everything. But Tony isn't anomalous. In a very real sense, we all lie like Tony Soprano.

In postmodern America,[1] of course, lying is no longer called lying. We have all become "value relativists," claims the *New York Times,* adding that both Tony Soprano and the American people now live by Tony's macho creed: "You gotta do what you gotta do."[2]

So how serious is this social problem of lying and deception? One survey from the early 1990s showed that 91 percent of Americans tell lies regularly, and two thirds see nothing wrong in telling a lie.[3] According to James Patterson and W. Kim, lying has become "an integral part of American culture, a trait of the American [social] character."[4]

At the beginning of season two, an Asian-American man takes a securities exchange licensing test under the name "Christopher Moltisanti," thereby setting Tony's nephew up with falsified credentials to run the Webistics stock scam. Similarly some half a million Americans use fraudulent credentials and diplomas, including 10,000 questionable medical degrees. As many as one in three employed Americans may have been hired with credentials that have been altered. An FBI undercover investigation, DIPSCAM (Diploma Scam), involved one agent who was able to obtain seventeen advanced degrees by mail for little or no coursework. The late Florida Democratic Congressman Claude Pepper, cooperating with the investigation, got a Ph.D. from a university in Los Angeles by paying $1,780 and mailing in four book reports.

Today, identity crime is the fastest-growing form of fraud in America. Indeed "deception regarding (individual) identity and biography [is one of the most] common, but little commented upon, features of American life."[5] After Tony Curtis played Waldo Demara in the 1961 movie *The Great Impostor*, Demara became a role model for other impostors. Demara had successfully passed himself off as a monk, a teacher, an assistant warden of a Texas prison, and a Royal Canadian Navy physician and surgeon—and, yes, he actually performed surgery on sailors. Inspired by the movie, one woman who lived in an eighteen-room mansion and owned a Rolls Royce, bilked the government out of $377,500 in welfare, medical payments, and food stamps. She opened twelve different welfare claims under phony names, claiming a total of forty-nine children.[6] Identity theft of Social Security numbers (SSNs), credit cards, and other documents now victimizes an estimated 500,000 to 700,000 Americans a year, according to the U.S. Department of Justice.[7]

National efforts to prevent identity theft have been relatively ineffective. In Oregon, seven defendants were sentenced to prison for their roles in a heroin/methamphetamine trafficking organization, which included entering the United States illegally from Mexico and obtaining the Social Security numbers of other persons. The SSNs were then used to get temporary employment and identification documents to facilitate distribution of the drugs. In getting jobs, the defendants used false alien registration receipt cards, in addition to the fraudulently obtained SSNs, which provided employers enough documentation to complete I-9 employment verification forms. Some of the defendants even used the fraudulently obtained SSNs to get earned income credits on tax returns fraudulently filed with the Internal Revenue Service. Some relatives of narcotics traffickers were arrested in possession of false documents and were charged with possessing false alien registration receipt cards and with using the fraudulently obtained SSNs to obtain employment. A total of twenty-seven defendants have been convicted in the case to date, fifteen federally and twelve at the state level.

New York State Attorney General Eliot Spitzer—joined by the New York State Police Special Investigations Unit, the State Inspector General's Office, and the New York State Insurance Fund—discovered that an employee of the Insurance Fund, who was subsequently charged, had pilfered personal data from office files and then used the stolen identities to obtain goods and services on credit. Some of the 9/11 terrorists also used falsified documents to enter the United States.

A Language of Lies

As noted, Tony Soprano's business necessitates much of his lying, but the essential dishonesty goes even deeper. Inspired in part by the need to communicate cryptically over the phone about criminal enterprises, the language of Tony and his cohorts seeks to conceal as much as it communicates. Tony's lieutenants often tell him that they've "taken care of that thing," when in fact "that thing" refers to a brutal murder. Christopher considers the senseless execution of a representative from an Eastern European gang as his having "taken initiative." Tony's mother Livia suggests to Uncle Junior that Christopher, whose friend Brendan has hijacked trucking shipments under Uncle Junior's control, be "taught a lesson." The lesson comes in the form of a mock execution in which Christopher begs for his life. The complicated, convoluted lives of the Sopranos operate on a foundation of lies that protect the members of the family not just from rivals or law enforcement, but even from their own consciences. The culture of lies applies not only to criminals intent on fraud for personal gain. Lying and deception are institutionalized behaviors among the American power elite, including major corporations, government, and, above all, the mass media. The English language, as used by these dominant institutions, has become thoroughly perverted by the use of "doublespeak." First coined by George Orwell in *1984*, his 1949 novel about a future totalitarian state, doublespeak uses language with incongruous and conflicting elements. With its effective obfuscation, doublespeak provides a dangerous weapon of social control, manipulation, and exploitation. Rutgers University English professor William Lutz has identified five kinds of doublespeak: euphemism, jargon, gobbledygook, puffery, and weasel words.

A euphemism is "an inoffensive or positive word or phrase used to avoid a harsh, unpleasant or distasteful reality." Corporate and government organizations often use euphemisms to deceive, mislead, and otherwise alter the public's perception of reality. Euphemisms designed to deny moral wrongs are used constantly. In 1984, the U.S. State Department decided that the word "killing" would no longer be used in reports about nations that violated human rights. Instead, the phrase "unlawful or arbitrary deprivation of life" became the preferred term when the nations received U.S. military aid—a potentially embarrassing situation.[8] In the Vietnam War, the killing of Vietnamese civilians by U.S. forces was called "pacification." Assassination has been dubbed "termination with extreme prejudice." Jargon is specialized language used in a trade or profession. When used to communicate with other members of the same profession, jargon can provide useful shorthand, but often it is used to deceive people negatively affected by organizations. Employees are often termed "associates," and when they are "laid off" (that is, fired) their "former employers call it downsizing, (or 'restructuring') and speak boldly of the company's bright future while voting themselves bonuses."[9]

Gobbledygook (also known as "bureaucratese") consists of words and sentences designed to overwhelm audiences or impress them with the speaker's apparent competence and expertise. Former Vice President Dan Quayle, a master of gobbledygook, intentional and otherwise, explaining the need for the Star Wars weapons system, noted: "Why wouldn't an enhanced deterrent, a more stable peace, a better prospect to denying the ones who enter the conflict in the first place to have a reduction of offensive systems and an introduction to defensive capability?"[10] Bureaucratese is commonly mixed with euphemisms and jargon of all kinds.

Puffery—inflated language, usually in the form of unprovable superlatives and overgeneralizations—is used endlessly in advertising and sales. We encounter puffery everyday.

"The Ultimate Driving Machine" (BMW)

"The Power to Be Your Best" (Apple Computers)

"The Greatest Show On Earth" (Ringling Brothers Barnum and Bailey Circus)[11]

Automobile dealers claim to be "number one" in their area, but they often fail to define what "number one" means—or define the space that comprises their "area."[12] Puffery is lingua franca in advertising.

Another type of deceptive language includes the use of weasel words. Weasels suck out the insides of eggs by making a small hole in the shell, then put the empty egg back in the raided nest. The egg still looks whole but has no substance. Weasel words appear to be making a claim but in reality have no substance or truth to them. The most commonly used of such words is "helps," as in "our cold medicine helps relieve your cold symptoms." Since "helps" does not mean cure, stop, or end, the word is practically meaningless. Nor does the claim specify how much the medicine "helps." Another such word is "virtually." A dishwasher soap can be advertised as leaving dishes "virtually spotless," yet leave plenty of spots.[13]

Newspeak, Doublethink, and the Clinton Scandal

In *1984*, Orwell also described an official state language called "newspeak," which limits the public's ability to view their government and its activities critically. Newspeak promotes belief in ideas that are inherently contradictory, such as:

"Nuclear war is winnable."

"We had to destroy the village in order to save it."

"Peace through war."

"Capital punishment enhances life."

Newspeak results in a type of illogic called "doublethink," the ability to hold two contradictory ideas in mind at the same time and believe both are true. The only way one can persist in believing the truth of both ideas is never to examine them side by side, which would reveal the contradiction. During the Clinton impeachment hearing, both the White House and the House Judiciary Committee engaged in newspeak.

- Clinton and Vernon Jordan tried to help secure a job for Monica, which was "totally unrelated to the scandal."
- Monica had sex with Bill, the public was told, but *he* did not have sex with *her*.
- Bill did touch Monica's breasts, but not for the purpose of sexual arousal.

For all the moral damage caused by the Clinton scandal, its impact pales in comparison to many other scandals, ones far more serious constitutionally but that did not result in presidential impeachment:

- President Johnson lied about an incident in the Tonkin Gulf that was used to start an undeclared war that killed 59,000

Americans, two million Vietnamese, and cost $150 billion in
U.S. treasure.

- Republican presidential nominee Ronald Reagan promised
  Iran that he would secretly sell it arms, if he became president, even though the U.S. government considered Iran a terrorist country. Once elected, Reagan used the proceeds for
  those sales to illegally finance a counterrevolution against
  Nicaragua, whose government was recognized by the United
  States. Reagan lied to the American public about these incidents, as did members of his administration—including his
  vice president, George H. W. Bush. Most of the key figures in
  the scandal were indicted but then given presidential pardons
  in the last month of the senior Bush term.

During Watergate, the Senate Judiciary Committee carefully
reviewed Richard Nixon's case before it was passed on to the Rodino
Committee in the House, introducing all manner of evidence against
Nixon. The Clinton hearings, in contrast, will go down as the most
nonsensical in our history:

- Not a single material witness was called.
- No direct evidence of any kind was introduced.
- The prosecutor in the case was turned into a witness.
- Convicted perjurers were converted into experts on perjury.

Clinton's prosecutors were self-proclaimed law-and-order zealots.
To them, Clinton's impeachment represented both a logical extension
of law-and-order rhetoric and a chance to lead the nation out of the
morass of sixties-inspired moral relativism, premarital sex, welfare
rights, and draft dodging. Clinton's dalliance and lies represented to
them the very incarnation of this amoral subculture.

During the trial, new doublespeak messages poured forth. The
Republicans insisted that Clinton's attorneys were the "best paid and
most skilled in the nation," whereas the House Managers were
merely "inexperienced citizen lawyers." The GOP Managers claimed

repeatedly that the scandal was not about Clinton's private life, but in fact all the lies of which he was accused were indeed about his private behavior. Representative Henry Hyde, Chair of the House Judiciary Committee, and one of Clinton's most relentless persecutors, admitted to having had an extramarital affair that broke up a marriage when he was in his forties, but fobbed it off as a "youthful" indiscretion that "didn't count." With the hypocritical Mr. Hyde, youth was obviously not wasted on the young. The price of this long, drawn-out, and ultimately pointless persecution was quite high.

The Clinton "Zippergate" scandal dominated the news and obsessed the nation for eighteen months, much as the O. J. Simpson case had a few years earlier. American obsession with sensationalized stories distracted the nation from really important matters. One such issue was the Clinton administration's warnings about Osama bin Laden's plans to hit U.S. targets and the dangers represented by radical Islamic terrorism, a matter with which the nation is only now obsessed. As Gore Vidal recently observed, the greatest point of this scandal is that it served as a gigantic distraction from our actually doing something to help the 80 percent of us who don't own the nation's wealth, who can't give big bucks to political campaigns, and whose welfare is threatened by congressional inaction on issues that matter, like health care and economic justice.[14]

C. Wright Mills believed that one of the great tasks of modern social science was the description of the effects that economic, social, and political institutions have on people's feelings, values, goals, and behaviors.[15] Indeed, the sociological imagination involves the ability to shift from one perspective to another, "from the political to the psychological . . . [the sociological imagination] is the capacity to range from the most impersonal and remote . . . to the most intimate features of the human self."[16] Mills believed that "it may well be that the most radical discovery [of] psychology and social science is the discovery of how so many intimate features of the person are socially patterned and even implanted."[17] Thus, many of the personality traits most people consider to be individual characteristics are actually widely shared products of mass socialization by the communications media and other bureaucratic institutions that dominate postmodern life. Tony Soprano—and the America that not so secretly admires him—did not just happen; they were created.

The Macro-Micro Link

In Tony Soprano's world, we see a community from the perspective of its criminal element, extending from organized criminal syndicates to greedy business owners to duplicitous community leaders to corrupt law-enforcement officials. The lies these groups and institutions perpetrate create an atmosphere that negatively influences those under their influence. How much is the Church's moral authority compromised when it accepts contributions from Paulie Walnuts or attempts to counsel Tony Soprano? What is the effect on the black community when a respected leader, the Reverend James, accepts a payoff for having organized African-American protestors as a work-slowdown ploy against a construction company Tony is shaking down? With all the lies flying about the Soprano household, is it any wonder that Meadow has learned how to manipulate her parents to reduce the severity of her punishments for misdeeds?

There is a link between societal institutions and micro-social problems like lying and deception, between alienating conditions of social structure and feelings of alienation experienced by the individuals. Such connections are often described as the "macro-micro link," implying a relationship between the most intimate of feelings and the most important structural features of modern life.

We need to understand that although institutions shape personality traits, they do not mold these traits by themselves. Often they have an indirect influence.[18] However, the characteristics molded within families and by schools, religious institutions, and such community organizations as the Boy Scouts, Little League, and Girl Scouts reinforce those traits that economic and political institutions require of us. In a nation as diverse as the United States, character traits differ widely among various social classes, racial and ethnic groups and geographic regions. Thus, it becomes difficult to speak of a "national character," a set of traits that applies equally to all Americans. It is reasonable, however, to describe traits for which there is solid empirical evidence, such as the United States having the highest percentage of people who believe in God of any industrial democracy. The issue is not which institutions have the most influence, but what kinds of social character our society as a whole produces, and what sort of social problems individuals experience within postmodern culture.

One central theme in the writing on American character has dominated literature since the 1940s: the picture of a lonely individual wishing to be liked by other people, someone who uses a "marketing personality," packaging and selling him or herself like a "handbag" on the job market. Life in postmodern society has become an act wherein people suppress their authentic needs—for love, self-esteem, and identity—in reaction to social pressures to conform and to achieve.[19] Even individuals as self-determined and unapologetic as career criminals learn to mask their needs in order to achieve their ends more easily. For all his rage and brutality, Tony Soprano often suppresses his true feelings—like his extreme distaste for the brutal and unreasonable Richie Aprile—in order not to jeopardize the stability of his operations.

The Nature of Alienation

The belief that human nature derives from a few basic human needs runs contrary to the notion perpetuated by the power elite that human nature is fundamentally violent and aggressive.[20] Evidence demonstrates that people in every type of social structure have needs for:

- Love, including physical affection and emotional cohesion with other people.

- Self-esteem, including recognition of achievement, approval, encouragement, and affirmation that results in a positive concept of oneself and one's abilities—a positive sense of "power, confidence, agency."[21]
- Identity, organizing principles that define who one is and where and how one fits into the social roles that make up one's environment. An identity gives one the ability to organize one's perceptions, emotions, and beliefs.

When these three emotional needs are met, people feel secure and believe that their lives have a meaningful purpose. These needs require ongoing, repeated gratification. However, individuals are to some extent unique in both interests and personality. The more a social structure allows for people's social roles to satisfy their basic needs, the lower that society's level of alienation.[22]

When these needs are not met, we, individually or as a culture, experience alienation. Excluded individuals and groups feel resentment and confusion, subjective reactions to an objective condition that exposes people to forces beyond their control and understanding. Thus, the negative feelings of the alienated individual are rooted in a societal base: "The roots of alienation do not reside in either intrapsychic [individual personality] processes or in interpersonal relationships, but in societal structures."[23]

Alienation is characterized by feelings of estrangement from either society or from oneself, often from both. The specific emotions associated with alienation[24] include powerlessness, meaninglessness, normlessness or anomie, loneliness, and both cultural and personal estrangement. By turns, Tony Soprano has exhibited all of these traits. With his need to lie about almost every facet of his life, it is little wonder that Tony experiences frequent bouts of alienation.

Although he has at his disposal many very effective recourses to his problems, Tony has often felt powerless in certain situations. Livia's personality prevented his having a fulfilling maternal relationship, and his inability to please her left him feeling frustrated and ineffective. The static between Tony and Uncle Junior elicited help-less feelings of being "in a box," being forced to react in ways he would rather avoid. After Christopher was shot by ambitious associates, Tony chose to avenge the shooting personally, but then found himself facing a possible murder charge that threatened to take him from his family.

Powerlessness is a feeling that results in people perceiving that they are helpless to achieve their goals or roles in life. People who experience powerlessness often see their future as shaped by forces beyond their control—the bureaucracy or work organization—and they see themselves as cogs in a wheel.[25] They do not feel in charge of their own lives and destinies. Tony, ignoring the fact that his own poor judgment led to the murder investigation involving Christopher's shooter, rants angrily to Dr. Melfi about the people conspiring to deprive him of his freedom.

People experiencing meaninglessness lack an understanding of the environment of which they are a part. They live in the present, without a sense of optimism about their future. During A.J.'s adoles-cent existential crisis, Tony finds himself at a loss to confront the moral issues that seem to be troubling his son. Tony complains to Dr. Melfi about a lack of meaning in life, of feeling that the only absolute truth is death. Dr. Melfi shows no surprise; she's heard about Tony's mother. In fact, Livia later imparts her own philosophy of meaning-lessness to A.J.: that the world is a jungle, that one can't expect hap-piness, that in the end we all die alone. "It's all a big nothing," she concludes.

Normlessness, or anomie, arises when people strive to achieve culturally prescribed goals, such as becoming successful by acquiring money and status but lack codes of standards, values, or ideals to influence their behavior. They have no guide for their behavior. This can result in an "adaptation mode" in which people choose deviant or criminal behavior over legal or societally approved means of achiev-ing their goals.

On *The Sopranos*, normlessness takes two forms. The broader form encompasses almost every character in the series as they lie, steal, and murder. Yet even within that group, Tony perceives a set of norms that he witnesses others abandon for their own ends. When he warns Richie Aprile against risking their waste management business by mixing it with drug sales, Richie allows that Tony, as the boss, gets to make the rules. "No, I don't make them," Tony insists. "They've always been there."

Another factor in alienation, loneliness results from feeling a lack of social acceptance by people within one's environment, feeling instead rejection and estrangement from others. Since loneliness is a feeling experienced by individuals, it is possible to feel lonely even in crowds. With the necessary suspicion any cautious Mafioso should have, Tony has often experienced loneliness. Not only must he shield himself from rivals and informants, he must even keep a certain distance from his family. Tony can't risk implicating his wife and children with certain facts about his work.

People with feelings of self-estrangement experience themselves as alien, and as a result have feelings of resentment and confusion. Self-estrangement often opens people to the possibility of self-deception. Self-estranged people often feel fragmented—and feel guilty for feeling that way. Self-estranged people often hide these feelings by putting on masks, called "impression management," "image construction," "acting," or "selling of the self." Being strangers to themselves, they lack a stable identity and often feel like frauds. Not trusting themselves, self-estranged people tend to be distrustful both of other people and society as a whole. Tony butts up against self-estrangement frequently as he attempts to face the disparity between the roles of his home life and the roles of his working life.

The characters in *The Sopranos* exhibit symptoms of alienation all the time. Tony's panic attacks stem in large measure from his feelings of powerlessness and meaninglessness over his inability to relate to his impossible-to-please mother. Tony's wife is so lonely that she looks to two men other than Tony for emotional intimacy. The old-school Mafiosi, especially Uncle Junior, complain of the lack of norms regarding the loyalty of the younger generation to the organization. Tony is also a study in self-estrangement, feeling unsure of his identity at home and virtually anywhere in life.

If members of American society are encouraged to develop certain personality traits, like chronic lying, then a condition of alienation may be said to exist. Alienation is directly related to a host of individual, micro-social problems, including suicide, drug abuse, delinquency, sexual deviance, and, most central to this discussion, mental illness. To be sure, alienation is not the only cause of these maladies, any more than any human behavior is caused by a single variable. Nevertheless, the more a group or groups become alienated, the more likely they are to suffer from micro-social problems. If alienation is socially patterned in various groups, it is, by definition, structurally caused.

Media Alienation

Putting aside the fact that *The Sopranos* is itself a part of the mass media, the show itself often portrays the effects of the media, television, music, newspapers, films. These things populate the background of *The Sopranos,* and they frequently enter the story. During A.J.'s existential crisis, he quotes a defiant line from a rap song. His friend is dubious, claiming that rap "is all about marketing now." The very structure of mass media alienates because the average person sits so far removed from its ownership and control. The dominant media institutions—television networks, major newspapers, recording companies, book and magazine publishing houses, movie studios—are huge, multinational corporations that either own or are owned by other corporations, banks, and insurance companies.

Media ownership and control are approaching monopolistic proportions. Competition among newspapers is nearly dead: 97 percent of all chain-owned newspapers have no competition from other newspapers. By the year 2005, it is estimated that ten multinational firms will control most of the world's mass media.[26] Nine global media firms dominate the commercial media—AOL-TimeWarner, Disney, Bertelsmann, Viacom, News Corporation, TCI Cable, General Electric (NBC/RCA), Sony (Columbia/Tristar), and Seagram (Universal). These nine and another thirteen companies accounted for half the worldwide media ownership, as of the early 1990s. Some Wall Street analysts predict that the number will soon be down from twenty to six. It already is in book publishing.[27]

Most observers fear that increased concentration of ownership restricts the content of news and political opinion allowed on the media. Although this is a serious concern, the content of media programming, movies, and advertising, and the effects of that content on audiences also present problems.

Teleculture

A half century ago, C. Wright Mills observed that no one knows all the functions served by the mass media. Today, the mass media not only keeps us informed of what's going on in the world but also shapes our perceptions of that world. Indeed, mass communications Professor Arthur Asa Berger believes that America has evolved into a "teleculture," wherein television "has become the most powerful socializing . . . force in society."[28] Its influence has replaced traditional sources of socialization and ethics: parents, priests, teachers, and peers. Debate also rages over the media's effects on people's values and behavior. To be sure, the media often influences people in subtle and indirect ways. Additionally, people's perceptions of media messages filter through a number of lenses, including social class, age, gender, race, ethnicity, and earlier socialization experiences with media. Nevertheless, considerable evidence supports Berger's notion of the media as the dominant socializing force in America.

In Tony Soprano's America, television is omnipresent, just as it is throughout the nation. The numbers regarding the ubiquity of television are staggering: by the early 1990s, 98 percent of American households owned television sets; 30 percent of households had two or more TV sets.[29] In America, even homes that lack hot running water or indoor toilets have a television. Since the mid-1980s, Americans have been spending fifty-two hours a week in front of the TV. Homes with three or more people have a TV on sixty-one hours per week. The average American encounters 100 television commercials, sixty radio commercials, and thirty print ads a day; 90,000 ads per year of various types.[30] The ads equate happiness with materialism, present sexist portrayals of women, and contribute to dependency, anxiety, and low self-esteem.

Some interesting links between certain media themes and various character traits are relatively undisputed, such as the relationship between the tremendous amount of violence seen in American media and experienced in American life. Thousands of studies have demonstrated that media violence can motivate individuals predisposed to commit violence to do so. Thus, after the movie *The Deer Hunter* premiered in 1979, at least twenty-five people in the United States committed suicide by imitating the movie's Russian roulette scenes. Suicides also increase significantly in the United States after a famous person, like Marilyn Monroe, is reported to have committed suicide. Homicide rates increase immediately after heavyweight boxing matches. America is the most violent industrial democracy in the world, with a homicide rate ten times higher than the entire continent of Europe. Half the American public reports having violent urges, with a fourth having acted on those impulses.[31] One out of three American adults now owns at least one gun, and, most frighteningly, 26 million Americans now carry guns with them when they leave home. As on *The Sopranos,* so in our everyday lives.

Media violence outpaces even the real violence in society. Movie and television role models have grown more violent since the 1950s. Heroes no longer need a reason to commit violent acts. Sylvester Stallone, Mel Gibson, Clint Eastwood, and Arnold Schwarzenegger usually play lone-wolf heroes, cynical macho types who have no respect for societal institutions. Tony Soprano is the culmination of a process, the apotheosis of a tradition, but, of course, also in himself a vast criticism of that process.

Children's television is the most violent of all categories of TV programming, averaging twenty-five violent acts an hour. Ninety-five percent of children's programming features violent acts. Moreover, studies reveal that children often believe as real what they see on television. The more time people spend watching television, the more they overestimate the actual amount of violent crime in American life.[32]

The mass media shape key sexual behaviors and attitudes, including the frequency of premarital and extramarital sex and the link between sex and violence. The year before *The Sopranos* premiered in 1999, HBO debuted another groundbreaking series. As *The Sopranos* examines the male underside of suburban America, *Sex and the City* looks at the sex lives of four middle-class Manhattan women, but both chart their characters as they navigate toward fulfillment of the basic human needs—love, self-esteem, and identity. A film from five years earlier, John Dahl's *The Last Seduction*, predicts the themes of both *The Sopranos* and *Sex and the City*, with an amoral, gangsterish, sexually predatory, homicidal heroine, played by Linda Fiorentino, fusing some of the worst elements of Tony and *Sex and the City*'s four heroines.

No doubt the naked go-go dancers at the Bada Bing do their part to attract heterosexual male viewers. Dramatically, they also demonstrate yet another aspect of Tony's contradictory adulterous amorality. Sexual symbols are now attached to every product and service in media advertising. Sex has become a commodity in itself, selling products in ads associated with youth, power, and success. Even children in ads have become sexual beings with little girls pictured wearing bras.[33] In movies, magazines, and television shows, sex is frequently separated from emotions and relationships. The media depicts sex as unrelated to personal responsibility for consequences, affection, intimacy, or commitment. Many movie heroes remain single and seduce multiple partners without ever becoming emotionally attached to a woman, the perennial James Bond being the template.

Studies of movies, television, men's magazines, and pornography during the past twenty years all indicate "increased depictions of violence against women,"[34] the main effect of which links sex and violence. Such images also reinforce myths about women and rape— that they like it and want it or, worse, that they deserve it. A meta-study (analysis of data contained in other studies) published in the year 2000[35] reviewed several decades of empirical studies and concludes that exposure to pornography correlates with sexual deviancy (early first intercourse, excessive masturbation), sexual perpetration (aggressive, sexually hostile, and violent behaviors), attitudes regarding intimate relationships (viewing persons as sexual objects), and belief in the rape myth (women cause rape and should resist or prevent it).

In May 1995, ABC's *Prime-Time Live* revealed that sexually charged entertainment and advertising were being watched by young children, making them far more aware of and eager for sex than many parents suspect. Hidden cameras showed seven-year-old girls "ogling photos of half naked male models. Teachers showed pictures drawn by first and second-graders—Cinderellas with breasts and nipples." Six-year old girls stated that girls should be sexually assertive in order to attract boys. Both little boys and girls told interviewers that the job of being sexually aggressive now belongs to girls. Children just over five years of age were shown simulating intercourse during recess in schools. America's obsession with sexual gratification has now filtered down to the youngest members of the society, and may lead to extremely dangerous results: increasing incidence of sexually transmitted diseases, illegitimate births, and other forms of sexual deviance, such as rape.[36]

Sex-crime statistics mirror the content of media's sexual presentations. During the third season of *The Sopranos*, not only did viewers witness the brutal death of a young woman at the hands of one of Tony's men, they also saw the rape of Dr. Melfi. The rate of rapes in the United States is twenty times higher than that in other industrialized countries like England, Spain, and Japan. Moreover, 52 percent of American women on college campuses report being victims of sexual victimization, double the reported rate from a decade ago.[37]

The Inauthentic Condition

Aside from portraying violence and sex, the American media tries to tell us what we should look like—essentially that young is beautiful. It recommends what goals in life to strive for—especially money, power, popularity, sexuality, status, and prestige—and offers techniques to achieve them.[38] By throwing these images at us, the media distracts us from the causes of social problems, while it actually perpetuates many such problems.

Almost all advertising and political propaganda appeals to the need to belong to a human collectivity in which one's needs for love, recognition, and identity are fulfilled. A hallmark of inauthenticity is the presence of positive, overt appearances, coupled with negative underlying realities.[39] Tony Soprano, of course, wanders through an inauthentic existence most every day. In the media, instances of inauthenticity appear in ads for cigarettes and liquor, with their implied promises of sex, success, and popularity. What are the consequences of regular smoking and drinking? Smoking kills 450,000 Americans a year and costs society over $50 billion annually in missed workdays, medical costs, and other expenses, which exceeds all profits and tax receipts from tobacco items. Tobacco use causes heart disease, 90 percent of all lung cancer (including about 6,000 annual cases from "passive smoking"), bronchitis, emphysema, birth defects, and osteoporosis.[40] Alcohol is a factor in 150,000 deaths annually, and about $120 billion in medical bills, lost work time, and related costs. It is a factor in about half of all homicides and is nearly always the first drug to which illegal-drug abusers become addicted. No one argues that all people who abuse alcohol and other drugs learn to do so from advertising. However, evidence indicates that the more heavily alcohol is advertised in a society, the more alcohol is consumed. Thus, the amount of alcohol consumed in a society is due not merely to genetic predisposition, ethnicity, or will power. There are also important sociological influences that affect alcohol consumption. No rational person argues that even moderate cigarette smoking is harmless. Throughout our history, alcohol and tobacco have killed tens of millions more Americans than all "illegal" drugs combined.

Advertising is not just a set of messages for products; it is a medium that socializes people to be consumers. It does so in a deceitful way most of the time. Most advertising appeals to people's fears about not being loved or to their low self-esteem or to their problems of identity—evidence that American culture and society are not meeting these basic human needs

Drugs of all types are heavily advertised on TV (about once every eleven minutes) and in magazines. These ads attempt to increase feelings of insecurity and low self-esteem in consumers, and, obviously, the people who feel most insecure are most vulnerable to such appeals. The message is: if you want to be confident, loved, and successful, if you want to know who you are, where you are going in life, and how to get there, you need us. In short, the media tries to instill dependency in consumers.

Everyone in the Soprano household has a dependency on consumerism. They live in a house far larger than they need, always have an overstocked refrigerator, drive fashionable new-model cars, and generally have their every material desire fulfilled. Carmela, when trying to cope with her strained marriage, goes on spending sprees for new furniture or redecorates her already flawless home.

Many people who read about the themes presented in lifestyle ads respond by saying something like, "Well, those may be the themes, but I don't take such appeals seriously, and neither does anyone else I know." Jeffrey Schrank has pointed out that 90 percent of America's television viewers consider themselves "personally immune" to commercial appeals, yet these viewers account for 90 percent of all sales of advertised products.[41]

Advertisers spend over $130 billion a year to get their deceptive messages across. Would they spend this gigantic amount of money on something that didn't work? Indeed, the most problematic and profound aspect of all media may be its constant mixing of fantasy and reality. There is evidence that mixing fantasy and reality causes confusion in vulnerable groups, especially teenagers.[42] Inauthenticity encompasses more than themes about unmet emotional needs; it is based on the logic of doublespeak: it requires us to believe in two contradictory things at once. We do the same with Tony Soprano, perceiving him as both hero and gangster.

Individual Inauthenticity

During an early session with Dr. Melfi, Tony confesses unexplainable feelings of hatred toward the average man, the "happy wanderer." Tony thinks he should be pleased to witness someone going merrily on his way, but he feels intense anger instead. But that same cheerful face may also remind him of his own face, as he admits to having to play "the sad clown" in his everyday life. Tony often smiles at the world even as he feels emotionally fragmented inside.

Over fifty years ago, C. Wright Mills[43] described the inauthenticity that takes place among the "cheerful robots," otherwise known as white-collar workers. At work, they must smile and be personable, courteous, and helpful. White-collar workers sell not only their energy and time to their organization, but also their personalities. They repress behind a carefully cultivated good humor their resentment and anger over having to interact with people they do not like.

Those who study the sociology of emotions have found some interesting evidence supporting Mills's claims. In 1983, sociologist Arlie Hochschild[44] estimated that a third of American jobs involved "emotional labor," positions that require inauthentic behavior in the form of acting. Since her now classic study, the United States has become much more of a service economy, with many more subs possessing this emotional content. Hochschild differentiates between superficial acting (pleasant facial expressions and gestures) and deep acting (expressions of feelings). Superficial acting requires putting on a pleasant expression and repeating the same pat phrases over and over. Sociologist George Ritzer has described the superficial acting by fast-food restaurant employees:

> Rule Number 17 for Burger King workers is "smile at all times." The Roy Rogers employees who used to say "Happy Trails" when I paid for my food really had no interest in what happened to me in the future, on the trail. (In fact, they were really saying, in a polite way, "get lost!") This phenomenon has been generalized to many workers who say "have a nice day" as one is departing— they have no interest in, or concern for, how the rest of one's day goes. Again, in a ritualized way they are really telling us to "get lost," to move on so someone else can be served.[45]

Tony Soprano fits right into the postmodern service economy. His services include prostitutes, illegal gambling, and a host of other vices. On occasion, like the time he hosted a rigged card game, Tony loves to play master of ceremonies. On such occasions, he poses as a respectable businessman, engaging in what is now called "impression management."

Half the positions requiring this kind of impression management are in service-sector jobs occupied by women: airline attendants, clerks, nurses, social and recreational workers, radio and television announcers, and college professors. Most important, Hochschild reports that both men and women who sell their emotions as commodities experience feelings of powerlessness, an important form of alienation, in reaction to the constant pressure to perform. The language, clothes, and "look" associated with these roles come from the inauthentic role models in the media. A *Good Housekeeping* story describing Mary Tyler Moore's different "faces" typifies the masks women wear. She has her "business face," which uses "golden, toasty" colors that are flattering, even in harsh fluorescent office lighting. Her "evening face" highlights her "flawless skin," smoldering dark eyes, and glistening, molded mouth, all worthy of a "round of applause."[46]

Unfortunately, life in mass organizations increasingly concerns itself with impression management and emotional acting.[47] Some students of bureaucracy[48] have noted that certain types of cynical and successful people at the top of organizational hierarchies exude charisma via a superficial sense of warmth and charm, yet make decisions based on an object-directed dehumanization that converts people into subhuman categories. Such leaders have few problems in making such decisions because they can think in nonhuman, black-and-white terms regarding plant closings, layoffs, manipulative advertising campaigns, or organizational deviance. Thus inauthenticity and dehumanization cause social problems because these behaviors are, at times, handsomely rewarded.

Despite his emotional crises arising from his own inauthenticity and ability to dehumanize others, Tony Soprano himself gets handsomely rewarded for having cultivated antisocial aspects of his personality. He makes life-and-death decisions all the time, then covers over his deeds with his intelligence and charm. Such impression management often becomes an important part of private life. "What began as the public and commercial relations of business have become deeply personal: there is a public relations aspect to private relations of all sorts, including even relations with oneself."[49] Young white-collar workers often spend much of private life in singles bars and other "meat markets," projecting false images about their personalities and statuses. *Sex and the City* is loaded with such scenes. They manipulate each other for monetary and sexual purposes, and many drink alcohol and use drugs in order to be accepted by others and to escape feelings of alienation. Their relationships, whether sexual or merely friendly in nature, tend to be shallow because they keep so many of their true feelings hidden from others and, most sadly, from themselves as well.[50]

In *The Sopranos*, Christopher, in his pursuit of a screenwriting career, has an affair with his cousin's girlfriend Amy, an ambitious film executive. Yet Amy is unable to step outside the image she has of her career role. She refers to celebrities she knows as "friends," compares a real-life anecdote to the plot point from a film, and even reduces an awkward emotional parting with Christopher to being "a William Inge moment." Although Christopher appears hurt that Amy appears to have used him primarily for his knowledge of Mob culture, he in turn most likely found her Hollywood connections as attractive as he found Amy herself.

Many people believe that their feelings of alienation are theirs alone, a personal trouble, but such feelings are so widespread they can be considered part of American social character. We live in a postmodern culture in which reason and freedom have become increasingly weakened, engendering an atmosphere of indifference, uneasiness, and cynicism. The social character of American life is dominated by the cheerful robot who puts in an eight-hour workday, mostly in white-collar jobs in bureaucratic organizations, and engages in escapist entertainment and alienated consumption during his or her leisure time. The cheerful robot is a product of mass, urban life, with its emphasis on status seeking, consumption, competition, and dependence on bureaucratic organizations for employment, goods, and services.

Micro-Social Problems and Alienating Conditions

Due to insecurity about personal identities and statuses, the social character of our age is overly sensitive to the opinions of others—a condition termed "other-directedness." All of these themes fly in the face of the American myth of rugged individualism. We cheer when take-charge Tony Soprano climbs behind the wheel and laughingly chases down a pedestrian delinquent on his loan payments, but we also see ourselves in the terrified face of the victim.

Objectively, there exists no given "human nature." There is no evidence to suggest that specific character traits, such as greed, aggression, or sin, are inborn in humans. Instead, we identify various values, beliefs, goals, attitudes, and norms prescribed by various cultures for their members.

Social character consists then of those traits widely "shared among significant social groups and which . . . is a product of the experience of those groups."[51] Social character emerges from the parts of our personalities we have in common with most other members of our society. In diverse, multicultural nations like the United States, there are also social characters specific to genders, ethnic groups, regional groups, and other influential group memberships.

Within this view, two components of character stand out: the structure of selfhood and the nature of a social character's value system. Within the realms of self and values, social character interrelates with social problems. The notion of selfhood is difficult to grasp because it is so taken for granted. Sociologically, selves are somewhat complex. Many of us possess an individualized sense of selfhood. We are aware of our existence as both psychologically and physically separate from other people. But not all people conceive of themselves in the same way.

Those in Tony Soprano's real and criminal families like to believe they have a collectivized sense of self, especially in their shared traditions as Italian Americans. Yet the dominant culture in America—and the nature of the work that supports the characters of *The Sopranos*—engenders individualism.

In the United States, there are few subjects more written about than the self. Go into any bookstore and you will find entire sections devoted to "Self Help," literally help for the self. Most of these books are written by psychologists and other members of the so-called helping professions, the colleagues of the fictional Dr. Melfi. Of interest to students of social problems is just why so many selves in America need help and with what.

Another important aspect of social character is the set of values in which a given culture believes. Values consist of general ideas that are widely shared by a social group about what is desirable or undesirable, good or bad, beautiful or ugly, and so on. Interrelated collections of such beliefs make up value systems, which come in two broad categories. Sets of values tend to be either stable and relatively unchanging over the centuries or fluid and prone to relatively rapid change. American culture is characterized by rapid social change, and American values change with astonishing rapidity. For example, in the 1950s, premarital sex was taboo; by the 1970s and before the AIDS crisis began in the mid-1980s, it had come to be considered the norm; since then, people's values and behavior about premarital sex have become more conservative. Doubtless when a vaccine for HIV finally becomes a reality, sexual norms will once again undergo a rapid change.

Dehumanization

The impersonal nature of bureaucratic structures, the values promoting materialism and status, and the decline of community make mass societies prone to another form of alienation: dehumanization, which exists in two interrelated forms, object-directed and self-directed.

Object-directed dehumanization occurs when people are labeled less than human for purposes of profit, exploitation, and manipulation. In Tony Soprano's world, that goes for almost everyone. The mass media, both programming and advertising, contains this type of dehumanization in the form of stereotypes. Social critic Michael Parenti notes that the mass media constructs an unreal world in which minorities and women are continually stereotyped as part of a greater set of ideological messages. Italian Americans like Tony Soprano frequently appear in the media as members of the Mafia or as dumb gluttons incapable of speaking correct English. Italian women are portrayed as shrieking hysterics. In fact, whereas *The Sopranos* addresses this tendency, both through a host of professional Italian-Americans—like Tony's neighbor Dr. Cusemano and Tony's therapist Dr. Melfi—and through direct commentary—Melfi's ex-husband rails against the common Italian stereotype of mobbed-up wiseguys—the show also plays directly to the stereotype.

American stereotypes portray working-class people as stupid and slovenly in speech and appearance (the work they do is almost never shown), labor unions as corrupt, and individual heroism as nearly always preferable to collective action or teamwork. American Indians become savages, barbarians, and "devils,"[52] possessed of a lust for killing, destruction, and a disregard for human life. *The Sopranos* may contribute to the stereotype of Italian Americans as gangsters. Thus the media do much more than entertain; they propagate "images and ideologies that are supportive of imperialism . . . capitalism, racism, sexism, militarism, . . . violence, vigilantism, and anti–working class attitudes."[53] Moreover, they do these things in ways that dehumanize us all.

Self-directed dehumanization, a symptom of self-alienation, involves turning oneself into a "cog in a wheel," a dehumanized machine. This results in stress and burnout. Not only has Tony experienced periods of dreary self-alienation in which he has merely gone through the motions of his day, but the stress of his job and family has frequently triggered his anxiety attacks. People who dehumanize themselves may also tend to stereotype other people,[54] interrelating object-directed dehumanization on the individual level. In postmodern mass society, both dehumanization and inauthenticity are an integral part of the social character.[55] In that sense, Tony Soprano is the poster boy for the postmodern social character.

The Individualized Self

The United States long ago proclaimed itself the land of individual rights, individual cases, individual personalities, and individual egos. As we have seen, the mass media constantly reinforces these notions, focusing especially on celebrities and individual heroes. America's concept of the individualized self is so extreme as to be unrealistic; it is a notion loaded with myths and contradictions, a major cause of many micro-social problems.

Americans may be the only people on earth who believe in "rugged individualism," imbuing people with nearly limitless free will. The exercise of this freedom requires that individuals become self-sufficient and psychologically secure so that they may compete against other individuals in seeking life's material rewards. The ideology of individualism is not just mythical; it is downright dangerous.

America's extreme view of individualism causes great problems when it comes to establishing intimate relations with others. In 1938, the psychologist Karen Horney wrote on this subject, noting that one of the great problems Americans face is deciding who they can trust. Her words could have been written yesterday:

> American culture is economically based on the principle of competition . . . the psychic result of this situation is a diffuse hostile tension between individuals . . . competitiveness and the potential hostility that accompanies it, pervades all human relationships . . . between men and men, between women and women and men and women, and whether the point of competition be popularity, competence, attractiveness, or any other social value it greatly impairs the possibilities of reliable friendship.[56]

One result of the potential hostility between individuals is fear, including the fear of others' anger and the fear of failure and lowered self-esteem. Together, competitiveness, the potential hostility it engenders between individuals, fear, and lowered self-esteem result in individuals feeling lonely and psychologically isolated. One reaction to loneliness concerns an intensified need for love and affection. Because it meets such vital needs, romantic love is overvalued in American culture, reaching mythic proportions as a cure-all. Because we have come to expect more than it can possibly deliver, romantic love has become an illusion that serves to cover up the destructive factors that created the exaggerated need for it in the first place: extreme individualism and competition.

The result is genuine contradiction. Americans, with their individualized selves, need a great deal of affection, but America's extreme individualism and competition make love difficult to find. Because love is both highly cherished and surprisingly scarce, this contradiction causes people to become neurotic—possessed with low self-esteem, destructiveness, anxiety, and an excessive need for attention, approval, and affection from others.

A second contradiction of the American self concerns a tension between the alleged freedom we enjoy and all of the factual limitations placed on that freedom. Our myths teach that anyone can grow up to be president or a millionaire. Yet, in reality, America has only one president at a time, and millionaires are literally fewer than one in a million. Thus individuals constantly drift between feeling great power in determining their own destinies and feeling powerless to accomplish much of anything by themselves.

From a sociological perspective, living in a culture that promises individual happiness and success but fails to provide the means for the vast majority to achieve it causes a great many social problems, including crime at all social class levels, alcoholism, and drug addiction. Choosing such deviant activities has been described as an adaptation to the reality of living in a society that prescribes the goal of material success but fails to provide the means to achieve it. This structural anomie is now playing an important role in shaping both social character and social problems.

Far from being simply individualistic, Americans are a living contradiction. They live in a homogeneous culture, constantly witness mass propaganda, frequently engage in the same spectator behavior—television, movies, sports, pop music—and yet persist in the belief that they are a nation of nonconformists. It is the nature of that conformity that is the issue; to many social critics it appears blind and unthinking.

Like Tony Soprano, many Americans reside in a superficial world in which they fear revealing their true identities. Most people's fears stem not from their membership in organized crime but in organized hypocrisies of daily life that involve the little deviancies necessary to get ahead. They respond to the fear of being found out by hiding behind multiple masks of inauthenticity and dehumanization in a culture that rewards both. Yet we all pay a high price for our deceptions. Tony cannot be honest with his family, his friends, or his therapist about many of his acts. Deceptive advertising and mass consumption bring us a culture of chronic indebtedness, stress-related diseases, record numbers of bankruptcies, and myriad fraud schemes. Government propaganda results in foreign and defense policies of secret wars conducted by secret agencies in a quest of victories over numberless enemies. Meanwhile, we grow ever more alienated from our work, our consumption, our politics, and our government.

Tony Soprano and the Crimeogenic Department Store

IN ANY EPISODE OF *The Sopranos*, the criminal operations of Tony and his associates form a major portion of the show. Yet crime also permeates the world in which the show takes place. New Jersey's *Star-Ledger* runs the kind of stories any American newspaper runs, a seemingly endless series of criminal acts locally, nationally, and internationally. Livia Soprano obsesses about the horrific crimes she reads about. On TV, Tony watches a former Mafia member appear on a talk show as an expert on organized crime. Characters make references to such Mafia-related films as *The Godfather*, *Scarface*, and *Analyze This*. In Tony Soprano's America, crime is one of the great national themes.

No other social problem preoccupies America like crime. Public opinion polls often rate it as the leading social problem facing the nation. Crime is also a leading topic on news broadcasts and in newspaper headlines, elbowing out human-interest and other positive news stories. American entertainment establishes crime as its favorite genre: crime movies and television shows abound, and crime provides an essential element of soap opera plots. Ratings for shows like *The Sopranos* are sky-high: well over 9.5 million viewers watched the third-season finale. Why are we so fascinated by this topic?

The characters on *The Sopranos* inarguably support crime as a way of life: Tony leads an organized-crime syndicate, whose "employees" make a living scheming about new ways to defraud legal businesses. Tony's strip joint Bada Bing, has a back room where clients pay for sex. Tony runs a numbers game from the basement of a local restaurant. His business associates, many of who are murderers and rapists, "take care" of anyone at whom Tony nods his head. Even his family is filled with criminals: Tony's sister literally got away with murder, his uncle is an old-school mafioso, and his mother took out a contract on her own son. Even Carmela, Tony's well-meaning wife, implicitly threatened her neighbor's sister to get her to write a college letter of recommendation for Meadow, Carmela and Tony's daughter.

It would be one thing if we watched this show and shook our heads disapprovingly, but we don't. We often cheer for these characters, we root them on as they enact vengeance upon one another, and we feel their losses as their plans go awry. Each week, we see another act of criminal behavior; each week, more of us watch. Sure, it's great entertainment. The production values are high, the writing strong, the actors talented, and the story lines compelling. But how do we reconcile our enjoyment in watching the show with the depravity of the characters? It's nothing new: we've done it for years as we flocked to *GoodFellas* and *The Godfather* trilogy. It's as if we condone their behavior, even if just for the fifty minutes we spend with them each week. How, as a society, did we get to this place? For an answer we need to take a look at the American crime problems' structure in all its forms, as well as the allied problem of drugs.

The War on Drugs

Drugs present an immensely harmful problem in and of themselves; couple drugs with crime, and the effect becomes explosive. America's drug problem has, to an unappreciated extent, become America's crime problem. Consider the case of *The Sopranos'* Jackie Aprile Jr. Early in the third season, we see him as a nice, clean, upstanding boy who everyone thought would make a nice match for Meadow Soprano. Unlike his goombah family members, Jackie wasn't part of the business; he was a student at Rutgers—possibly he would become a doctor. Yet when we see him pop methamphetamines, we know he's doomed. Sure enough, his habit leads him to gamble and soon he flunks out of school. He sees his dreams of following in his late father's Mafioso footsteps destroyed when Christopher Moltisanti vetoes Jackie's request that his associate be allowed to sell Ecstasy in Adriana La Cerva's new nightclub. After that, Jackie spirals even further downward into drug addiction and erratic behavior, holding up a poker game of well-connected criminals, robbing his business associates, and performing other criminal acts, until Tony finally orders that he be killed.

Aside from their link with crime, drugs, both legal and illicit, inflict much social harm. Drug abuse in the American workplace is becoming increasingly common: lost workdays due to drug and alcohol abuse cost American business an estimated $246 billion a year.[1] Hospital treatment for the victims of crimes by street-level drug dealers stands at an estimated $1 billion. Annual court costs for illicit drug trafficking cases run $30 billion. In 1990, it was estimated that a fifth of all children in Oakland, California, were being raised by their grandparents, due in large part to their parents' involvement with drugs. One study at that time found that thousands of grandparents in New York City were also raising their grandchildren, because the children's mothers were either drug addicts, in prison, or dead from AIDS.[2]

Although America is in a continual state of war against drugs, we never seem to win. Tony Soprano's insistence that his men steer clear of drugs dissuades no one. Even his friend Big Pussy Bompensiero dealt heroin until the law caught up with him and convinced him to inform on Tony. The money in drug sales is just too good, and despite efforts by law enforcement that make it a riskier racket than most, both the supply and the market remain consistently strong. New laws and initiatives crop up constantly, yet none prove effective. In 1993, former Drug Enforcement Administration head John Long and former DEA Deputy Chief Thomas Kelly claimed that the demand for cocaine in America was so great and the money involved so substantial that new drug supply networks cropped up almost daily.[3] By the most optimistic estimates, law-enforcement officials seize only 10–15 percent of illegal drug shipments imported into the United States; in a 1988 *National Law Journal* poll of 181 prosecutors, two thirds of those interviewed stated they were having little or no impact against the sale and trafficking of illegal narcotics.[4] Recent movies like *Traffic* and *Blow* show that the fourth war on drugs within a century was lost before it began. Ironically, a number of members of Congress confessed that they did not realize that we were losing the war on drugs until they saw *Traffic!*

The most seriously addicting illegal drugs in America are heroin and cocaine, which kill 2,000–3,000 people a year. Due to unsanitary needles, injectable drugs cause about a third of the nation's cases of HIV infection. Together, all illegal drugs combined are thought to be responsible for perhaps 7,500 deaths each year in America. Yet alcohol, a legal drug, is implicated in 150,000 deaths a year, and cigarettes kill an estimated 460,000 Americans a year.[5] Thus, the legal drugs of tobacco and alcohol kill 570 times the number of people that illegal drugs kill—a most interesting irony of the war on drugs.

Although Tony Soprano does not condone trafficking in illegal drugs, he has no problem with stolen cigarettes or alcohol. However, some of his crew regularly take cocaine, methamphetamines, and marijuana. In the first season, Meadow asks Christopher for some crank to help her study for the SATs. Christopher—himself a frequent drug user—rationalizes that to protect Meadow from buying drugs from strangers, he'll give her some "just this one time." We've also seen several instances when Mafia family members were itching to branch out into heroin trafficking, only to be told no by Tony. This behavior isn't altruistic: government retaliation for dealing with stolen alcohol and tobacco pales in comparison to what the Feds do to drug traffickers.

Street Crime and Drugs: The Chicken or the Egg?

America's violent street-crime and drug problems are inseparable. It has never been completely clear if drug users who commit street crimes begin using drugs first and then begin committing crimes or if they start with criminal activity and then enter into drug use as part of a criminal subculture.

The examples on *The Sopranos* provide a skewed view of the situation, as most of the characters were born into a life of crime. As Tony Soprano's nephew, Christopher gravitated toward crime, although it seems possible that both Meadow and A.J. may escape. Jackie Aprile Jr. seemed destined for better things, but after his father's death he began the slow descent from academic achievement to illegal, more immediate gains. However, even though Tony's kids have avoided both crime and drugs and Christopher and Jackie Jr. have avoided neither, the conclusions about the connection remain vague. Often the connection differs with each type of substance abused. Most often, criminals who begin their drug abuse with alcohol are alcohol abusers first, and then engage in crime. Criminals addicted to heroin or cocaine largely begin by committing crimes and then becoming addicted to drugs. One survey of U.S. prisoners found that 60 percent of the prison population who had ever abused drugs did so only after their first arrest.[6] However, there is little doubt that drug use makes the crime problem in America much worse than it would be otherwise.

The vast majority of street criminals who use drugs are poly-drug users—marijuana, alcohol, cocaine, heroin, or sedatives—and are often addicted to more than one drug. Because one drug alleviates the undesired side effects of the other, heroin and cocaine are commonly used together. What may be surprising to realize is the unappreciated relationship between the use of legal substances—especially alco-hol—and the use of illegal drugs—especially heroin and cocaine. These findings present alarming implications for our children, who learn their behavior from what they see and what they are surrounded by. They begin drinking early, rapidly move on to illegal drug use, and wind up using more than one drug on a regular basis—all the while increasing the odds that they will commit one or more crimes.

Besides drug selling, street crime tends toward petty property crime, which usually "pays" much better than other kinds of small crime—it's tax-free and offenders tend to get away with it more fre-quently. The type of crime represented most frequently on *The Sopra-nos* falls into this category: DVD players "fall" off a truck and into the hands of Tony's crew, Christopher showers Adriana with piles of stolen designer shoes, the characters deal in hot cars, fenced jewelry, and stolen cartons of cigarettes.

However, drug-using street criminals commit more frequent and serious crimes than do non–drug-using street criminals. Several years' worth of studies conducted on weekends by the Department of Jus-tice in major American cities during the past dozen years confirm this, showing that between 60 to 90 percent of people arrested for felony crimes test positive for illegal drugs. And those addicts who are criminals commit a tremendous amount of crime. In California, for example, in 2001, a mere 6 percent of the criminals accounted for fully 60 percent of all violent felonies. Data have long existed con-firming the vast majority of these felonies as drug related.

The relationship between drugs and crime does not stop at the street-crime level, however; according to the news media, the public, and politicians seeking office, street crime is just the most visible form of crime. In fact, other forms of drug-related crime are far more common—yet infrequently discussed, even though they involve far higher levels of money and corruption. The drug-crime relationship creates a "crimeogenic department store," where crime and drugs form a complex, interrelated web in which criminals of all stripes exist without ever meeting each other. Junkies, street gangs, Tony

Soprano–type syndicate members, corrupt cops and politicians, money launderers, and even members of the CIA all play their roles, but rarely meet each other face-to-face. Yet the whole system functions with corporate-like precision much of the time.

One way to picture the interrelated nature of the crime and drug problems is to view it as a department store with different floors. The department store deals in two products: drugs and money. Both are manufactured at each floor—with different levels of involvement, a broader reach, escalating quantities, and a fatter wallet at each floor. Drug users who commit street crimes make up the department store's ground floor. Let's take a look at the recent history of the other floors of the store.

The Crimeogenic Department Store:
First Floor: Street Gangs

The first floor of the Crimeogenic Department Store houses street gangs made up of youthful offenders involved in the manufacture and distribution of crack cocaine. After making its debut in America in 1985, crack cocaine became a staple product of many street gangs throughout the United States. With regular cocaine going for $100 or more a gram in the mid-1980s, crack provided a cheap alternative— about $5 to $10 a dose. After crack was introduced, cocaine-related deaths increased four-fold in the United States.

The lucrative crack trade created a huge market for street gangs in large urban areas, especially Los Angeles, where substantial increases in gang membership in the Crips and Bloods followed the introduction of crack. Between 1985 and 1988, the Los Angeles Police Department noted a 71 percent increase in the number of gangs in LA. Contemporary studies reported the presence of over 100 gangs in Chicago, fifteen to twenty in Cleveland, fifteen in Columbus, Ohio, thirty-one in Phoenix, sixty-six in New York City, eight in Dade County, Florida, and thirty-five in San Diego. Gangs tend to be about 90 percent male, although the percentage of female members is growing. Ethnically, the

gangs are homogeneous, reflecting the ethnic composition of the segregated neighborhoods from which they arise. Thus, African-American
neighborhoods—such as South Central LA—give rise to African-
American gangs, Asian neighborhoods—heavily concentrated on the
West Coast—to Asian gangs, Puerto Rican communities—found
along the East Coast—to Puerto Rican gangs, and so on. Admittedly,
the market has shrunk since its zenith in the 1980s.

Contemporary street gangs operate with bureaucratic efficiency,
possess powerful weapons, such as Uzi submachine guns, and use
state-of-the-art technology, cell phones, laptops, PDAs, and pagers.
Gangs are set up in the same type of hierarchies as are Soprano-style
Mafia-type syndicates: lieutenants reporting to capos reporting to one
central head. This structure allows gangs not only to stay organized,
but also to flourish: by their 1991 apexes, the Crips had 30,000 members and the Bloods 9,000.[7] Before heading east, the LA gangs
quickly spread their operations to major cities on the West Coast and
then inland to places like Denver. The DEA claims that LA gang
members have branched out into virtually every state, with Crips
being arrested for drug-related shootings as far away as Buffalo.[8]
Miami-based gangs have also branched out to cities in the South, like
Atlanta and Savannah, Georgia, and Mobile and Montgomery,
Alabama. Their spread was not necessarily conspiratorial; often they
went where they found fewer law-enforcement officials and cheaper
drug products available for purchase.

Crime in these cities—especially weapons offenses and drug-
related homicides from battles over territory—increased in the 1980s
and early 1990s before leveling off and then declining. Many innocent people, including children, were gunned down in the crossfire.
In 1991, after crack-dealing gangs entered Chicago neighborhoods,
623 drug-related murders were committed by August of that year.[9]
This example typifies the relationship between drugs and violent
crime, especially homicide. In 1988, at the height of New York City's
crack epidemic, the body count reached an all-time high—1,896
murders in a single year.

A study of 414 of these homicides found that over half of the murders were primarily drug related.[10] Moreover, a third of the victims were drug dealers. Although in the vast majority of these cases, the murderers were not high on drugs—these homicides being about the struggle for neighborhood territories for the street-level trade—these homicides were definitely drug related.

Street gangs represent only the first level of organization in the crime-drug hierarchy. However, the first floor of the Crimeogenic Department Store is an important one in the evolution of a career criminal: gang-related crime is one step up from disorganized, solitary street crime. Tony Soprano's nephew Christopher, for instance, participated in crimes perpetrated by small gangs of his friends looking to work their way up to a more elevated criminal status. Gang members often recruit youthful offenders and street-crime veterans, so gangs form an important bridge to higher levels of organized crime, where they have the opportunity to advance in rank, make more money, and sell more drugs. Street gangs might be a vital link in the drug distribution process, but they generally do not grow or import drugs into the United States; that floor of the Crimeogenic Department Store belongs to members of organized-crime syndicates.

Second Floor: Organized Crime

Unlike street gangs, whose members tend to be teens or young adults who eventually quit gang life, die, or are promoted to higher ranks, members of organized-crime syndicates tend to start as adults—and their membership is for life. However, street gang members often join organized-crime syndicates upon reaching adulthood. For example, the late Gambino family godfather John Gotti and his brother began their organized-crime careers with membership in a street gang that specialized in robbery. In January 1992, a two-year federal investigation found that LA's Crips had direct ties to the Medellín cocaine cartel, a leading organized-crime syndicate.[11] Likewise, several of Christopher Moltisanti's younger associates on *The Sopranos*, either street criminals or street gang members, hope for initiation into Tony's crew as a reward for their laudable street and gang crime efforts. Although their eagerness and ambition often prove their undoing—as when two members of Christopher's gang are killed after trying to kill him to impress Tony's rival Richie Aprile—Christopher himself eventually proves himself worthy and is inducted as a made man. In our Crimeogenic Department Store, the first floor often leads directly to the second.

The definition of organized crime has always been controversial, the exact structure of organized crime itself steeped in myth and heated debate. Most experts view organized-crime syndicates as possessing common traits including:

- An organized hierarchy
- Profits made through criminal activity enterprise
- Threats or actual use of force
- Corruption of public officials, law-enforcement agents, and politicians
- Trafficking in illegal goods and services: drugs, prostitution, illegal gambling, loan-sharking, illegally dumping toxic waste

However, organized-crime syndicates frequently engage in a host of legitimate business activities, everything from owning car dealerships and pizza parlors to real estate development and property management.[12] Many of these businesses serve as fronts to hide profits and criminal acts connected with illegal enterprises.

In *The Sopranos*, for example, Tony runs a waste management facility that serves to account for his annual income. In fact, when asked what her father does for a living, Meadow usually replies that he's in waste management, although as the show develops, she appears increasingly uncomfortable doing so. Other crew members operate restaurants, manage stores, run bars, host clubs, and engage in a number of other legal activities to keep a clean front for the Feds.

These legitimate businesses serve a dual purpose: they not only explain the crew's income to the IRS but also serve as locations for clandestine meetings and illegal activities.

While organized criminal syndicates engage in a host of illegal activities, none is more profitable than the importation and selling of illegal drugs. In 1986, it was estimated that the worldwide illicit drug market grosses anywhere from $500 billion to $750 billion a year, an amount larger than the gross national product of many nations.[13] The figure today is probably around $400 billion. The American Mafia, in its heyday from the 1960s to the 1980s, realized an estimated annual profit of $78 billion from the drug trade. Compare this to the $200 million income it receives from bootlegged cigarettes, and the immense profits to be made by keeping drugs illegal become obvious. Even though Tony Soprano still refuses to claim drug trafficking as part of his many illegal activities, many rival families have not followed suit—the profits are just too big.

The Italian-American Mafia

Different crime syndicates sometimes specialize in different types of drug sales. Italo-Sicilian crime families got into the heroin trade in the late 1940s and still import heroin into the United States from Europe, especially Italy, concentrating primarily on the East Coast market. In the 1980s, the Mafia also began selling cocaine. The American Mafia is linked to the modern-day Sicilian Mafia via the Sicilian Zips, Mafia members sent to the United States as transporters of heroin and cocaine to supply the New York–New Jersey Mafia families. The Zips are linked to the American Mafia by blood and include two of the Gambino brothers, relatives of the heads of one of New York's most powerful crime families. Tony and his crew, fictionalized representations of an anonymous branch of the Italo-Sicilian Mafia, most closely resemble the American Mafia, although, as mentioned earlier, the show does not yet have them involved in the drug trade.

The Latin-American Drug Cartels

Most of America's heroin and cocaine comes from Latin American syndicates. The Herrera Family, a Mexican organized-crime syndicate, operates in cocaine and Mexican brown heroin. Consisting of six interrelated familial groups, about 2,000 of whom are related by marriage or blood, the Herrera family is centered in the Mexican state of Durango. In the United States, the Herreras have headquarters in Chicago, where they have now allied with the Colombian cocaine cartel. The Herreras illustrate the "organized" aspect of organized crime. In 1985, 135 of their members were indicted in Chicago; over eighty Herreras were convicted and dozens became fugitives. By 1988, all those convicted or on the run had been replaced.[14] This ability of organized-crime syndicates to guarantee succession makes them extremely difficult to eliminate completely.

The famous Colombian drug cartel is known as the Cali group. Most cocaine destined for the U.S. is shipped from Colombia by way of Mexico to satisfy the 2.5 to 3 million cocaine users in the U.S.

The Japanese Yakuza

A Japanese crime syndicate, the Yakuza—meaning "good-for-nothing"—specializes in methamphetamine production in Korea, Japan, and the Philippines. Over 300 years old, this group lives by a code established in feudal times by Japan's Samurai warriors. Yakuza are famous for rituals involving cutting off fingers and tattooing their bodies from ankle to neck to demonstrate their loyalty to the group.

In Japan, the Yakuza hold influence with the police and politicians at the highest levels of government. Their relationship with Japan's police involves an arrangement whereby the Yakuza escape prosecution in exchange for literally policing Japan's street criminals. As a result, Japan's street-crime rate remains very low, and its organized-crime syndicates run in such an open fashion that some even have phone book listings, member newsletters, and office buildings complete with the organization's logo. The Yakuza helped derail the Japanese economy in 2001 via massive bank frauds, and they maintain active interests in the global sexual slavery trade as well.

The African-American El Rukins

African-American organized crime began when African-American soldiers in Vietnam experienced the Southeast Asian heroin market firsthand in the early 1970s. They learned that they could purchase heroin directly from Asian suppliers, bypassing the Italian-American Mafia. The most prominent African-American crime organization is El Rukins, which was founded by Jeff Fort in 1970 while serving a prison sentence for contempt of Congress and embezzling funds from an Office of Economic Opportunity federal grant. El Rukins have dealt in cocaine smuggling and have assisted Libya's Muammar al-Qaddafi in terrorist activities. They have been employed by Chicago's Cook County Democratic Organization to campaign in African-American wards and served as poll watchers in the 1983 Chicago mayoral election.[15] Other African organized-crime families are of Nigerian and Haitian origin and usually supply heroin to cities in the East and Midwest.

These are just the largest groups; smaller drug-dealing syndicates abound. Jamaican gangs—also known as posses—comprise thirty different groups with an estimated 10,000 members. The posses in the 1980s operated fifty-five crack cocaine houses in as many American cities, some of which brought in $9 million a month. America's prisons also house organized criminal syndicates—including the Mexican Mafia, La Nuestra Familia, the Aryan Brotherhood, the African

American Guerrilla Family, and the Texas Syndicate—that distribute drugs, especially heroin, in some of the largest prisons in the United States. American-based Russian organized-crime groups smuggle narcotics into the country from the former Soviet bloc. Heroin from Afghanistan and Pakistan frequently ends up in the hands of Russian Mafia members. A Cuban organized-crime group grew out of the failed invasion of Cuba's Bay of Pigs in 1961. Trained by the CIA, some of its members went into cocaine trafficking after the failed invasion, but they were taken over in 1976 after a bloody war with the Colombian cartel. Finally, motorcycle gangs—Hell's Angels, Outlaws, Pagans, and Banditos—deal in methamphetamines and phenycline (PCP or angel dust).

Although many theories and myths about the structure and causes of organized crime abound, solid empirical evidence exists to show that, in America's Crimeogenic Department Store, organized crime occupies a unique position. In essence, organized criminal syndicates provide the bridge, a vital link between "underworld" crime committed by drug gangs and street addicts and "upper-world" crime engaged in by white-collar professionals and legitimate corporate and governmental organizations.[16]

Third Floor: White-Collar Crime

Most media presentations, like the *Godfather* movies, portray white-collar criminals as a super-secret conspiratorial set of organized-crime families who, through force and threat, bully their way into whatever endeavors they choose. Hence, the public understands "making you an offer you can't refuse" as the modus operandi of the Mafia. Much empirical evidence points in another direction, however.

White-collar occupations include business owners, professionals, lawyers, bankers, and doctors; the term "white-collar crime" refers to the illegal activities these otherwise respectable citizens commit. White-collar crime can take about any shape and form imaginable, but a few types seem to be most prevalent. White-collar criminals often agree to launder drug money for criminal syndicates, accepting huge amounts of cash, typically in small denominations in exchange for cashier's checks or other liquid assets, such as bonds, stocks, and money orders. Colombian drug traffickers, through wholesale jewelry markets in New York, Los Angeles, and Houston, laundered an estimated $1 billion in cash in the late 1980s. Those convicted in the scheme included two gold traders.[17]

Neither organized crime nor the illegal drug business could exist without the cooperation of legitimate elites in government, the criminal justice system, and businesses. In fact, much evidence suggests that organized criminal syndicates, corporations, and government agencies have cooperated with each other throughout the postmodern era, 1945 to the present.

In *The Sopranos*, legitimate businesses owned or operated by members of Tony's crew actually serve to launder money for Tony's and other syndicates. Although we haven't seen Tony's direct interaction with white-collar businesspeople, we know he's been in contact with them: during the first season, at Dr. Melfi's urging, Tony considered joining a country club, only to be pestered by dentists, doctors, and other white-collar professionals—none of whom were condemning his Mafia roots but rather dying to hear stories about his wicked ways. Their eagerness to hear about Tony's Mafia exploits can perhaps explain why professional people choose to risk financial and personal ruin to engage in money laundering and other types of drug-related crime: the risks, the thrill of it all, the glory.

Fourth Floor: Banks and Major Corporations

When organized-crime members need to launder a few hundred thousand dollars, they look to white-collar criminals. When they need to clean several million dollars, the syndicate looks a little higher, to large investment firms, national banks, and major corporations, such as American Express, Merrill Lynch, and various other financial institutions. These large, sometimes multinational firms have a broader global reach, more financial power, and a greater number of individual—potentially bribable—arms, making it easier for the Mob to launder with impunity. Regardless of the institution's ethical stance on, direct participation in, or knowledge of money laundering, these banks and corporations are still involved. One doesn't have to be a willing participant to have a workstation in the Crimeogenic Department Store.

Federal law requires that banks report all cash deposits of $10,000 to the Internal Revenue Service. In 1975, only 3,000 such deposits were reported. In 1988, the number had soared to 5.5 million. A number of major American banks have willingly overlooked the IRS's reporting requirement, sometimes receiving a 1.5 to 2 percent commission from drug-trafficking depositors for doing so. Estimates suggest that the total amount of money laundered each year is immense. It has increased from an estimated $300 billion in the early 1990s to around $1.2 trillion in 2001, about half of all funds connected to the worldwide drug trade. Of this amount, $100 billion is laundered in the United States. Nine tenths of this amount ends up overseas, often in secret Swiss accounts, where it can then be freely moved.

In the 1980s, the famous "Pizza Connection" case resulted in the conviction of over 400 Mafia members in Sicily and the United States on numerous charges, including heroin trafficking. Gangsters had laundered tens of millions of dollars in cash through a number of New York City banks, which then electronically wired the money into secret, untraceable accounts in Swiss banks. Although the banks could claim innocence of the drug connection to these funds, they should have had some suspicion that these large, routine deposits, made by numerous Mafia goombahs, were specious in nature.

The Pizza Connection traffickers also deposited $5 million in cash with the Merrill Lynch brokerage firm in $5, $10, and $20 bills over a six-week period. Merrill Lynch not only accepted these dubious deposits but also provided the couriers to transport the money with extra security. The same couriers helped launder $13.5 million through accounts at the E. F. Hutton investment firm, which also provided security for them.[18]

It's easy to look at these patterns of big business and banking crime and be skeptical of yet one more half-baked conspiracy theory surrounding them. However, consider these other schemes committed by big businesses and financial institutions:

- In 1991, the National Mortgage Bank of Greece was fined a record $1.8 million by a Brooklyn federal judge because the bank's American branch engaged in one of the largest money-laundering schemes in U.S. history.[19]
- In the 1980s, CIA associates used Florida's Castle Bank to launder drug money for organized-crime figures.[20]
- Also in the 1980s, another Florida bank with CIA ties, the Bank of Perrine, was purchased by the Colombian cocaine cartel to launder drug money.[21]
- The CIA and the Mafia both played an important role in establishing the World Finance Corporation, a Florida-based company that laundered drug money and supported terrorist activities in the early 1970s.[22]

Finally, consider perhaps the most scandalous example of cooperation between legitimate corporations and global crime syndicates: for years during the 1990s, big tobacco firms hired global organized-crime syndicates in North and South America, Asia, and elsewhere to sell cigarettes on the African-American market. In addition, as many as one in every three cigarettes may have been sold this way worldwide. In return, some of the tobacco firms agreed to launder drug money for the Latin American cocaine cartels.[23]

Fifth Floor: The Criminal Justice System

Although Tony Soprano worries about federal investigations into his activities and frets over the fine details of the RICO predicates, he has no fear of local authorities. In his world, police are easily bribed or lured into cooperation. In the first season, police detective Vin Makazian helpfully watches for Tony the happenings at police head-quarters. He goes even further, trailing Dr. Melfi to assure Tony that she can be trusted, and even beating up her date in the belief that Tony and Dr. Melfi are romantically involved. When Tony takes over his Uncle Junior's high-stakes poker game, Paulie pays off the beat cop to make sure the authorities keep clear of the action. Tony has nothing to fear from the police in his own backyard. Organized crim-inal syndicates are a chief source of corruption among federal, state, and local criminal justice personnel. The United States has a long history of police corruption, so long that every source investigating the problem since the 1890s has unearthed substantial and wide-ranging forms of police bribery. About 100 drug-related bribery cases involving police at all levels of the criminal justice system now come before American courts each year. For example:

- Seven Boston police detectives were convicted on fifty-seven bribery counts involving $18,000 over eight years.
- Sheriffs in several rural Georgia counties accepted bribes of $50,000 each to permit drug smugglers to land airplanes on abandoned roads.
- In 1990, federal agents arrested sheriffs in four Kentucky coun-ties for taking money from cocaine traffickers in exchange for safe passage through their state.[24]

As much as we'd like to believe that law-enforcement officials are above corruption and drug trafficking, there is just too much evidence to the contrary. In 1991, a Los Angeles grand jury indicted seven members of an elite police narcotics squad unit for stealing tens of thousands of dollars from drug seizure money and for falsely accus-ing defendants. The seven deputies from the Narcotics Division of the LA County Sheriff's Department were ultimately convicted of skimming $1.4 million from drug seizures.[25] In this case, we have cor-ruption on so many levels that we can't begin to trace the roots.

As mentioned, Tony Soprano is no stranger to police corruption. He and his crew make regular payments to local law-enforcement agencies so they will steer clear of Tony's underworld dealings. The main crime-prevention presence on the show is the FBI, whose constant, bumbling attempts at indicting Tony provide a source of comic relief. Even Agent Harris, who frequently appears to question and sometimes to arrest Tony, comes across as nothing more than a bland bureaucrat wearily discharging his duties. The only time we see the police is when they are interacting with Tony and his crew on a personal level. For example, during the third season, Tony receives a moving violation from an honest cop. Tony's attitude is incredulous: doesn't the cop know whom he's ticketing? After verbally insulting the officer, Tony pays the ticket, but follows up with a city official, who demotes the officer. As seasoned viewers of crime-family movies and films, we expect this behavior from Tony and are appalled that the officer would think of ticketing someone with Tony's power.

Police corruption occurs most often with the enforcement of so-called victimless crimes, especially narcotics and other drugs. Legislatures have typically enacted laws to enforce the morality of the majority, making criminal certain offensive acts that may harm the individual who performs them. Laws prohibiting gambling, sex between consenting adults, pornography, liquor, and drug use create such victimless crimes. Over 80 percent of the police work in the United States deals with the regulation of private morals. Although many police officers refuse to accept bribes from murderers and thieves, they may accept them from the perpetrators of victimless crimes. This occurs for several reasons: they believe these crimes are harmless and impossible to control anyway; they may feel strong community pressures against enforcement of such laws; and they face organized crime, with its threats and enticements, which encourages cooperation. Many police departments manufacture ideologies, which neutralize any guilt about taking payoffs, making distinctions between "clean" money (for example, from drugs sold to adults or minorities of any age) and "dirty" money (for example, from drugs sold to white children).

Between 1994 and 1997, some 508 people were convicted of law-enforcement corruption in cases investigated by the FBI.[26] A partial list of cases reveals the presence of organized crime and illegal drugs in American society.

- In 1987, Mike "Mad Dog" Roark (so named for his fierce pursuit of drug dealers while outfitted in combat fatigues and packing a pistol, prosecutor and mayor of Charleston, West Virginia, pleaded guilty to six counts of cocaine possession.
- In 1990, the FBI produced a forty-two-count indictment of Kentucky law officers for conspiracy to extort and protect illegal drug traffickers.
- In 1993, thirty-five New York City police officers were arrested for preying on drug dealers. The officers would rob the drug dealers of cocaine, guns, and money. A commission headed by Judge Milton Mollen released a preliminary report on New York City Police corruption, drug trafficking, police brutality, and so on, condemning the "blue wall of silence" that police erect during investigations of police corruption.
- In 1995, an investigation by author Anthony Summers concluded that former FBI Director J. Edgar Hoover protected organized crime for years because the Mafia knew about Hoover's homosexuality, including his cross-dressing and participation in orgies. Mafia bosses Frank Costello and Meyer Lansky allegedly had obtained photographs of the FBI director having sex with his aide and lover Clyde Tolson.

Although no major metropolitan police department is completely free of police misconduct, a handful of U.S. cities have developed well-deserved reputations of rampant corruption. Some of worst problems face five cities that have had the lion's share of bad press regarding police corruption: New York, Los Angeles, Miami, Philadelphia, and New Orleans.

New York

The New York Police Department (NYPD) has a distinct and enduring reputation of police corruption and excessive force spanning many decades. Two independent commissions have been organized to investigate New York's problem: the Knapp Commission of the 1970s and the Mollen Commission of the 1990s. At one time, police corruption in the NYPD was so uncontrollable that a Special State Prosecutor for Corruption was appointed in 1972 by Governor Nelson Rockefeller. Governor Mario Cuomo later abolished the position due largely to costs. The Mollen Commission was formed in the early 1990s. Independent investigatory committees such as these have become quite controversial in a city where politicians and law-enforcement officials disagree whether something in addition to the NYPD's Internal Affairs Division is needed.

The Knapp Commission report of 1972 exposed major corruption in the NYPD. It was publicized by the 1973 movie *Serpico*, in which a real-life NYPD officer, Frank Serpico (played by Al Pacino), exposed the policemen taking bribes and sharing the take with supervisors. The commission investigated the widespread practice, which led to the dismissal of officers and a change in policy. Officers were literally taken off the streets and encouraged to stay in their cars to discourage the temptation of accepting bribes.

The Mollen Commission operated for twenty-two months in 1993 and 1994. The group discovered rampant police corruption, especially in the West Harlem precinct, where officers had been terrorizing minorities and participating in drug trafficking. The commission's report resulted in the arrest of fourteen NYPD officers, who were charged with various crimes. One particularly surprising charge was the shooting and serious wounding of a drug dealer while officers stole the dealer's cocaine supply and $100,000 in cash during an illegal search. One officer testified during the Mollen Commission hearings that officers kept guns seized from suspects and used them as "throwaway" guns to plant on suspects in the event of a questionable arrest. The report claimed that officers found to be corrupt were more likely to be brutal as well.

The Mollen report uncovered forty corruption cases that were never fully prosecuted and more than 100 that were simply ignored. The report suggested corruption existed in the department's Internal Affairs Division and discovered a common pattern of bribery and "look-the-other-way" schemes previously thought extinct. This misbehavior was supplemented by a new offense: officers acting as criminal conspirators. Perjury by NYPD officers was so common that some have referred to it as "testilying."[27]

By the time the Mollen report was released, more than fifty NYPD officers had been arrested on charges such as drug trafficking, extortion, brutality, and civil rights violations. The central figure of the largest corruption scandal was an officer named Michael Dowd, who led a group of officers who extorted protection money from dealers and sold cocaine to youths. Dowd reportedly received $5,000 to $8,000 a week in payments from drug gangs. Dowd and four other officers were also arrested. Reportedly, the U.S. Attorney had obtained evidence necessary for indictment in 1988 but delayed the arrests for four years for unexplained reasons.[28] Dowd was convicted and sentenced to fourteen years in prison for organizing groups of officers in the raids of Brooklyn drug dealers' apartments for cash and drugs.

In response, the NYPD began to take measures against the problem, such as requiring two years of armed forces or college experience for new recruits to prevent those with discipline problems from entering the force. Independent investigative committees such as the Mollen Commission coupled with corrective actions the department took against corrupt officers made some headway in the fight against corruption, although the NYPD continues to be plagued with the problem. The latest breach in the blue wall of silence was the conviction of three officers in the torture of Abner Louima, a Haitian immigrant, due to testimony by fellow officers.[29]

Los Angeles

In 1992 the Christopher Commission, formed to identify problem areas in policing, identified forty-four problem officers who had histories of excessive force, forging evidence, and murder. The commission was established after police were caught on videotape brutally beating an African American, Rodney King. The acquittal of the officer accused of the beating set off one of the worst riots in American history, with dozens killed and over $1 billion in property damages.

In the early 1990s, the Los Angeles County Sheriff's Department was rocked by a scandal in which $1.4 million was skimmed by the departmental drug squad. Thirty indictments were issued. This source of revenue spread from the Los Angeles Police Department to the Feds. Then in 1995 came the acquittal of O. J. Simpson in the murder of his wife, Nicole, and Ron Goldman, in part due to racist statements made on tape by one of the investigating officers, Los Angeles Police Detective Mark Fuhrman.

In September 1999, another scandal unraveled in the Los Angeles Police Department. It was revealed that a judge had sent Javier Ovando, an Hispanic male, to prison in 1997 for twenty-three years after two anti-gang squad officers, who had shot Ovando, claimed that he had threatened the officers with a gun. The shooting left Ovando paralyzed for life. In 1999, one of the officers involved admitted they had framed Ovando. Not only had Ovando been unarmed, but the officers—who were being investigated for stealing from drug dealers—had planted a gun on him after shooting him. The case against Ovando was dismissed, and because he admitted to framing Ovando, Officer Rafael Perez had his sentence for stealing cocaine reduced. In addition, over a dozen other officers were relieved of duty and put under investigation for selling drugs, using excessive force, and/or covering up the scandal within the anti-gang division.

According to the National Association of Criminal Defense Attorneys:

> Rafael Perez was an officer in the Los Angeles Police Department's Rampart Division's anti-gang unit, until he was charged with stealing eight pounds of cocaine from department evidence storage. As part of his plea agreement for reduced time, he gave, and may still give, a series of statements about wrongdoing by officers in the unit.
>
> In Los Angeles the District Attorney asked the court to set aside more than a hundred convictions. The LA City Attorney recommended and the city council approved a $15 million settlement for Javier Ovando, one of the Rampart victims. The Los Angeles Police Department has been placed under federal supervision. This is just the beginning.
>
> The court-appointed lawyers for citizen/victims of the Rampart police are reviewing thousands of cases, in an effort to identify and correct all of the abuses of the Rampart police. The city anticipates that damages payments to victims will exceed $100 million. Damage to the criminal justice system and people's confidence in it may be irreparable.
>
> The magnitude of Rampart police misconduct is astonishing. Equally astonishing is the fact that the police crimes went unnoticed by the authorities for years. They became public only when Det. Perez was arrested for his own crimes. In a successful effort to reduce the years in prison that awaited him, Perez turned on his criminal colleagues. The "blue wall of silence" was breached, but for all the wrong reasons.[30]

Miami

Miami has a notorious reputation for police corruption due to the remarkable amount of drug business that infiltrates the city. Crime related to the drug trade overwhelms department policemen and provides temptations involving large amounts of cash. During the mid- to late 1980s, the Miami Police Department developed corruption problems that continue to this day.

Much of Miami's drug-related crime centers around the cocaine trade. Cases involving Miami police officers have included cocaine shipments stolen from lobster boats, officers selling badges to criminals, robbery, kidnapping, cocaine possession, and attempted murder. In a highly publicized 1986 case, seven Miami police officers were indicted on charges including racketeering, drug possession, robbery, cocaine trafficking, aggravated battery, and murder when they stole cocaine from a boat while the drug smugglers, who were hiding below, drowned; the officers later sold the drugs and kept the profit. Three officers were charged with the smugglers' murders. The officers were members of a ring called The Enterprise, a gang of ten former and current Miami policemen.

In the mid-1980s, 10 percent of Miami's police force were jailed, fired, or disciplined in connection with a scheme where officers robbed and sometimes killed cocaine smugglers, then resold the stolen drugs.

Things have only gotten worse since the 1980s. In 2001, thirteen current and former officers were charged with conspiracy and other crimes related to planting guns at crime scenes, imitating the TV show *Miami Vice*.[31]

Philadelphia

In 1974, the Pennsylvania Crime Commission concluded that the Philadelphia Police Department was plagued with corruption. Officers were accepting free food and money from businesses in return for extra police protection and were taking payoffs from bars and clubs to overlook state liquor code violations. Officers were taking bribes to protect drug trafficking, prostitution rings, and gambling dens.

The Philadelphia Police Department has an impressive history of police corruption involving a wide variety of offenses. In 1984, seven policemen (including the former chief) were convicted of accepting $350,000 in bribes from gamblers trying to avoid arrest. More than thirty Philadelphia officers were convicted of extorting or scheming to extort money from drug dealers in the 1980s.

Former Police Commissioner Frank Rizzo seemingly tolerated a brutal police force. He was known to say, "The way to treat criminals is *spacco il capa* (bust their heads)."[32] Under Rizzo's command in the 1970s (as compared with that of his predecessor), Philadelphia policemen were thirty-seven times more likely to shoot unarmed citizens fleeing the scenes of nonviolent offenses.

In another corruption exposure, a well-organized group of six Philadelphia officers admitted in 1995 to lying, obtaining false search warrants, and planting false evidence as well as stealing money from suspects. Their guilty pleas resulted in the reversal of 116 convictions. A typical action by the group was to steal money from younger African-American males in poor neighborhoods and fake evidence of drug dealing. They also burglarized businesses, trafficked heroin, sold police files, and ran prostitution rings. In 1996 the Philadelphia district attorney stated that about 1,400 convictions would have to be reconsidered due to the corrupt cop's activities.

New Orleans

Notorious for corrupt police officers and low wages, the New Orleans Police Department has yet to outgrow its reputation as one of the most corrupt, brutal, and incompetent departments in the nation. A 1980 incident leading to the resignation of the police superintendent occurred over the shooting of a white officer. Mobs of police entered a predominantly African-American area of town and killed four, injured fifty, and carried out mock executions on two more.[33]

In 1995, it was reported that fifty New Orleans police officers had been arrested, indicted, or convicted over the previous two years for rape, bank robbery, aggravated battery, drug trafficking, and homicide. Two shocking cases of murder committed by officers occurred less than a year apart. New Orleans police officer Len Davis faced the death penalty after ordering the murder of a woman, Kim Groves, who had filed a brutality complaint against him (for allegedly pistol whipping her friend) in October 1994. Although the complaint was confidential, Davis somehow discovered it and put out a hit on the woman. In 1995, Davis was sentenced to life plus five years in prison.[34] In March of that year, officer Antoinette Frank shot and killed a fellow officer while she was robbing a restaurant. She also killed two others working at the restaurant, execution-style. Unbelievably, during the year before Frank's arrest, four other New Orleans police officers were also arrested for murder.

An outside reformer appointed in 1994 as police chief, Richard Pennington fired and disciplined a number of officers, improved background checks for recruits, and instituted a system to identify repeat offenders.

Sixth Floor: Crime in Government Intelligence Agencies

Members of the CIA may not be peddling drugs on American street corners, but in the name of anticommunism, world power, and acquired wealth, it has indirectly helped the global drug trade for years. U.S. intelligence agencies have a long history of accepting assistance from and providing logistical support to some of the world's largest drug-trafficking syndicates.[35]

The CIA helped build what became known as the "French connection," the enterprise primarily responsible for the U.S. heroin market from the 1950s to the 1970s. In 1950, the CIA recruited Corsican gangsters, the Ferri-Pisani family, to form an elite terror squad to break a strike by Marseilles dockworkers who had refused to ship arms to Indochina in support of the French military presence there. Corsican gangsters assaulted communist union picket lines and harassed union officials. In return for stopping the strike, the Ferri-Pisani family was allowed to use Marseilles as a shipping center for Corsican heroin en route to the United States.[36]

The U.S. government also supported opium production in South-east Asia's Golden Triangle (poppy-growing regions in Thailand, Burma, and Laos) for over thirty years by providing arms, military support, and protection of corrupt officials—all in the name of anti-communism. This relationship began in the 1950s, after Mao Zedong's Chinese Communists defeated Chiang Kai-shek's National-ist Chinese army, the Kuomintang (KMT), in 1949. The CIA helped the KMT regroup and settle in a region bordering China, Burma's Shan States, one of the richest sources of opium poppies in the world. By 1959, opium production in the region had increased nearly tenfold, and the leading Chinese organized-crime operation, the Cholon Triad, was born. The CIA helped the KMT ferry opium to Laos, where the CIA taught farmers to grow opium. Between 1964 and 1975, CIA-funded Laotian tribe members processed opium into heroin—the CIA even helped smuggle the heroin out of Laos on its own airline, Air America.[37]

Much of this effort backfired. In 1970 the Cholon Triad began producing and importing into Vietnam injectable heroin, sold to American military personnel by poor street kids, South Vietnamese soldiers, and prostitutes. Street peddlers gave away free samples. By mid-1971, the U.S. Army estimated that 15 percent of its members, 40,000 of the 267,000 GIs in Vietnam, were heroin addicts. By 1974, an estimated 100,000 American soldiers in Vietnam were addicted to heroin, consuming as much heroin as would 2 million users in the United States.[38]

In the 1950s, the CIA aided Chinese organized crime by bribing the head of the Thai police, General Phao Srivanonda, who went into partnership with Cholon Triad in vice operations, extorted money from wealthy citizens, and rigged Bangkok's gold exchange before being ousted in 1957. The Thai government gave exclusive drug-trafficking rights to remnants of Chiang Kai-shek's KMT, now the world's largest heroin-trafficking army.[39] All of this was made pos-sible by the CIA, unbeknownst to U.S. taxpayers, who of course footed the bill.

The Crimeogenic Department Store's Closet:
Civil Rights Abuses

One of Tony Soprano's smartest moves—better than any numbers racket, high-stakes gambling, or major heist—is his maintenance of a family-man image. As much friction as it causes with his underlings, his attempt to keep clear of the drug business means that the authorities have fewer pretenses on which to arrest or investigate him. Although in light of the many other illegal operations that Tony oversees, this may seem only a slight concession, it allows him to stay away from an area of law enforcement that engenders routine civil rights abuses. Therefore, the FBI maintains a plodding pace when it comes to building evidence against Tony. Without the cover of a hot-button issue like drug sales (and of course considering the highly paid legal counsel Tony keeps on retainer), the agents must be careful to make sure that they follow protocol carefully to avoid abuses of Tony's civil rights.

Many legal experts have remarked that one of the first casualties of the war on drugs may be the civil liberties guaranteed to Americans in the U.S. Constitution.[40] In other words, in our fervor to rid the nation of illegal drugs, we may take shortcuts similar to those that Tony Soprano takes in his pursuit of the American Dream. Why adhere to constitutional protections when the persons violated are drug criminals? We may choose to ignore the finer points of our laws if we see the traffickers as part of a minority group—those marginalized, second-class citizens who make up the largest body count in the drug trade—or better yet, the poor, who have neither a voice in our legal system, nor the money to purchase one.

The enforcement of drug laws has always been closely tied to the social control and repression of the rights of minority groups:

- The anti-opium laws of the 1870s were the first narcotics laws in the United States. These amounted to a direct attack on the working-class Chinese immigrants on the West and East

Coasts, many of whom participated in the building of the American railroads.

- In 1914, the Harrison Act outlawed cocaine, a very popular drug among the middle class; it was an ingredient in Coca-Cola, and Sears even sold it by mail order. But American racists convinced the federal government that African Americans, high on cocaine, were busily committing violence and sexual assaults.

- From 1919 to 1933, liquor was outlawed because upper-class WASP reformers feared that the newly arrived Catholic working class would use the neighborhood bar to foment revolution.

- In 1937, the Marijuana Tax Act outlawed marijuana, the outcome of a campaign by people convinced that "lazy Mexican workers" were the primary users of marijuana.

- William Bennett, drug czar in the first Bush administration, ordered sixty low-income residents of a Washington, D.C., public housing project evicted for reported drug use in their apartments.[41] Police sweeps in African-American communities remain common in large cities. As of June 2000, there was no legal requirement to inform public housing tenants of their rights to a grievance hearing when allegations of drug activities are made against them or a member of their family living with them.[42]

Since the 1960s, these same anti-drug laws have been used against young middle-class whites and others whose alternative lifestyles pose a threat to an economic system based on the work ethic, with its stress on punctuality, stability, and conformity. Thousands of members of these groups have been arrested and/or deported from the United States under these laws.

The current war on drugs likewise threatens the civil rights of millions of Americans, both in their homes and in the workplace. Each state in the union has laws punishing cocaine possession, but the penalties vary widely. When a young woman was arrested in Texas in 1987 for speeding and running red lights, police found three vials of crack in her purse. The penalty for first-offense cocaine possession in Texas carries a twenty-year maximum sentence. The same offense in Virginia, the woman's home state, could have resulted in her being released with a mere warning.[43] Beginning in August 1987, federal workers in sensitive jobs had to undergo mandatory drug testing. This policy has been upheld by courts, and by 1992 meant that an estimated 22 million workers inside and outside government were subject to drug testing. Almost immediately, an underground "clean urine" industry sprang up whereby people could purchase samples of clean urine to pass such tests. The temptation to do so may not be confined just to drug users. The urine tests are not always reliable and may show false positives if the tested urine's owner has eaten such foods as poppy seed bagels. False positives can occur in 3 to 5 percent of cases.[44] Urine tests cannot tell when someone has taken a drug, or if the drug has affected job performance.

Despite all these pitfalls in the war on drugs, the government still insists on fighting it with the same old policy of punishment. The result is an actual worsening of both the crime and the drug problems. There were more people in federal prison on drug charges when Ronald Reagan left office in 1989 than there were people in federal prison for all offenses when he took office in 1981. These policies do not work because they do not address the causes of crime and drug abuse in America. As of 2000, "Government data report that 75 million Americans have used illegal drugs; about 40 million continue to use illegal drugs."[45]

The Culture of More

From a sociological perspective, the causes of crime and drug problems are located within the institutional and cultural contradictions of American society and social character. Crime and, to a substantial degree, drug abuse, can be traced to the nature of America's social structure with its competitive capitalism and immense inequalities of wealth and power, and the values surrounding the American Dream—money and success.

In 1990, *U.S. News & World Report* claimed that America has a serious addiction to addictions in general. Each week in the United States over 2,000 groups catering to sex and love addicts met and discussed their addictions, as well as a like number of meetings for those describing themselves as codependents.[46] Americans spend $49 billion on illegal drugs each year. Clearly, this cannot be explained solely by notions such as addictive personalities, people whose lack of self-control leads to drug abuse. No one has yet explained how all of these addictive personalities happened to end up in the same country. A more fruitful area of inquiry concerns the many sources of cultural encouragement present in American society to use drugs.

Advertising continually urges people to purchase items they do not need with money they do not have, as Stanford sociologist Alex Inkeles once observed.[47] One of the most interesting facts about modern advertising is that it began with the promotion of drugs that were basically snake oil concoctions.[48] This fact speaks volumes about the relationship between material culture and addiction. Today, legal drugs remain among the most heavily advertised items. Advertisers ask us to consume legal drugs when we can't sleep or can't stay awake, when we want to celebrate, mourn, lose or gain weight, raise our spirits, kill our pain, and treat hundreds of additional psycho-physiological conditions. As Barbara Ehrenreich writes: "Drugs . . . symbolize the larger and thoroughly legal consumer culture with its addictive appeal and harsh consequences for those who cannot keep up or default on their debts." [49]

Alcohol ads, for example, are loaded with implied promises of popularity, friendship, sexual attractiveness, and success.[50] The products advertised in commercials and various lifestyle magazines show up in soap operas, prime-time TV shows, and movies as composing a lifestyle to be emulated. Many of the same products are given away as prizes on game shows and in mail-order contests.[51] More to the point, the relationship between legal and illegal drug use is at once subtle and profound: studies demonstrate that people who begin smoking cigarettes in their teens are 100 times more likely to encounter an abuse problem with illegal substances than nonsmokers.[52]

Tony Soprano embodies the essence of the culture of more. He wants only the best, for himself and his family. His wife has every material thing, including a beautiful, tastefully decorated home in the suburbs, a closet full of designer clothes, jewelry, fur, and money to take expensive trips. His children are getting educations at first-rate institutions. Meadow has a gorgeous SUV and more than ample spending money, A.J. has all the sports equipment, video games, and electronic toys he could ever want. As for Tony, he indulges in his own culture of more by eating to his heart's content: every episode shows him standing in front of the refrigerator eating prosciutto and other snacks. And he has several mistresses and indulges in the free sex that the Bada Bing provides. He has everything an American is supposed to want and need. So, why does he feel so empty? Why do depression and fainting spells send him to Dr. Melfi? Does popping Prozac help?

Drug Treatment: Not for America

One of the most tragic aspects of the American drug-abuse problem is that other nations have demonstrated it can be brought under control. There will probably always be a minority of people who, for various reasons, will consume drugs, no matter how harsh the penalties. Such democracies as the Netherlands provide maintenance doses of drugs to addicts and offer free treatment for those who want to kick the habit altogether. In fact, between 1982 (when the Dutch treatment policy went into effect) and 1986, the number of addicts requesting drug-free treatment for their abuse doubled. Under this policy, 60 to 80 percent of all of Holland's addicts receive some kind of assistance, and the number of cocaine and heroin addicts appears to have stabilized.

U.S. drug policy emphasizes punishment and seizure of property rather than treatment. Both of these policies have managed to make things worse. As of 2000, prisons in most states have become dangerously overcrowded, filled with drug abusers.[53] Adding hundreds of new U.S. Customs and Border Patrol officers in the early 1990s has made no appreciable dent in the supply of drugs being smuggled into the United States. Each year in the United States, about 800,000 addicts undergo some kind of treatment, but an additional million have no means to get treated. Medicalizing the drug problem—prescribing doses of addictive drugs for users unable to benefit from drug-treatment programs—not wholesale legalization, appears to offer the best hope for taking the profit out of the drug trade and reducing the number of addicts through treatment.

The odds are not good that the United States will adopt such a policy. There are several reasons for American reluctance to do so. First, our puritanical heritage fools us into believing that addiction is a problem of moral weakness, an inability to control one's appetites and demonstrate one's will power. Second, policies that work elsewhere are always viewed as suspect and un-American. Finally, Americans labor under a myth that supposes millions of unaddicted people are waiting for easy access to drugs under a doctor's care. These pre-addict folks, the myth goes, are poised to sign up to become drug addicts as soon as they can legally do so. They will go to their physicians in large numbers to have drugs prescribed for them, feigning addiction, just so they can become addicts in earnest. That medicalization works in other advanced industrial democracies in no way sways American prejudices to the contrary.

The Crime/Drug Connection

Crime and drug abuse, in all forms, represent two of the most serious social problems facing American society today. Street crime costs 25,000 lives a year and accounts for $20 billion in property losses. Drug abuse kills 600,000 people a year (98 percent of it from alcohol and tobacco, not illegal drugs) and probably tolls around $200 billion in financial harm from medical bills, lost work productivity, and criminal-justice system expenditures.

Crime and drug abuse are intimately interrelated social problems. Most street property and violent crime is now drug and alcohol related. Drug abuse is also related to every other major form of crime in America and internationally as well. The 400 billion annual drug trade is widely shared by street gangs that distribute illegal drugs to street users. Organized criminal syndicates on all inhabited continents manufacture illegal drugs and sell them to street gangs for distribution. White-collar criminals put up finance capital for drug shipments and launder drug profits. Some large corporate banks and investment firms have been involved in multimillion-dollar money-laundering schemes and have even provided security for money launderers. Organized criminal syndicates also account for a major source of corruption of law-enforcement personnel and politicians. The CIA and other government agencies have demonstrated a surprising willingness to aid organized criminal syndicates in the establishment of drug territories in the name of foreign-policy objectives.

Thus the crime problem in America is more like a crime-producing department store wherein all floors are interconnected with dark stairways. So are the real causes of crime and drug abuse. Although they are somewhat complex, among the most important factors are a society characterized by extreme inequalities of wealth and power, inducements to use drugs to solve personal and social problems, and a set of cultural values that contains a surprising admiration of successful criminals. Could a show featuring Tony Soprano be as popular in a society that didn't have these values? But one of the saddest aspects of the drug problem is that other modern democracies, like the Netherlands, have brought drug abuse under control by viewing the solution in pragmatic, medical terms. Meanwhile the United States still insists on viewing drug abuse as a crime, a policy that has indubitably failed. Tony Soprano hasn't embraced drug trafficking yet. Perhaps he's smarter than the Feds he so fears.

The Sopranos'
Family Life. . . and Ours

Dᴜʀɪɴɢ ᴀ ᴅᴀɴɢᴇʀᴏᴜs ᴛʜᴜɴᴅᴇʀsᴛᴏʀᴍ, Tony and his family find themselves in Tony's SUV, desperately hoping to make it home through the driving rain. Finally Tony pulls over, and he, Carmela, Meadow, and A.J. pile out to head for the shelter of Artie Bucco's restaurant, Nuovo Vesuvio. Despite a power failure and the late hour, Artie ushers the Sopranos into the warmly lit establishment and seats them for dinner. Sheltered from the storm outside, Tony smiles and proposes a toast to his family, telling his children that if they're lucky, when they have families of their own, they will "remember the little moments, like this, that were good." After thirteen episodes full of theft, brutality, betrayal, and murder, *The Sopranos* concludes its first season with a heartfelt family moment.

Many Americans enjoy *The Sopranos* and Mafia pop culture because of the family themes involved: the families presented in these shows and films may be dysfunctional, but at least they stay together. Many of the scenes in such fare take place in the kitchen or dining room, the symbolic hearts of family homes. Aside from making many of us hungry for Italian food, these scenes convey a sense of solidarity and togetherness lacking in so many families today.

Sure, there has been a lot of talk for decades about family values and the family as the backbone of American life. But the family is the most vulnerable of all American institutions. *The Sopranos* represent a family on the edge of destruction, a scandalous American skeleton in its national closet. Despite all the rhetoric about family values and community after September 11, 2001, many facts undercut such warm notions:

- Only 6 percent of African-American children and only 30 percent of white children in America will grow up with two parents.

- The American divorce rate increased from 25 percent in the 1950s to 50 percent of first-time marriages in the 1990s and has remained steady. Since the late 1980s, two thirds of all U.S. marriages have ended in separation or divorce.[1]

- In 1993, some 28 percent of babies were born to women who had never been married. By 2001, that figure was one in three, despite incentives in the new welfare reform laws to curb such births.[2] Currently, 25 percent of pregnant women, many of them teens, get no prenatal care at all.

Even many families who do stay together, however, do not have a high quality of life. Ten million children in the United States—42 percent of all American children between five and nine years old, and 77 percent of children between ages ten and eighteen—are now described as latchkey kids, children lacking adult supervision on an occasional or frequent basis.[3] A half a million teenagers give birth each year in the United States, and most of these births are in poor families. Teen pregnancy costs the United States $19 billion in health care and social services each year; U.S. teen birth rate—eighty-three teen births for every 1,000 births—is the highest in the industrialized world.[4]

Some 3.6 million men and women with children under age fifteen also take care of a disabled parent. Nearly a third of married women in America with children under age fifteen also give care both to an elderly parent and to children.[5] This extension of care represents an enormous source of psychological stress, as working women try to balance work and family roles.

The Myth of the American Family

When Tony Soprano's sister Janice gets punched in the face by her boyfriend, she shoots him dead. Most women in such situations can't retaliate that way. Each year, 4 million women are battered by their husbands or lovers, and 4,000 are beaten to death.[6] Moreover, familial abuse is a very underreported crime, and most doctors are not sensitized to spot it.

Sadly, there has been a significant increase in reported abuse cases since 1990, and most of this increase is real, not merely the product of encouraging abuse victims to come forward. An estimated 95 percent of the victims of this violence are women. In homes where women are abused, children are abused at a rate fifteen times higher than the national average. About one in every six American children is a victim of incest or abuse. A third of the victims of physical abuse in the United States are babies! Due in part to the toll taken by violence within families, the percentage of children not living with either natural parent doubled in the United States between 1987 and 1991, and, as a result, over half a million children lived with foster parents as of 1998.[7/8]

Some 5,000 Americans are murdered each year by someone in their own families, in half the cases by a spouse or a sibling.[9] The FBI estimates that in the United States, a wife is beaten every thirty seconds, and more than 40 percent of them are pregnant at the time of the beating. Over 160,000 children are abducted by their parents each year, and 60,000 children are expelled from homes by their parents. There are 1.5 million cases of elder abuse by family members reported each year. Many of the elderly are imprisoned in their own homes, beaten, and have their bank accounts raided by family members for their Social Security checks. These statistics do not convey the harms connected with these incidents. The toll taken by child abuse, incest, and neglect is staggering, and in many ways incalculable. Thus the violence presented on *The Sopranos* is in many ways representative of the violence that takes place within the American family.

Millions of American children now come from divorced families. A study of 699 families in thirty-eight states found that children of divorce are significantly more likely, five times more likely, in fact, than children from intact families to engage in drug abuse, violence, suicide, and out-of-wedlock childbirth. The changes children experience after divorce, especially during the first two years, are profound. Over half of the children interviewed in a 1992 study viewed divorce as the central experience of their lives. The great contradiction involving children and divorce concerns a perverse form of timing: what children of divorce need is increased parental nurturing and attention during the divorce process. However, during the divorce parents are more likely to focus on their own traumatic problems and, thus, may be unavailable to give children the emotional support they need. The Sopranos are immune to this particular dysfunction because, being Catholics, they can't divorce like most other Americans. They may kill their lovers, but they won't divorce their spouses.

The fictional perfect family of the 1950s was a middle-class unit consisting of an employed father and a full-time mother/homemaker. Tony Soprano, despite the very plain contradictions between his family and work lives, wants his own family to resemble this ideal. He even balks at discussions by his teenage children of sex, proclaiming that whereas in the rest of the world it may be the 1990s, in his house it would always remain 1954. Although such perfect families as Tony imagines he remembers existed in the fifties, they were the great exception in American familial history. The United States had the world's highest divorce rate in 1889 and has had the highest rate ever since. Even in the idealized fifties, about one in four American marriages ended in divorce.[10] In the fifties, a third of American children lived in poverty, hardly evidence supporting notions of another myth of the fifties, the affluent society.

However, perhaps the most idealized notion stemming from the 1950s myths concerns the idea that married women, especially mothers, did not work outside the home. Fewer women had careers during the 1950s because many were forced out of jobs they had held during World War II. Returning servicemen received preference over working women. Nevertheless, by the end of 1959, 40 percent of women over age sixteen had full-time jobs. Between 1940 and 1960, America experienced a 400 percent growth in the number of working mothers, and by 1960, women with children under eighteen accounted for nearly a third of female workers.[11] This trend in employment continued into the mid-1990s: as of 1993, 60 percent of mothers with children under six years of age and 75 percent of mothers with children between six and twelve years old had jobs.[12] Today, only 4 percent of American families feature the father as the lone breadwinner and mother as a full-time homemaker.

Why all the concern about women working outside the home? The reason is largely ideological. Conservatives claim that full-time motherhood is essential for raising emotionally healthy children, as are two-parent families. Not only does this place most of the blame for family ills on women, it is also largely wrong. There is no evidence that employed mothers produce children with more emotional problems than do full-time homemakers. Nor is there much evidence that two-parent families are necessary for raising emotionally healthy children.

Carmela Soprano, for example, serves her family in a very traditional role, but her efforts have not ensured that she and Tony have trouble-free kids. Meadow has used drugs, abused alcohol, and allowed her friends to wreck her grandmother's vacant house for a party. A.J. damaged his mother's car while joyriding, broke into a church to steal sacramental wine, and vandalized his school. Meadow and A.J. don't act out just because of their father's criminal world; they are also reacting to the temptations and values of the larger world around them. By the standards of prescribed family values, Carmela does all she can for her children: providing a clean and loving home and nutritious meals and keeping involved in her children's schools.

What seems to have shifted so much responsibility onto mothers was that they began working outside the home just as numerous other socioeconomic changes were taking place in the United States. Vietnam, Watergate, and the scandals of the 1980s created a pervasive distrust of government, economic institutions, and adult authority in general. Inflation during the 1970s and 1980s forced large numbers of women into the workplace. The unemployment rate went from 3 percent in the 1950s to above 10 percent in the 1970s and 1980s and 6 percent in the 1990s. Violent crime rates, drug abuse, and rates of mental illness all dramatically increased between 1960 and 1990. Sexual mores also underwent a profound change, beginning with the popularization of birth control in the 1960s. Thus, many trends have contributed to the problems of the American family.

As mentioned, the United States is one of the few industrialized nations that does not provide paid family leave of four months of the year at 80 to 90 percent pay; nor does the United States provide ten weeks parental leave, subsidized day care, free preschool, and public day-care centers.[13] In contrast, French families receive an annual $1,100 child-care allowance. With so many serious problems facing the American family and so few steps taken to alleviate these ills, there appears no truth whatever that the family is treated as the backbone of American institutions by either our economic or political system.

Alienation, Courtship, and Marriage

Dehumanization and inauthenticity also characterize relations between the sexes. These forms of alienation figure directly in divorce statistics. One problem is that both men and women are taught to perceive each other as objects—albeit different kinds of objects. One enduring stereotype has been that men have been socialized to see women as sex objects and "darling little slaves" who do domestic work.[14] Women, meanwhile, are socialized to view men as success objects. Along with these images have come others. Arlie Hochschild[15] has documented a profound change in the relationship between the sexes. The rise of the service economy, coupled with severe inflation in the 1970s and increasing numbers of married women in the workplace, redefined the concept of happiness for women. Marital contentment for wives now seems to revolve around the willingness of their husbands to do housework. One study of 600 couples documented that men's failure to help with household chores was the second-most-common reason for divorce.[16] Thus, the role of homemaker continues to be devalued in American society, and working couples often try to pass it on to low-paid domestic help. This is certainly the case in the Soprano household, even though Carmela holds no job outside the home. Otherwise, the wife still gets stuck doing most of the work. In fact, women who work outside the home work an average of fifteen more hours per week at home than do their male counterparts. Even when husbands share some of the housework, wives feel more responsible for it, especially for checking on children's safety while at work. Moreover, men have more power over the housework they do perform, such as changing the oil in the car or repairing appliances. Husbands tend to do fewer of the least desirable tasks associated with housework, such as scrubbing the toilet.

The housework issue, which makes women into unpaid commodities, is also reflected in each gender's view of marriage itself. A 1993 national poll revealed that almost half of America's single women do not want to get married. Many have become disillusioned by the high divorce rate. Men, on the other hand, are significantly more likely to want marriage. Two thirds of unmarried men claim they are seeking wives, and men are twice as likely as single women to believe that people who live alone are unhappy,[17] reflecting the fact that men have few close male friends.

Men are also dehumanized in the mate-selection process and in the work roles they play in American life. Women who work still marry men who make more money than they do, so the success object stereotype still holds. If women work more at home, it is also true that men work more than working women do, eight hours more per week on average, to be exact.[18] Men still feel responsible for the family finances in the same way that women feel more responsible for the family housework. If women are sex objects and darling little slaves, men then are not chosen for their humanity but for their material potential.

For all the rhetoric about the wonders of romantic love and the sanctity of marriage, the sad truth is that America is experiencing something brand new in the history of civilization. Some are calling it the "postmodern family"; others view it as the breakdown of civilization itself. The Sopranos' dysfunctions represent our societal anxieties over the ungluing of our own familial stability—and with good reason:

- Couples marrying today who are between the ages of eighteen and twenty-four have a 75 percent chance of divorcing.
- The average first-time marriage of the above-described couple will last approximately seven years.
- Those remarrying will have an even greater chance of divorce the second time around.
- Over 30 million people in America now live alone.
- The number of single-parent households is one third the number of two-parent households.

As Charles Derber notes, there has been no recorded situation like this in the last 2,000 years.[19]

The Paradox of Ageism

Tony's mother, Livia, took out a contract on her son because he put her in a nursing home against her will, thus reinforcing many of the stereotypes associated with ageism in the United States. Ageism is generally thought of as being associated with "old age," but there is plenty of ageism involving the young as well as the old in America.

Stages of life, such as youth and old age, are social roles that are socially constructed and defined. Being old was regarded as a special status 200 years ago in the United States. Many Americans lied about their ages in the 1776 Census, telling census-takers they were actually older than they were.[20] In part, the elderly were respected because there were so few of them, and thus living to an old age was considered a great accomplishment.[21] Today being old, which is defined as age sixty-five or older, is increasingly common.

Indeed, according to the U.S. Census Bureau, America is an aging society. In colonial America, half the people were age sixteen or younger; in 1990, less than a fourth of Americans were under age sixteen, and half were thirty-three or older, and by 2050, at least half could be thirty-nine or older. Thus, older people cannot easily be accurately perceived as a numerical minority. Their numbers are growing, as is their political influence. Millions of people belong to groups like the American Association of Retired Persons (AARP), a powerful Washington lobby group influential in policy matters affecting elderly people: Social Security reform, health care reform, and tax laws relevant to retired persons.

Respect for elderly people is common in agricultural societies but declines dramatically when societies industrialize. This is because older people often own a good deal of land in agricultural economies, where status is heavily dependent on land ownership. By contrast, in industrial societies, status is more a function of the job one holds and one's ability to be a productive member of the economy. Thus the elderly, rather than being respected, are often viewed as nonproductive and in a state of deterioration.

Ageism arose in America once industrialization began, shortly after the Civil War. By 1900, the elderly were frequently viewed as physically and mentally degenerated. This came about when the medical profession began concluding that older people suffer from specific diseases related to aging, like hardening of the arteries and gout. These diseases were thought to be incurable and resulted in many elderly people being placed in nursing homes. This view reached its zenith when a 1907 veterans' law declared that all people over age sixty-two, regardless of their actual state of health, were disabled.

Another important cause of ageism was nineteenth-century fundamentalist Christianity, which defined older people as morally degenerate, incapable of attaining salvation. This, of course, was a form of emotional blackmail against the elderly, who often converted to born-again Christianity in order to save themselves, creating a lively market for Bible-thumping preachers who pitched their revival tents all over America after 1865. The final nail in the coffin that is ageism was probably the Social Security Act of 1935. Ironically, the law was designed to help older people enjoy their "golden years" by providing them with a guaranteed, but meager, pension. Unfortunately, the law had the effect of forcing many older Americans out of the labor force at age sixty-five, a practice made illegal in 1967, with passage of the Federal Age Discrimination Act.

Most people who are not elderly feel ambivalence about older people. Many perceive the elderly as dependent, rigidly conservative, and asexual, on the one hand, and, on the other, as trustworthy, friendly, and knowledgeable. Studies demonstrate that people are more likely to offer help to elderly citizens because of these positive qualities. Unfortunately, industrial society tends to separate the elderly from everyone else, primarily because many people move away from their parents in pursuit of education, careers, or other goals.

The great paradox of ageism is that everyone, if they are fortunate, becomes old. This is very different than racism; whites won't become blacks and vice versa, but both African Americans and whites, if lucky, will become old.

If we were to put some prejudiced white people in with some African Americans and lead a discussion about race, there is a good chance that the white people would emerge less prejudiced and more sympathetic toward African Americans than they had been before the discussion. However, if we gathered a sample of ageist persons, persons prejudiced against the elderly, and took them to a nursing home populated by older residents for a chat, there is little probability they would emerge more sympathetic toward the elderly. Indeed, putting prejudiced people in contact with any repressed minority tends to reduce levels of prejudice in all but one case—the elderly. The great paradox, of course, is that this is the only "minority" (and there is considerable debate concerning whether the elderly are a minority) group that all who are lucky enough to reach old age will join.

This prejudice of ageism is so unyielding in part because the United States is a youth-obsessed culture. The fear of aging itself is a commonplace neurosis in American life. Americans of almost every age, except the very young, possess a terror of being perceived as older than they are, making the United States the most age-conscious society in the world. Youth obsession is a major trait of the American social character, with millions of Americans spending billions of dollars on pills and elixirs to retard the aging process and plastic surgery to retain a youthful appearance. We lap up books that promise to make us forever young. If we are seventy-two years old, we say we are "seventy-two years young."

Treating oppressed minorities in a childlike fashion is nothing new, as African Americans found during slavery and after. However, this and other equally damaging stereotypes about the elderly are what the media purvey. Livia Soprano displays many of these characteristics:

- Senility, mental illness, declining intelligence
- Unhappiness to the point of misery
- Loneliness
- Chronic illness
- An inability to live alone
- Illness upon retirement
- Poverty

- Asexuality, disinterest in sex, impotence
- Residence in nursing homes and other long-term care institutions.[22]

The facts belie each of these beliefs. Most elderly people are not mentally ill or senile. Many older people in their seventies and eighties are world leaders. Most elderly people can still learn quite well, as long as they are encouraged to see themselves as vibrant, alive, and physically active. Thus, in 1990, of the 30 million Americans who were age sixty-five and older, only 4.4 million—fewer than one in seven—experienced some sort of impairment in their daily activity level, which includes eating, bathing, dressing, walking, or using the bathroom.[23] Unfortunately, mental deterioration among the elderly is something of a self-fulfilling prophecy: many assume they cannot learn or be active and, therefore, do not try.

There is no evidence that most elderly people are lonely and miserable. According to a Harris poll taken in 1965 and repeated in 1981, most people ages eighteen to sixty-four believed that people over sixty-five are lonely, whereas about half of the people over sixty-five thought older Americans suffer from loneliness. However, loneliness was not among the problems reported as personally experienced by those over sixty-five. Indeed, most older Americans describe themselves as satisfied.[24]

Most people over sixty-five do not suffer from chronic illnesses that limit their ability to work or engage in most other satisfying activities. However, because the stereotype of the elderly as "sick and tired" is so popular, it results in discrimination against them in the workplace. Likewise, there is evidence that intelligence in most elderly people systematically increases with age.[25]

Although most elderly Americans are not chronically ill, American society perpetuates the stereotype of the sick elderly through mass media warnings to elderly people to have their blood pressure checked, get flu shots, and keep a close watch for subtle signs of heart disease, osteoporosis, and Alzheimer's. Thus, although most cultures distinguish between the healthy and productive elderly and the debilitated and dependent elderly,[26] the United States assumes that the vast majority of elderly persons are chronically ill and dependent, making America "one of the worst countries in the world in which to grow old."[27] Although the vast majority of older Americans are financially secure, a large number do live in poverty, their economic plight causing them serious problems. About 5 percent of elderly males and 14 percent of elderly females live in poverty. Two thirds of the elderly poor are widows. Older people who live alone are five times more likely to be poor than couples, and four fifths of the elderly people living alone are widows.[28] Moreover, it is the most elderly of the elderly who are often the poorest, due to the devastating effect of retirement in working and lower-class elderly. On the other hand, a large portion of America's millionaires are over age sixty. Thus, social class, gender, and ethnicity are as important as age in determining income level in later life.

Many elderly Americans do live near the poverty level, with nearly two thirds of Americans over sixty-five receiving over half of their income from Social Security, which tends to be detrimental to the economic well-being of the elderly in a number of ways: people on Social Security are permitted to keep only $1 in every $2 they earn over $5,000. Moreover, most private pension plans do not adjust payments for inflation, and workers who work part-time, change jobs, or have not worked enough consecutive years often do not qualify for private-plan benefits. Thus, people over sixty-five have a lower median income than people age twenty-five to sixty-four in the United States. Minority elderly people have even lower median incomes than non-minority elderly.

It is likewise untrue that most elderly citizens live in institutions. Over 90 percent of older males and 81 percent of older females live with a spouse or by themselves and not in an institution. Similarly, there is no evidence that deterioration and illness follow immediately

upon retirement. It is true that retirement requires a major psychological adjustment, and for most people it takes time to find comfort
in it,[29] but that does not make retirement a death sentence, as the
stereotype holds. The crucial variable in retirement concerns a person's economic, physical, and mental state upon retirement, and not
retirement itself.

Asexuality is one of the most interesting stereotypes about the
elderly. The idea that many Americans believe older people incapable of sex is really our sexually repressed society's way of letting
older people know we disapprove of them even thinking about sex.
In nursing homes and other institutions, if older people are "caught"
having sex, they are viewed as immoral or naughty children. Thus,
there is a contradiction concerning the sexuality of the elderly. If
they refrain from sexual activity, they are viewed as physically deteriorating. If they engage in sex, they are often viewed as morally
deteriorating. The fact is the human body has a lifelong potential for
sexual enjoyment. One study of 244 married couples, with an average age of seventy-two, found that two thirds were still sexually
active on a weekly basis.[30]

Finally, only about 5 percent of older Americans live in institutional settings. While major harms are perpetuated in some of these
places, they are largely a symbol of how the elderly are segregated
from everyone else in society, especially the young. This is probably a
cause of the high suicide rate among elderly persons: the older the
person, the more likely he or she is to be alone and, thus, to commit
suicide. The suicide rate among elderly people aged eighty-five and
over is 55.5 per 100,000, compared with a rate of twenty-five to thirty
per 100,000 for people ages sixty-five to seventy-four.[31] The rates for
people ages twenty to sixty-four is about twenty per 100,000.

Just because the negative images concerning older Americans are
mythical does not mean that the elderly do not suffer from serious
social problems. They do. Among the most serious of these are economic discrimination in work and consumption, criminal victimization, inadequate housing, and abuse and neglect.

Criminal Victimization and the Elderly

Criminal victimization is a complex and interesting problem among older Americans. *The Sopranos* defied the stereotype when Livia tries to have her son murdered. But at the same time, Livia is obsessed with the possibility of being victimized, accusing her housekeeper of stealing, harping on news stories about horrific crimes, and issuing cautions about crime to her neighbors. Surveys indicate that older people fear criminal victimization more than any other problem, even health care, lack of money, and loneliness.[32] Ironically, official statistics demonstrate that the rate of victimization among elderly citizens is among the lowest of any American group. Research also shows that elderly women fear crime more than elderly men, but this might be due to the reluctance of males to admit fear.

How realistic are the fears of the elderly? The problem is complex. Official data show the elderly are the least likely of all adult groups to be victimized by violent street crime, but these data may be misleading. Some criminologists insist that the elderly underreport criminal victimization—in fact, half to two thirds of all crime against all age groups goes unreported. Robbery and larceny are the two most common crimes against elderly people—especially pickpocketing and purse snatching—and rates of theft are higher among the elderly than for any other group in America. The most likely victims among the elderly are the urban poor, especially minority poor, who experience the highest rates of violent crimes, including robbery and assault. The non-poor elderly suffer the highest rates of larceny, and the African-American elderly suffer the highest rates of assault and robbery.

Thus the fear of crime expressed in polls by elderly people is justified. They are more likely to experience being assaulted or shoved around. Victimization is more of a direct threat to their personal safety, and they have fewer personal or financial resources with which to protect themselves or to recover losses due to crime.

Moreover, the elderly are most likely to be assaulted in their own neighborhoods, to have their own immediate physical space and sense of well-being violated. Their losses are more devastating due to their own meager resources. The fear of crime by older Americans is more pronounced precisely because many older people live alone and are isolated in their own neighborhoods, and unlikely to belong to various community groups.[33] Moreover, the elderly who live alone suffer much higher rates of violence and theft than do married older people.

Finally, the elderly suffer very high rates of victimization from white-collar crimes, especially scams, confidence games, and frauds. Amazingly, nine of ten fraud victims do not report crimes against them to the police, largely due to personal embarrassment or the smallness of the loss.

Inadequate Housing and Abuse

Although she was too smart to abuse her mother outright, Tony's sister Janice maintained a very tense relationship while she cared for her mother in her final months of life. When Janice pushed to have a "Do Not Resuscitate" order placed on Livia's hospital chart, Livia put up resistance to Janice's efforts at loving overtures. In a moment of repressed rage at her mother's willfulness, Janice sees a safety sign on a stairwell change into an image of Livia plummeting down a flight of stairs. But with a mother as formidable as Livia, Janice was wise to resist her matricidal urges.

The abuse of elderly people in America is a recently discovered and serious social problem that includes several forms of maltreatment. Physical abuse can include everything from pushing and shoving to rape and assault. Psychological abuse consists of threats, verbal intimidation, and isolation. Many elderly also suffer from neglect and deprivation of adequate medical care, nutrition, and other essential goods and services. Finally, the elderly are vulnerable to financial exploitation, wherein their money is mismanaged, misused, squandered, or stolen.[34] In 1989, the *New York Times* featured an article titled "Granny Bashing," which claimed that over 500,000 elderly people in the United States suffered from physical abuse at the hands of their own children. If verbal abuse and financial exploitation are included in definitions of elder abuse, the estimates climb to between 700,000 and 2.5 million cases a year.[35]

Although the true extent of all forms of elder abuse is impossible to measure because it is so easily covered up, and the definitions defy precise measurement, there are some important findings that have recently emerged. Passive neglect, the most common form of elder abuse, consists of cutting off food and medical care and leaving elders alone. Active neglect, also common, involves tying elderly persons to a bed or a chair or locking them in a room while the caregiver goes out. One study by the University of New Hampshire's Family Research Laboratory found that children of elderly parents were abusers in 23 percent of cases, but spouses were abusers in 58 percent of cases.[36] Part of this pattern concerns residency. Some 40 percent of elderly Americans live with their spouses, whereas only 10 percent of the elderly live with their children. Thus spouses have much more opportunity to engage in abuse than do children of the elderly.[37] Likewise, although nearly three fourths of elderly couples own their own homes, and 85 percent of elderly homeowners have paid off their mortgages, these statistics reflect the lifestyles of middle-class and upper-class elderly people. Some 4 to 6 million older Americans—20 to 30 percent of elderly people—live in inadequate structures, including units that lack indoor flush toilets, hot running water, sufficient heat, and/or are in conditions of disrepair.

Finally, there are serious problematic conditions within the nation's nursing home system. Although there are many fine nursing residence units in the United States, a minority have been involved in scandals that have made the entire industry distrusted in the public mind.[38] Negligence, careless conduct resulting in injury, or violations of a person's rights, can have dire consequences.

Nursing home patients may find themselves subject to dozens of adverse conditions through no fault of their own—bed injuries, pressure ulcers, falls, fractures, malnutrition, and dehydration are some of the more common conditions.

Some nursing homes suffer from notoriously unsanitary conditions. Fecal matter is left on stairs. Dirty laundry is carried through kitchens when food is about to be served. Patients are left to sit on their beds in their own waste.

Another problem in nursing homes concerns the misuse of drugs. Often inadequate medication records are kept. Patients are given medicine that has not been prescribed for them, and unqualified personnel, even patients themselves, can obtain access to narcotics and drugs. Other times, drugs that have been prescribed by a doctor are not dispensed. Other problems include the use of drugs past their expiration dates and drugs being dispensed with nonsterile needles.

Nursing homes also suffer from physically unsafe conditions. Air conditioners break down during heat waves, sometimes suffocating patients. Fires, when started, often kill frail residents due to smoke inhalation. Conditions like lice and tuberculosis erupt, requiring patients to be quarantined in their rooms. This isolation, if prolonged, sometimes produces mental instability. Finally, nursing homes also suffer from a host of related problems, such as the cruel use of unauthorized restraints, including handcuffs and straightjackets, forced tranquilizing of patients, and reprisals against patients who complain about conditions and maltreatment, including sexual abuse.[39]

What all of the examples concerning the elderly indicate is how much victimization can take place when a group is perceived as "useless" and rendered invisible to the rest of society. The tragic truth is that the elderly do not have a meaningful place in the social order, are alienated from other groups, and, as a consequence, their victimization tends to go unnoticed. Much the same is also true of America's youth.

Youth and the "Family Values" Debate

As New York University communications professor Neil Postman has noted, childhood as a recognized stage of life is only about 400 years old.[40] Lower-class children in many industrializing nations are treated like little adults, working side by side with adults in factories and frequently getting injured or killed from working with dangerous machines or breathing coal dust while sweeping chimneys.

These days, young people and children are at the center of a confusing debate about family values, raising responsible children, and the family as the backbone of American life. Parents in the 1990s and early 2000s spend 40 percent less time with their children than did parents in 1965; parents spent about thirty hours a week with children in 1965 and only seventeen hours a week in the 1990s. Indeed, a 1989 poll found that two thirds of all full-time working mothers would like to work fewer hours in order to devote more time to their children. Two thirds of parents polled in a nationwide survey also agreed that the most effective way to strengthen the family was to spend more time together. And children agree. When asked what makes for a happy family they most frequently answer "doing things together."[41] Unfortunately, pressures and cultural changes keep families from spending time together. Single mothers spend 33 percent less time than their married counterparts engaging with their children in primary-care activities, like bathing, dressing, and chauffeuring. The percentage of families who regularly eat dinner together has declined from 75 percent to less than 35 percent since 1976. The Sopranos continue to sit down for meals together, but not without a great deal of effort from Carmela to maintain the tradition.

There are also severe economic pressures on many American families. Since the 1960s, real incomes have fallen, taxes and inflation have increased, and the average unemployment rate has risen from 3 to around 6 percent (with damaging spikes of over 10 percent in the 1970s and 1980s). Between 1965 and 1995, the costs of major family expenditures, like health care, housing, transportation, and higher education, rose faster than general price increases. In 1973 a thirty-year-old paid 21 percent of his or her annual income for mortgage payments; by 1987, that figure had risen to 40 percent.

As a result, it is not unusual for intact families to contain a working mother and father, who between them may hold down three or four jobs.

Another subtle, yet major, cultural change has occurred with the prevalence of a "me first," antisocial selfishness in the American social character. Within the family, this has translated into workaholism for both males and females pursuing careers. American culture has always placed more status on making money than on raising healthy families, as is evident in today's career patterns. Today, women are more likely to be admired and appreciated for launching a catchy new ad campaign for toothpaste than they are for nurturing and shaping an original personality. This has had a detrimental impact on fatherhood, as well. So long as child rearing is viewed as a lowly calling for women, it is unlikely that it will take on increased significance for men.[42]

Rampant careerism has also been accompanied by the rise of the yuppie (young urban professional) lifestyle, with its materialism and neglect of emotional attachments. Television programming and dramatic increases in all types of advertising have created an ethic espousing personal happiness as the greatest good and consumption of material goods as the way to achieve it. As a result, many middle-class parents pursue money so they can keep up with their credit card payments, and turn child rearing over to video games.

Although such changes in American culture may account for some of the family's problems, they clearly do not account for all of them. Important as well is the lowly place given the family in the institutional order of American society. A more plausible explanation for the problems of youth and family crises lies in the contradiction between America's professed value of the sacred family and the dominance over family life by other institutions in America, especially the political economy. What all of this indicates is that the family is the weakest of all American institutions. Moreover, it is the young who are the primary victims of its instability.

Children: The Leading Victims

America probably leads the world in the number of politicians who claim that the family is an important institution, but it is actually woefully neglectful of families and children. The United States remains the only modern democracy without national health insurance, without subsidized day care, and without paid family leave. In America, people who work with children are paid only two thirds as much as bartenders.[43]

Moreover, the family is in many ways an invisible institution in the American power structure. The nation sets aside one day to honor mothers and one day for fathers, but no day to honor children. There are no Washington lobbies and political action committees for families possessing the kind of influence as those enjoyed by business lobbies in the United States. Without the protections and supports enjoyed by families in other advanced nations, American families are vulnerable to disruptions that overpower their often inadequate resources.

Over 3 million American children (one in six under age seven) have dangerous levels of lead in their bodies from paint chips and dust. Each year, gunshots, drowning, and injuries kill 8,000 American children and permanently disable 50,000. Much of this suffering could be prevented by proper safety measures.[44] Within the family, children are most vulnerable to child abuse at frighteningly young ages—from birth to five years of age. They are most vulnerable to sexual abuse between ages nine to fifteen, but cases of sexual abuse of children five years and younger have been reported.[45]

The harms perpetrated by child abuse, incest, and neglect are, in many ways, incalculable. Take, for example, what is termed "reactive attachment disorder,"[46] a condition that affects 30 million children in America. These children are the victims of incest, abuse, and neglect. They are unable to bond—to become attached to—other human beings. As children, they often strangle animals, start fires, try to drown their playmates, steal, lie, and inflict physical damage on other people's belongings. The symptoms associated with attachment disorder involve severe forms of inauthenticity and dehumanization. Disordered children do not treat themselves or other people as human beings with needs for love and recognition. Consequently, their symptoms reflect extreme forms of alienation.

Disordered children often stab themselves with knives and exhibit no fear of dangerous heights or other risky situations, such as reckless driving or robbing convenience stores. In adulthood, these people become salespeople who sell unsafe used cars, bosses who steal their subordinate's ideas, consumers who fail to pay their debts, and serial killers. Attachment disorder begins in the first three years of life. It is estimated that all 30,000 children eligible for adoption in the United States have some degree of this syndrome, as do most of the almost 500,000 children living with foster parents, which represents a doubling of the number of children not living with either parent between 1987 and 1991.[47]

Attachment-disordered children have no idea how to relate to other people. Consequently, they behave insincerely when expressing love or other emotions. They tend to be perceived as untrustworthy, and come across as manipulators.

Stealing, hoarding, and gorging of food and possessions are also common among attachment-disordered children. Not knowing how to form attachments to other people, disordered children experience severe unmet emotional needs. As a substitute for needs involving love and human contact, disordered children often steal and hoard items like food, even if they are not hungry.

Acts of deception take place in both childhood and adulthood. As children, disordered persons often feign helplessness, or act loving or cute, smart or beguiling—whatever suits their need at the time to get what they want. In adulthood, such behavior many manifest itself as fraud and con games. A final symptom of attachment disorder involves what is termed chronic lying. Such children lie even under extreme circumstances, especially when they are caught directly in the act of misbehaving. They continue to lie even when it is obvious a lie is being told.

Attachment disorder is also associated with the most serious social problems of youth, including delinquency, drug abuse, and, most harmful, perhaps, criminal victimization and suicide.

Runaways, Criminals, and Victims

Each year, an estimated 1.3 million children run away from home. A growing number (around 10 percent) are "pushouts," who leave because their parents refuse to let them live at home, but most leave without parental permission. The number of runaways is evenly divided between girls and boys, cutting across all social class lines.[48] Although most go less than ten miles away and return home within three weeks, about three fourths are escaping parental abuse, rejection, or alienation from school. Many former runaways were labeled stupid or lazy by teachers at an early age and reacted by being truant, not doing homework, or becoming detached from or hostile to school. Less than half of former runaways are regularly employed; middle-class runaways usually have a deep feeling of failure as well as major problems in getting along with parents. Nearly all former runaways had problems with the law for offenses ranging from public drunkenness to assault and battery. At least 50 percent of homeless children were physically or sexually abused before leaving home, and "pushout" runaways report more violence and conflict with parents than children who left without parental permission.[49]

Crime and criminal victimization are serious problems for runaway children. A large number of teen girls go into prostitution, experience drug abuse, or become rape victims, and both runaway boys and girls are frequent targets of robberies and assaults. One study of 576 runaways found that 44 percent were school dropouts, 14 percent had been arrested, 10 percent had destroyed property, and 8 percent were gang members. Over half reported they were in some kind of trouble with the law at home before running away. One study reports that runaways who stay on the streets two or more weeks have a 75 to 90 percent chance of becoming involved in illegal activity. Runaways are also frequent victims of both other runaways and various youthful criminals, a large percentage of whom (50 to 80 percent) are seeking money in support of drug addiction.[50]

Finally, runaways have the highest suicide rate of any adolescent group. The suicide rates among all teens tripled between 1968 and 1993. Today, suicide is the leading cause of death for fifteen-to-twenty-four-year-olds. All told, about 500,000 adolescents attempt suicide each year, and about 5,000 actually kill themselves. Today, 60 percent of high school students know someone who has attempted suicide and 15 percent say they have considered it themselves. The leading causes of suicide among the young concern problems with grades in school, confusion over career choices they are often pressured to make, and problems in getting along with parents. Of those who attempt suicide, 87 percent report being influenced to do so by peer group members, 57 percent claim they were influenced by their parents, and 47 percent were influenced by conditions at school.[51] These tragic numbers indicate a strong link between suicidal behavior and a profound alienation from the institutions of everyday life.

Concerning youth crime—delinquency and crimes by young adults—slightly over half of all street crimes of violence and crimes against property are committed by young people ages fourteen to twenty-four. Juveniles between ages fourteen to twenty account for over 25 percent of all arrests and almost 40 percent of arrests for the most serious street crimes, such as homicide, rape, burglary, robbery, larceny, aggravated assault, vehicle theft, and arson. Between 1987 and 1991, the number of juveniles arrested for serious crimes—murder, rape, robbery, and assault—rose by almost 50 percent, according to the FBI.[52] Much delinquency stems from the fact that American society does not have a meaningful role for the young; their unemployment rates are much higher than those of adults, and teen unemployment is highly correlated with property crimes by juveniles. Thus the higher the teen unemployment rate, the more property crime is committed by the young.[53]

Most frightening, perhaps, 90 percent of all young people murdered in industrialized nations are killed in the United States. The U.S. homicide rate for youths ages fifteen to twenty-four is five times higher than that of Canada, which is the second-highest country for youth homicide. A series of incidents in 1993 finally forced the mass media to pay attention to the murder of young Americans:

- In Petaluma, California, twelve-year-old Polly Klaas was kidnapped and later found murdered.
- In St. Louis, two young girls, Cassidy Senter (ten) and Angie Housman (nine) were kidnapped at different times and later found murdered.
- In Southern California, a serial child molester, responsible for thirty-two separate attacks in the San Fernando Valley, continued a rampage that has resulted in a widespread police dragnet.
- One foundation president told a *Children's Express* reporter that in Washington, D.C., it is not unusual for children living in some high crime areas to go to two or three funerals a week for friends who have been murdered.

Aside from facing potential homicide, some 13 million young people now go hungry on a regular basis in the United States. The poverty rate for children in the United States is more than double that of any industrialized nation, and as of 1998 in the United States the percentage of children living in poverty has actually been increasing over the past quarter century.[54]

Drug Abuse and the Young

Alcohol abuse and its problematic consequences, including drug abuse, are major social problems in the lives of millions of American adolescents. A 1992 survey by the Department of Health and Human Services found that 8 million high school students out of 20.7 million (nearly 40 percent!) are weekly users of alcohol, and that includes 454,000 "binge" drinkers, who average fifteen drinks a week. Estimates are that 5.4 million students have binged at least once and that more than 3 million have binged within the last month surveyed.[55] It is also estimated that 6.9 million teens, some as young as thirteen have no trouble obtaining alcohol, despite laws in all fifty states making the legal drinking age twenty-one. In 2000, almost 7 million young people aged twelve to twenty were binge drinkers—that is, a fifth of all people under the legal drinking age.[56] The rate of binge drinking among underage people (19 percent) was almost as high as among adults aged twenty-one or older (21 percent). Underage people who reported binge drinking were seven times more likely to report using illicit drugs during the previous month than underage persons who did not binge drink.

- Heavy drinking was reported by 5.6 percent of the population aged twelve and older, or 12.6 million people. These 2000 estimates were nearly identical to the 1999 estimates.
- About 9.7 million persons aged twelve to twenty reported drinking alcohol in the month prior to the survey interview in 2000 (27.5 percent of this age group). An estimated 6.6 million (18.7 percent) were binge drinkers and 2.1 million (6.0 percent) were heavy drinkers. All of these 2000 rates were similar to rates observed in 1999.
- Males aged twelve to twenty were more likely than their female peers to report binge drinking in 2000 (21.3 percent compared to 15.9 percent).
- Young adults aged eighteen to twenty-two enrolled full-time in college were more likely than their peers not enrolled full-time to report any use, binge use, or heavy use of alcohol in 2000. Past-month alcohol use was reported by 62 percent of full-time college students compared to 50.8 percent of their

counterparts who were not currently enrolled full-time. Binge and heavy-use rates for college students were 41.4 percent and 16.4 percent, respectively, compared with 35.9 percent and 12.1 percent, respectively, for other persons aged eighteen to twenty-two.

In 2000, one in ten Americans twelve and older (22.3 million persons) had driven under the influence of alcohol at least once in the year before the interview, and among young adults eighteen to twenty-five, 20 percent had driven under the influence of alcohol.

According to the 2000 National Household Survey on Drug Abuse (NHSDA), a project of the Substance Abuse and Mental Health Services Administration (SAMHSA):

- In calendar year 2000, an estimated 14.0 million Americans were current illicit drug users, meaning they had used an illicit drug during the month prior to interview. This estimate represents 6.3 percent of the population twelve years old and older.
- Between 1999 and 2000, the rate of past-month marijuana use among women twelve and older increased from 3.1 percent to 3.5 percent. This increase was primarily due to an increase in use among women twenty-six and older, from 1.4 percent in 1999 to 2 percent in 2000.
- In 2000 among youth twelve to seventeen, 9.7 percent had used an illicit drug within the thirty days prior to interview. This rate is almost identical to the rate for youth in 1999 (9.8 percent).
- Over 2 million youths twelve to seventeen had used inhalants at some time in their lives as of 2000. This constituted 8.9 percent of youths. Of all youths, 3.9 percent had used glue, shoe polish, or Toluene, and 3.3 percent had used gasoline or lighter fluid.
- Among youths twelve to seventeen in 2000, the rate of current illicit drug use was similar for boys (9.8 percent) and girls (9.5

percent). Although boys twelve to seventeen had a slightly higher rate of marijuana use than girls in the same age category (7.7 percent compared to 6.6 percent), girls were somewhat more likely to use psychotherapeutics nonmedically than boys (3.3 percent compared to 2.7 percent).

- In 2000 among youths who were heavy drinkers, 65.5 percent were also current illicit drug users. Among nondrinkers, only 4.2 percent were current illicit drug users. Similarly, among youths who smoked cigarettes, the rate of past-month illicit drug use was 42.7 percent, compared with 4.6 percent for nonsmokers.

- An estimated 7 million persons reported driving under the influence of an illicit drug at some time in the past year. This figure corresponds to 3.1 percent of the population age twelve and older and is significantly lower than the rate in 1999 (3.4 percent). Among young adults aged eighteen to twenty-five, 10.7 percent drove under the influence of illicit drugs at least once in the past year.

- Although the nonmedical use of Oxycontin (a narcotic used for severe pain) was rare in 2000, the NHSDA data show evidence of an emerging problem. The estimated number of lifetime nonmedical Oxycontin users increased from 221,000 in 1999 to 399,000 in 2000. The 2000 NHSDA was not designed to report the current use of Oxycontin.

- An estimated 65.5 million Americans twelve and older (29.3 percent of the total population) reported current use of a tobacco product in 2000. An estimated 55.7 million (24.9 percent) smoked cigarettes, 10.7 million (4.8 percent) smoked cigars, 7.6 million (3.4 percent) used smokeless tobacco, and 2.1 million (1.0 percent) smoked tobacco in pipes.

- Among youth smokers twelve to seventeen in 2000, more than half (59.4 percent) reported that they personally bought cigarettes at least once in the past month. Approximately a third of youth smokers (33.8 percent) reported buying cigarettes at a store where the clerk hands out the cigarettes. About two-thirds (65.2 percent) of youth smokers twelve to seventeen reported that friends or relatives bought cigarettes for them at least one time in the past month.

- Between 1999 and 2000, the percent of Hispanic youth smokers who reported Newport as their usual brand increased from 18.7 percent to 31.4 percent.

Trends in Initiation of Substance Use (Incidence)

Trends in new use of substances are estimated using the data reported on age at first use from the 1999 and the 2000 NHSDA. Because information on when people first used a substance is collected on a retrospective basis, estimates of first time use or incidence are always one year behind estimates of current use.

- Approximately 1.5 million persons used pain relievers non-medically for the first time in 1999. The number of initiates has been increasing since the mid-1980s, when it was below 400,000 per year. Youth twelve to seventeen constitute the majority of this increase, from 78,000 initiates in 1985 to 722,000 in 1999.
- New use of cigarettes on a daily basis has decreased since its recent peak in 1997 at 1.9 million new users. In 1998, the number of initiates dropped to about 1.7 million, and it dropped again in 1999 to about 1.4 million. Contributing to this decrease was the smaller number of new daily smokers among youths twelve to seventeen, falling from about 1,163,000 in 1997 to 783,000 in 1999. Translated to a per-day basis, the number decreased from 3,186 youths per day in 1997 to 2,145 per day in 1999.[57]

A number of studies have found that drug users are

- Twice as likely to get into fights as nonusers.
- Three times more likely to be truant from school.
- Twice as likely to have trouble concentrating in class.

There is a problem with some of the drug and alcohol abuse surveys. Many are based on household samples or on high school student use. Many youth drug addicts and alcohol abusers are runaways and high school dropouts, and would tend to be missed in such polls. Likewise, many are poor, and lack telephones, another reason that would exclude them from such data gathering. Nevertheless, there is ample evidence of the links between drug and alcohol abuse and other forms of deviant behavior among the nation's youth. Finally, the NHSDA finds the heaviest drug use is frequently found in the eighteen to twenty-five age group, not among high school students.

Employment and the Young

Nothing quite attests to the fact that America has no real place for its youth as much as the high unemployment rates among teens. For example, in the final quarter of 2001, the teenage unemployment rate was three times that of adults women—15.8 percent and 5 percent, respectively.[58]

The Myth of the Family Debunked

For all the political rhetoric about family values, what exists in America in many ways is an institution threatened both from without and within. Lacking social supports necessary for survival, families are often vulnerable to dissolution from poverty, unemployment, debilitating diseases, and deaths. Postmodern courtship and marriage are now characterized by serial monogamy, a charge previously reserved only for relationships among the poor. The consequences of frequent divorce for children make them prone to feel unloved and alienated, and likely to engage in a wide variety of antisocial behaviors.

One of the reasons that Mafia fare, like *The Sopranos,* is cemented in the public mind is that family is such a central theme. But the Sopranos are a family that both somehow remains together and yet is replete with the most divisive of conflicts and dysfunctions. Livia's hit on her own son reminds us that the American family itself has become a dangerous institution. It is now the seat of a quarter of the nation's homicides. Tony's mother's great fear of the nursing home was not all caused by senility; much elderly abuse and death from such causes as prescription drug side effects takes place in nursing homes. Likewise, the relationship between Tony's sister, Janice, and her abusive boyfriend, Richie Aprile, whom she kills, reminds us of the incalculable damage from spousal abuse. Until something much more meaningful is done about these horrific social problems, all the political rhetoric about family values will remain part of a gigantic apology for what amounts to a national crisis.

Everyday Life in Tony Soprano's America

ALTHOUGH HE CAME TO THERAPY with reluctance and fear, Tony Soprano nevertheless has learned to accept some help and has come to make realizations about his own case. He attempts to keep the contradictory portions of his life separate, striving for "total control," which to him means being able to direct his power and anger only against the people in his life he thinks "deserve it." Yet he also frequently proves his own undoing, taking risks when he knows he should be cautious, allowing trivial matters to trigger his anger, finding dissatisfaction when he can't indulge in his criminal pursuits. While in Italy, Tony meets a shrewd and beautiful business associate who tells him he's his own worst enemy. Later, Tony brings up the subject with Dr. Melfi, explaining, "I bring all this on myself. I mean, that's what you keep telling me." Melfi counters. "Yes, I suppose it is . . . at root," she says. "The question is: How do you stop?" Until Tony learns more about the forces that drive his behavior, however, that remains the unanswered question at the heart of *The Sopranos.*

The crises of daily life are made up of seemingly personal troubles encountered in the immediate environments of neighborhood, work, school, church, and, for Americans like Tony Soprano, therapy—in which we discuss the impact these environments have on us. Feelings of alienation motivate individuals like Tony to commit antisocial acts, such as adultery. Some sell or take illegal drugs. Some commit murder. Alienated from other people and from social institutions, we engage in deviant acts that harm both.

Religious institutions, which might be expected to avoid or alleviate such acts, increasingly suffer the traumas of deviance. Scandal tears through the Catholic Church as more and more priests are charged with molesting children. A rabbi is convicted of money laundering. A minister has an affair with a member of the congregation. In all these cases, officials knew what was happening but preferred to cover it up. Why do these episodes take place?

What is it about the structure of modern life that regularly produces contradictions in the form of deviant behavior? From the viewpoint of the sociological imagination, what is the link between seemingly personal troubles and institutional contradictions?

Dehumanization and inauthenticity are the dominant alienating conditions of modern life, but each elicits different feelings of alienation in individuals. Dehumanization is closely linked to powerlessness, loneliness, meaninglessness, and feelings of isolation. It often motivates angry reactions against specific targets: sabotage at work, strikes by unions, revolutionary movements against repressive governments. Inauthenticity, in contrast, often results in a state of confusion, unspecified anger, and many forms of deviant behavior, from drug abuse, to con games, to homicide. Erich Fromm's classic works *Escape from Freedom* (1941) and *The Sane Society* (1955)[1] first analyzed the roots of modern dehumanization and inauthenticity. Fromm studied the rise of individualism in Western cultures. During the Middle Ages, he argued, there was no such thing as freedom or individualism. A person's identity was at one with the social role one played. One's entire life was spent in work, family, and religious roles. With the rise of capitalism came the rise of individualism. For the first time, people regarded themselves as psychologically and physically separate from one another. With individualism came the advent of freedom. Individuals could be masters of their own fate, could make their own decisions concerning work, marriage, and the form of government under which they would live. The great problem with individual freedom was that the ties that had once provided people with security and a sense of belonging had also disappeared.

The rise of capitalism also saw the rise of the wealthy elite, emerging with a huge mass of economically propertyless people. There was no unemployment insurance, no health insurance, no welfare state, and no other social supports that could provide a basis for individualism rooted in security. All workers became potential competitors for factory jobs. The individual was free, but also alone, isolated, and "overwhelmed by a sense of individual nothingness and helplessness."[2] Feelings associated with dehumanization, especially insecurity, loneliness, powerlessness, and anxiety, became widespread.

Under capitalism, labor, like the sense of self, became individualistic and atomistic—alone and isolated.[3] People lost control over both the conditions and fruits of their labor. Factory owners determined virtually all conditions of work: quality of product, wages, pace, and circumstances of the work process itself. Work rapidly became an empty experience, merely a means to an end, making money in order to survive.

Bureaucracy became the dominant form of social organization, exerting its grasp over individuals. Conduct became subject to rules, regulations, hierarchies of power, and, most important, emotional detachment. In factories, bureaucratic procedures meant that work became broken down into minute tasks, monotonous, repetitive, and requiring little skill. For white-collar workers, the challenge became one of "selling themselves on the personality market,"[4] putting on phony masks in order to manipulate workers and customers. This, coupled with the growth of consumer advertising, marked the birth of inauthenticity.

These changes in the structure of the workplace meant that work became something toward which people were, at best, indifferent and, at worst, hostile. Fromm believed the alienation experienced at work spills over into all areas of daily life, including family relations, religion, and education.[5] No one can argue that Tony Soprano doesn't experience this spillover to a greater degree than the average American. Without his difficult and untenable balancing act between his work as a criminal and his duties as a father, husband, and member of the community, Tony would at worst have serious mother issues to work out, and little more. But the dehumanization and inauthenticity inherent in his work cannot help but fragment him, sometimes to the point of debilitation.

Work Alienation: Dehumanization and Inauthenticity

A good deal of evidence confirms the powerlessness felt by workers, especially shop-floor and manufacturing workers, employees who traditionally have the least control over their working conditions. Sociologist Robert Blauner's early study of blue-collar workers of different professions found that workers with the least control over their working conditions experienced alienation as powerlessness, meaninglessness, isolation, and self-estrangement. Blauner[6] found that even among working-class employees, those who viewed their job as a craft, such as printers, felt a sense of control and involvement with their work that assembly line workers and miners lacked. Powerlessness within organizations is caused by hierarchical rule from the top, with employees having little input on managerial decisions. Meaninglessness is contributed to when work is divided up into minute tasks, fragmented, so that the worker is alienated from the overall product and from the work process. A sense of isolation is frequently found among assembly line workers, who perform monotonous, routine tasks working alone.[7]

The American Workplace: Blue-Collar Workers

Sociologist Kai Erikson[8] noted that the modern workplace is so characterized by worker separation from product and process that many workers never see raw materials that enter into the production cycle. Instead of making products, workers perceive that they are producing "stuff." Creativity is nonexistent, and the mentality of the worker is described as "lobotomized," made mentally dull and uncreative.[9] People who dislike their jobs, who feel they have no control over their working conditions, often experience declining physical and mental health, family instability, disillusionment with the political system, increased risk of alcohol and drug addiction, and violent forms of aggression, including insubordination or sabotage at work.[10] At the very bottom of the bureaucratic system are unskilled and shop-floor workers, who are often members of the working poor.

Resentment of repressive bosses sometimes spills over in extreme forms of workplace deviance. Murder in the American workplace was virtually unheard of from 1980 to 1988. Since then, there have been nearly twenty workplace murders a year in the United States, affecting some of the largest corporations and government agencies, such as the U.S. Postal Service. The most frequent motive given for workers killing their bosses and co-workers is resentment over having been laid off. Workplace murders are but one symptom of the changing conditions in today's America, especially job insecurity due to layoffs and the explosive growth of part-time jobs with no security.

Studies by Melvin Kohn and his colleagues established a link between the effects of work and a sense of self-esteem. Lower self-esteem is associated with low rank in organizational hierarchies, a lack of self-direction in working conditions, low complexity of job tasks, closeness of supervision, job-related stress—especially time pressures, dirtiness of working conditions, and the number of hours worked in an average week.[11] Kohn notes that these job conditions are intimately bound up with "the class and stratification system of industrial society."[12] Thus, the lower down one is in the class system, the more one's job is likely to contribute to low self-esteem.

Even in a job as apart from the norm as organized crime, such resentments surface. Aside from the usual avarice and ambition that drive Tony and his rivals to face off against one another, frustration over working conditions leads to deviant acts even among the deviants. Tony's friend and underling Big Pussy Bompensiero in part justifies his cooperation with the Feds by finding fault with Tony's leadership, as when Tony directs Pussy to track down a car stolen from one of A.J.'s teachers. At the end of the third season of the show, Tony's longtime lieutenant Paulie Walnuts looks to shift his loyalties over a series of slights from his boss. His dissatisfaction with his place in the hierarchy, his frustration at being assigned tasks he considers beneath him, and his perception that Tony does not have the will to hold onto his power all stand to push Paulie into a conspiratorial rebellion against Tony's authority.

The Modern Workplace: White-Collar Workers

White-collar workers exhibit somewhat different yet related forms of alienation. Middle- and upper-middle-class workers generally perform their work as cheerful robots, involving a constant sale of the self in the personality market. Their real purpose is one of manipulation for personal gain. Many of Tony's neighbors operate on this level, which may in part explain why they find Tony more tolerable than one might expect.

The white-collar worker is often alienated from himself and other people. Personal relationships come to resemble work relationships, wherein the sexes manipulate each other for purposes of sex and money. Boston University Professors Donald Kanter and Philip Mirvis have substantiated that such attitudes are surprisingly widespread in America. About half of their national sample agrees with the statement that "most people are only out for themselves and that you are better off zapping them before they do it to you."[13] Among their most important findings are that many people in America take a cynical approach to the work they do, and that this cynicism extends from the very top to the lowly bottom of the American occupational structure.

Even in the Mafia, with its code of silence and long-standing rules about its operations, this cynical selfishness holds sway. Numerous times over the course of *The Sopranos*, Tony has made references to those traditional rules to force rivals back in line. But even those closest to him push their own agendas: Christopher with his dreams of being a screenwriter, Pussy with his attempts to strike a deal with the Feds, Paulie with his resentment over Tony's management style, Uncle Junior with his willful defiance of Tony's ban on drug sales. Despite the need for cooperation in order to keep their operations going, the gangsters on *The Sopranos* frequently work against one another to further their own aims—even as they condemn other Mafia figures in the news as rats and sellouts when they do the same.

At the zenith of corporate America are so-called command cynics, senior managers who see themselves as animals in a corporate jungle. They believe that since they are on top, those beneath them must be "weak, naïve, inept, or just plain dumb." Command cynics also hold that everyone has their price, and everyone can be had. Beneath the "command cynics" are the "administrative sideliners," middle managers and upper-level government bureaucrats who view human nature as being cold and uncaring, and who have no genuine concern for people, except as means for their own ends. Next are a group of young game players, self-absorbed professionals who became visible symbols of the greed and narcissism of the 1980s. What these self-centered people have in common is a willingness to do whatever it takes to move up the bureaucratic ladder.

In the middle levels of the bureaucratic layers of business and government sit so-called "squeezed cynics," usually the sons and daughters of skilled factory workers and working-class clericals. This once upwardly mobile working-class group has been made cynical by the loss of manufacturing jobs and the decline of heavy industry. The job they once expected to give them security has been sent overseas, automated, or completely eliminated. They are now downwardly mobile Americans who have lost faith in the American Dream and whose cynicism stems from a belief that their careers have reached a dead end. These sad people are hard-bitten cynics, who believe they cannot trust anyone at work or in business, and that "expecting anyone to help you makes you a damn fool."

The Part-Time Explosion

The contemporary workplace is increasingly characterized by fewer full-time workers and large numbers of increasingly alienated part-time employees, especially among white-collar workers at all bureaucratic levels. Since 1982, temporary employment in the United States has increased nearly 250 percent, while overall employment grew only 20 percent. As a result, these workers suffer the increased stress that comes with a lack of job security and benefits, and their numbers are increasing. Thus over 60 percent of the jobs created in 1993 were for "temps," and any type of worker, even bosses, may now be hired part-time.[14] Many temporary workers complain of feeling like dehumanized objects, mere "fixtures."[15] Sadly, temporary employees have become attractive to companies in large part because they lack the rights enjoyed by full-time workers. They save employers a great deal in labor costs because they rarely receive benefits such as medical, dental, or eyecare insurance, have no pension plans, and sometimes earn minimum wage or below. The part-time explosion is a matter of heated debate, with one side finding part-timers liking their positions and the other side claiming exploitation and urging part-timers to assert their rights.

Interestingly enough, global crime syndicates have begun to follow the same model, but for different reasons. They frequently contract with one another on a job-by-job basis, hiring each other's services on a part-time basis. They have done this for drug deals, contract murders, and other business deals, thus mirroring the practices of the mainstream economy and alienation among executives.

White-Collar Alienation

Moreover, if Fromm's analysis is correct, we would expect that white-collar workers suffer from self-estrangement and other ills associated with inauthenticity. Jan Halper's book *Quiet Desperation*[16] found that professionals and executives believe that America is a society that tries to quantify everything. Thus, white-collar professionals often act as if subjective reasoning—one's preferences, desires, values, and beliefs—have no place in decision making or behavior. However, Halper found that many of the individuals she interviewed did use their intuition and preferences as a basis for decision making but were reluctant to admit it.

Halper found that a large portion of these men, almost two thirds, were tired of being dutiful, loyal employees, with no control over their jobs. Most of these men also suffer from numerous contradictions, one of the most common being a need to prove that they are both tough and nice guys at the same time. Halper found that 57 percent of managers don't delegate authority because they fear giving up control over decisions. As a result, many feel great stress over being constantly responsible for what takes place inside their firms.

Related to this need to control decision making is the fact that many corporate executives find it difficult to trust their fellow employees. They feel a good deal of hostility and resentment, as well as a fear of betrayal. The sad result of this distrust is that few male workers over age thirty have any male friends. Despite their considerable accomplishments, in many cases, a large number of these professionals suffer from low self-esteem. Many also confessed that their personal lives were dull, unfulfilling, and alienating. Frustrated at work, not intimately related to their wives, many of these men lead rich fantasy lives, preferring to see themselves as who they want to be, rather than who they really are. No matter how successful they are, many feel that they've failed to achieve success. Many suffer from reactions to denying their feelings for so long. Depression, feeling out of control, and other stress reactions are common. Some commit suicide.

Because men are not supposed to have emotional needs, they rarely bond with each other by sharing their feelings. If men do have other male friends, they are often accused of being irresponsible, neglecting their wives and children. Spending time with friends is viewed as time wasted, time not spent getting to the top of their profession. Thus, what few male friendships American men do have are superficial relationships undertaken for business purposes or purposes of convenience, such as neighbors or fellow churchgoers

Again, there is a parallel with the world inhabited by Tony Soprano. Tony doesn't know who he can really trust, who his real friends are. He lives in constant fear of being ratted out to the Feds by his fellow mob members, of being challenged for control of the activities in New Jersey, or of being whacked by rivals or even one of his own relatives! All of this is reflective *in extremis* of contemporary workplace problems in mainstream American life.

Contemporary Workplace Ills

Because of the massive layoffs that have taken place in recent years in corporate America, the distrust between workers has increased since the 1990s. No job seems safe anymore. Frequently, those not laid off feel the guilt, irritability, fatigue, and stress that accompany being left on a job that requires more hands. Moreover, corporations in the United States are now eliminating some 2 million full-time jobs a year, and most newly created jobs are located in the low-wage service sector, McDonald's-type positions.

Capitalist economies are in the early stages of a long-term shift from a mass manufacturing to an elite, highly educated labor force. In 1933, a third of the labor force was involved in manufacturing. By 1990, only 17 percent was so engaged. By 2005, a mere 12 percent of the American labor force will manufacture anything. Between 30 to 40 percent of all banking jobs will be eliminated by 2002. New jobs are likely to be in science, engineering, management, consulting, teaching, media, entertainment, and a few other highly complex fields.

Workers who remain on the job are increasingly likely to experience clinical depression as a response to increased stress. The increase in workplace stress has resulted in a dramatic increase in stress-related illnesses; an increasing number of employees are now suing and being compensated for work-related mental disabilities. Many factors are contributing to increased feelings of powerlessness by workers who feel they are being robbed of control over how to do their jobs.

The alienation felt by unemployed workers is even more profound. Studies reveal that unemployment for white-collar workers is an exceptionally traumatic event, accompanied by worry over finances and lowered self-esteem. During the recession of the early 1990s, nearly 30 percent of laid-off employees were white-collar professionals. Many unemployed white-collar workers report feeling the alienation associated with inauthenticity. These workers were implicitly promised careers and the long-term job security that comes with a profession. Once fired, dismissed employees are likely to feel the resentment that comes with feeling betrayed. Many former white-collar workers report that former employers violated their needs for security and justice.

As of 1993, there were 23 million part-time workers in the United States, and as of 2002 only 10 percent of Fortune 500 corporations were composed of full-time employees.[17] In a workforce that has become "fluid, flexible, and disposable," most temporary workers have no sense of security or identity and no benefits.

Alienation and Religion: Authoritarianism and Dehumanization

One of the most interesting aspects of Mafia life concerns the place of religion and the Catholic Church. Nothing has more dramatically symbolized the contradictions therein than the famous, breathtaking scene at the end of *The Godfather*. Don Michael Corleone attends the baptism of his new nephew and becomes the boy's godfather. As the officiating priest asks Michael to make a series of promises involving the renouncing of Satan and all of the evils attached thereto, cutaway shots show the Don's buttonmen eliminating all of his vicious rivals. In the movie's final scene, Michael lies to his wife about having his sister Connie's husband, Carlo, murdered as retaliation for her husband's setting up Michael's brother, Sonny, for a Mob hit. The *Godfather Part II* opens with a scene depicting Michael's son first communion. *Part III* opens with Michael receiving an award from the Catholic Church for his family foundation's generous charitable donations, which total in the hundreds of millions. In the *Godfather* saga, the Mafia is clearly shown as attempting to buy respect and influence via its relationship with the Church while committing heinous crimes and sins.

The same contradiction pervades *The Sopranos*. Carmela and Tony belong to and support the Church. Carmela knows what Tony does and still considers herself a good Catholic. In fact, in her loneliness she turns to her priest, and almost has an affair with him. The characters on *The Sopranos* seem to want it both ways with their Catholicism. On the one hand, they treat the forgiveness associated with Christianity as a license to sin. On the other hand, they sometimes ask, as does Paulie when Christopher has a near-death vision of Hell, why the Church does not watch out more for their interests, implying that the Church should stop them from sinning. Or in Paulie's case, he'd be happy for blanket immunity from divine justice.

The Church, for its part, has also used the Mafia for its own purposes. The scenes in *The Godfather Part III* with the Vatican Bank borrowing huge sums of money from the Mafia to avoid financial meltdown were based in fact. All of the contradictions involving the Mafia and the Church are symptoms of a more widespread condition, one worthy of closer examination.

Religion has undergone great changes in modern Western societies since the Middle Ages. In Erich Fromm's eyes, the concept of God has become a form of reification, which takes place when human beings invest powers and magical qualities in what are really human creations. These artificial creations are then worshipped as if they were real.[18]

The greatest change concerning idolatry began at the end of the Middle Ages. At that time, the writings of Martin Luther and John Calvin appealed to the urban middle class and the poor for whom freedom had become so problematic. The Protestant doctrines offered relief from the loneliness and anxiety brought about by the rise of industrial capitalism. Luther envisioned a religion in which human nature was considered sinful and freedom something that humans were incapable of handling. God became an all-powerful force who required complete submission. Lutheran and Calvinist theology made people dependent on sources outside themselves for salvation and security.

Today such complete submission is a sign of religious extremism. Extreme religious sects and fundamentalists of all types constitute a major source of social harm. One study of the leading textbooks used in fundamentalist Christian schools in the United States found some interesting patterns. It found that the books promoted religious intolerance, anti-intellectualism, and a disdain for science if it contradicts the fundamentalists' reading of the Bible. Humans are viewed as "imperfectible" until Christ returns during the last days of the earth. God, not humankind, is viewed as the source of good. The devil is seen as in control of the physical world. War is viewed as necessary in a world corrupted by evil. Darwinism and evolution are viewed as causing a breakdown of morality because they are "Godless" notions.

Most significantly, the same study found that fundamentalist texts do not condemn slavery, view Native Americans as immoral heathens, label the civil rights movement of the 1960s as "militant," and categorize all Democratic administrations in American history as "socialistic." All other religions except fundamentalist Christianity are labeled as cults and idol worshipers. The Jews are specifically blamed for Jesus' crucifixion, and Catholics are resented as intrusive immigrants. The texts also claim that most Americans have rejected God, despite great evidence to the contrary.

Another study concluded that fundamentalists tend to fit the profile of authoritarian personalities. Some recent studies[19] found that fundamentalist Christians feel threatened by open expressions of any values and lifestyles that are counter to their own. They are especially intolerant of feminists, pro-choice advocates, gays, and lesbians. A number of fundamentalists have been convicted of bombing abortion clinics and murdering doctors who perform abortions, thus underscoring the lengths to which some of them will go in opposing people whose views are contrary to theirs.

Because of their extreme ideology and the unquestioning manner in which they hold it, fundamentalists are easy prey to those willing to manipulate and defraud them for personal gain. Reverend Jimmy Swaggert, after being secretly photographed by a rival minister's son, confessed on television to hiring prostitutes to disrobe in front of him while he masturbated. Another fundamentalist, Oral Roberts, whose "ministry" is worth $500 million, told his television viewers that God would "call him home" (cause his death) if his followers did not immediately send in $4.5 million. Some of the people who gave money to these preachers were elderly people, whose only support was Social Security. Some went without heat in the winter for a time in order to send money to these churches.

Besides extremism, a second harmful condition troubling some religions these days is child molestation. Between 1984 and 1993, the American Catholic Church paid out $400 million in settlements of child molestation incidents by priests. Over 400 priests were accused of sexual acts with children during this period.[20] By 2002, the figure had reached approximately $1 billion. This great harm was, in many instances, aided and abetted by the Church itself. Between 1964 and 1987, at least thirty-six students in a Catholic school in Santa Barbara, California, were molested by eleven friars. One priest molested sixteen different boys and girls between fourteen and sixteen years of age. In a number of these incidents, Church officials were aware of the problems but let them continue for fear of scandal. The students waited until adulthood to lodge the complaints because they were convinced that they would not be believed over the word of clergy.[21]

In 2002, Cardinal Bernard Law of Boston became involved in one of the most serious sex scandals in the history of the American Catholic Church. Cardinal Law personally knew of one priest's pedophilia problems in 1984, but nevertheless granted the now-convicted molester's transfer to another parish. Throughout the next decade, the priest continued to fondle and rape some 130 children. The priest, Father John J. Geoghan, first came to the Church's official attention in the late 1960s and early 1970s, when accusations were made that he abused a young male. The Boston archdiocese not only neglected to respond to such charges decades ago but also failed to punish dozens of priests in the Boston archdiocese, despite their knowledge of the priests' potential threat to the young.

In the 1990s, the Church made promises that it would make sure it didn't happen again. The growing scandal also led, in February 2002, to a shameful Church admission that eighty priests, including eight still active, have been charged with child abuse in the past forty years in the Boston archdiocese alone. The Boston scandal mushroomed into evidence that child molestation by Catholic clergy in America is a widespread condition, a genuine social problem throughout the nation. The Philadelphia archdiocese discovered "credible evidence" that thirty-five of its priests sexually abused fifty children over five decades. However, since the statute of limitations has run out, the priests' names won't be given to the police.

For its part, Vatican officials hinted that the issue isn't pedophiles at all. Vatican officials are now laying the blame at the doorsteps of homosexual priests, who they say must be kicked out of the Church. The witch-hunt for gay priests within the Church has begun, and it threatens to ruin the reputations and lives of numerous innocent homosexual clergy, perhaps including hero Father Michael Judge, one of the first casualties of the World Trade Center terrorist attack of September 11, 2001. The real issue, of course, remains the Vatican's total misperception of the nature of the scandal of which it stands accused. This means that pedophile priests may end up being able to continue molesting children.

The Church itself is engaging in a cover-up of the true facts in the case. Yet, we should not be terribly surprised. Over forty years ago, distinguished sociologist Howard Becker argued that sociologists have two choices in life: they can either serve the interests of those who are in charge of bureaucracies (managerial elites) or those who are supposedly served by those bureaucracies (clientele). The problem, as Becker perceived it, is that those in charge of bureaucratic organizations always have to lie. Prisons do not rehabilitate. Mental institutions do not cure psychological illnesses. The Catholic Church does not always serve the best interest of its parishioners. In order to rationalize, cover up, and shift the blame for such failures, those elites in charge of various institutions have to lie, and they do.[22] This reality is also true in the case of educational institutions.

Alienation and Education

A great deal has been written concerning both the manifest and latent functions of education in the United States, functions important to understand as causes of alienation. The great contradictions of American education stem from the fact that schools do much more than just impart facts. They also shape personalities in ways that are antidemocratic.

Take, for example, the simple procedures necessary to secure order in the classroom. From their first days in school, students learn to stand in line without speaking, to raise their hands when they want to make question or comment, to take turns at the chalkboard, and to ask permission to engage in the most natural bodily functions. Students are increasingly socialized to take one standardized, objective test (true/false, multiple choice) after another. At first glance, these do not seem like character-shaping activities, but "the hidden lesson of such (rules) is to obey teachers (and other authority figures) and to follow rules without question."[23] Another crucial aspect of education concerns the ideology of capitalism, especially competition. Education researcher Alfie Kohn has written what is perhaps the definitive book concerning the pitfalls of competition in America. Reviewing hundreds of scholarly studies, Kohn makes an eloquent argument concerning the idea that competition is intimately related to self-esteem. One of his conclusions is that most highly competitive people suffer from low self-esteem. Such people feel the need not only to "win" but also to put down those they defeat in the process. Unfortunately, American education is based on individual competition for grades, scholarships, and admission to graduate, law, medical, and business schools.[24]

Finally, Kohn cites dozens of studies that confirm that cooperation works much more effectively in building self-esteem, friendships, productivity, and reducing aggression than does competition.[25] Unfortunately, American schools stress competition on tests, in sports, and in many facets of the educational experience. Critics of education have long held that schools at all levels of society function to do two things: act as a gatekeeper of the social class system and engage in various forms of political socialization designed to convince students to accept inequality. Thus, despite Head Start and other programs designed to help poor minorities obtain equal educational opportunities, 33.5 percent of white children ages three and four attend preschool classes, compared with only 27.1 percent of African-American children, and 20.3 percent of Hispanic children. Moreover, 80 percent of African-American and white children attend kindergarten, compared to only 76.6 percent of Hispanic children.[26]

Meadow and A.J., Tony Soprano's kids, benefit from their father's ill-gotten wealth. Both of them have had first-rate educations at private schools, and thanks largely to the influence of Carmela, their parents have remained involved in assuring their success. Meadow has proven herself a worthy student, studying hard, completing extracurricular activities to enhance her college applications, and choosing carefully between prestigious universities. A.J. remains a more uncertain student, showing signs of impulsivity and hyperactivity, perhaps similar to his sometimes self-destructive father. Yet even if A.J. never attains the academic success of his sister, the Soprano children have been given a significant advantage for success by virtue of the schooling their parents provide.

One major study found that students at private schools score higher on standard achievement tests than do students at public schools. Due to high costs, especially for tuition, private schools are much too expensive for poor, working-class, and many middle-class families. In 1966, James Coleman studied nearly 650,000 students in over 4,000 American schools. His report noted that the best-equipped public schools were predominately white. Yet a number of studies confirm that it is not the amount of money but rather social class variables that affect the educational aspirations that students have. These variables include the number of books in students' homes, the social class of their parents, and their parents' attitude regarding education. [27]

Summarizing a number of studies on the subject, economists Herbert Gintis and Samuel Bowles[28] noted, in the 1980s, that children whose parents are at the top of the occupational structure in the United States get more education than working-class and lower-class children do. These unequal educational levels are functions of expectations on the part of teachers and parents and student responses to institutionalized patterns of teaching and control. These patterns are reinforced by the differential amounts of financial resources different social classes are able to devote to educational expenditures. Thus, as of the mid-1980s, working-class children were over 2.5 times less likely to go to college than are middle- and upper-class children.[29] There is no reason to believe the odds have gotten any better.

Studies of school guidance personnel reveal that children of working-class parents are expected to do poorly in school, to terminate school early, and to follow their parents' example by ending up in similar jobs. Thus students are labeled as potentially "successful" or "unsuccessful" according to their social class, and, once labeled, they are treated in accordance with such expectations. Numerous additional studies have confirmed that the tracking system, placing students perceived to have similar intelligence and academic abilities in the same classroom, is heavily influenced by the dehumanization so widespread in bureaucratic institutions. In this case, studies confirm the existence of racial, class, and gender stereotypes among teachers at elementary, secondary, and university educational levels.[30] Worse, the tracking system is furthered by patterns of institutional segregation that have nothing to do with teacher expectations. A 1993 study by the Harvard Educational Project found that 66 percent of all African-American students and 74.3 percent of all Hispanic students attending public schools in 1991 to 1992 went to schools whose student populations were at least 50 percent minority students.[31] As a result of this study and others, civil rights organizations in twenty-eight states filed lawsuits over the financing of public schools in minority areas.

These days, high school students face forms of alienation not found in earlier years. Brent Collins, a high school teacher in Milwaukee who teaches creative writing and has won teacher of the year honors, concluded in 1990 after over a decade of teaching that a great problem faced by students is apathy. Some students simply do not care about learning, due to several important factors. Many hold part-time jobs after school, and studies have shown the more time students spend engaged in outside work, the lower their grade-point averages. Over two thirds of the students in Collins's classes never even bothered to turn in their homework assignments. Most of these students tend to be average students from average families. Because they are average, they do not receive the special attention heaped upon the gifted, who are literally "programmed for success."[32]

What this forgotten majority of students lack is any pressure to succeed either from parents or peers. Indeed, one study of 58,000 high school students revealed that 88 percent of "A" students reported a high degree of parental supervision in their schoolwork, and 80 percent of them came from two-parent families. Likewise, only 66 percent of "D" students reported a high degree of parental involvement in their schoolwork.[33] Aside from a lack of parental involvement, students also suffer from declining standards in teacher quality. For example, half of junior and senior high school English teachers did not major in English in college. A study by the Educational Testing Service (ETS), based on student papers corrected by ETS, found that the average English teacher is "barely literate."[34]

Another study, from 1993, of 140,000 fourth-, eighth-, and twelfth-grade students found that a quarter of high school seniors have not achieved even the most basic level of reading comprehension and that two thirds of all students do not have more than a superficial understanding of what they read. The same study also found that the more television students watch, the worse they read.[35] Most students watch a lot of TV, about fifty-five hours per week in most cases.

Some parents are so disgusted with public schools that 1.5 million of their children are now being educated at home. More surprisingly, the average student receiving a home-based education is five to ten years ahead of his or her public school counterpart. Award-winning teacher John Taylor Gatto has concluded that the great problem with high schools is simply that they have become irrelevant. Schools no longer teach the kinds of science, math, and language skills necessary for success in the global service economy of the new millennium.[36]

The relatively few people who read, write, and do math well get little respect. A 1993 study of nineteen industrial democracies found that the United States spends less of its gross domestic product on teachers than all but two other nations, Norway and Italy. American teachers also work harder and plan less than teachers in other nations. American teachers spend an average of thirty hours a week in the classroom, versus just eighteen in Japan and twenty-one in Germany. America's high school teachers average four years of higher education, versus five to six years of education training in European countries.[37]

Alienation and the University

The alienating conditions at universities stem from the same bureaucratic processes that affect other forms of education. According to education professors Arthur Lean and William Eaton, "the structure of the modern university with its departmental separations and its total lack of order among its specialized disciplines represents perfectly the disunity and chaos of modern culture."[38]

The nation's junior colleges reflect this alienation. Community colleges have long been criticized for their lowering of students' aspirations from four-year degrees to terminal vocational degrees in subjects like computer programming. This "cooling-out" function is part of the class-based tracking system that channels working-class community-college students into low-prestige majors and low-paying jobs. Such tracking also preserves elite colleges for more highly educated students from more affluent families. There is a debate over whether community colleges deliberately undertook this role under pressure from corporate America

There is little doubt, however, that contemporary junior colleges continue to perform an important gate-keeping function by channeling students into transfer programs to four-year colleges, or into vocational education. There is also evidence that students at community colleges are alienated from their teachers. Studies of junior college faculty confirm that most students are virtual strangers to their teachers. This is primarily due to large classes and heavy teaching loads at community colleges. College students at large universities frequently complain of feeling dehumanized. Many never see their department's most famous professors. This faculty has made their names through their research and publication, not with their teaching. In many large universities, it is not uncommon for one half to two thirds of all undergraduate courses to be taught by part-time faculty and graduate teaching assistants. Professors in most universities are primarily rewarded for their publications and for the research grants they bring into the university, not for their ability to teach students.

The Therapeutic State

The most controversial aspect of *The Sopranos* is probably the relationship between Tony and his therapist, Dr. Jennifer Melfi. Mafiosi take a blood oath of secrecy not to disclose anything that goes on outside their "families." Dr. Melfi's treatment of Tony raises constant moral issues. When Melfi tells her family that she is treating a gangster, her brother accuses her of taking moral relativism to an extreme, not merely using her amoral approach to therapy as a tool.[39] There is the possibility that rather than helping Tony's condition, Melfi is making him a more proficient gangster. Her early efforts to advise Tony how to deal effectively with Uncle Junior lead him to placate his uncle while he runs his criminal operations unhindered behind his back. Like Paulie, who admits to having seen a therapist when Tony finally chooses to share the news with his crew, Tony primarily wants to learn coping skills to better get him through his day.

The moral nature of the very relationship between Tony and Dr. Melfi is a matter of heated debate, and for good reason. During the show's first three seasons, Tony has had Dr. Melfi followed on a date, had her boyfriend intimidated, stormed into her office in the middle of other patients' sessions, exited angrily in the middle of his own sessions, and lied to her about having an affair with a fellow patient. The climactic events of the show's first season even forced Melfi to abandon her office and operate her practice out of a motel room.

So upset have these and other antisocial actions made her, that Melfi's own psychiatrist has observed her grow increasingly dependent on alcohol to get her through her sessions with Tony, and he prescribes medication to help her cope with the situation. Yet psychiatrists from around the nation praise the interaction between Tony and the good doctor as something as a model of a therapeutic relationship. One group of psychiatrists in the San Francisco Bay

Area watches the show each week in order to observe the doctor-patient relationship. "Dr. Melfi," who, lest we forget, is not a real person, now gets invited, in the person of the actress who plays her, Lorraine Bracco, to be on panels at American Psychiatric Association meetings![40]

Tony Soprano is a gangster who suffers from panic attacks. Why? His initial visit to Dr. Melfi was triggered by an attack after he observed the departure of a family of ducks living in his swimming pool. Yet, the root cause of his malady is a matter of some controversy in the social critical press. To paraphrase one author: Could you imagine Al Capone on Prozac or Lucky Luciano going to a psychiatrist?

The retort to this has been that the Mafia itself is on the verge of a nervous breakdown. This theory holds that the real reasons for Tony's panic attacks are that the mob faces unprecedented stress, both from within and without. From within, the loyalty oath of *omertà*—which viewers observed Christopher take during the show's third season—no longer holds sway over many of its members. Contemporary Mafiosi easily embrace the extreme greed and narcissism present in American life since the 1980s.[41] Some are lost in an orgy of drugs, sex, gambling, and other self-indulgences. If the Feds come calling, they will be the first to whack or rat out their fellow family members. Tony's longtime friend Pussy did as much when he found himself facing charges of drug dealing.

The Russian Mafia, various Asian syndicates, and other syndicates of Hispanic or African-American origin have either infringed upon or taken over significant portions of traditional Mafia markets. In some cases, the Mob has made alliances with these crime families. In other cases, they have simply lost certain markets to them due to attrition. During the 1980s and early 1990s, well over a thousand organized-crime figures in New York City and Italy alone were sent to prison, severely diminishing the ranks of traditional organized crime's five families in the greater New York Area. Little wonder *The Sopranos* is located in New Jersey.

The "breakdown" theory of the Mob is but one view of Tony's mental anguish. After all, Tony's own mother tried to have him bumped off by his uncle, an oedipal nightmare if ever there was one. Here was a mother who was impossible to please and an uncle who was jealous and vindictive enough to make any nephew paranoid. The theory emerges, therefore, that there are two Tony Sopranos: one who hates his mother and is full of violent rage and masculine toughness, and one who works to be a benevolent husband and father. It is when these two roles are brought into sharp conflict that Tony, so the theory goes, experiences panic.

Although there is some truth in both of these theories, each being something of a contributory factor to Tony's great angst, there are also additional considerations. Instead of looking at Tony Soprano as a Mafia capo or someone suffering from some personal psychiatric trouble, it is useful to view him as a representation of the American social character in the early twenty-first century. A 2002 article in the *San Francisco Chronicle* observed that many of the most notable movies of 2001 and 2002 featured main characters in various states of mental confusion: from *The Majestic* (about a man suffering from amnesia) to *A Beautiful Mind* (about a professor suffering from severe mental illness), both movies were about their main characters' extreme crisis of the psyche. Viewed in this context, why are we Americans so fascinated by people experiencing such altered states?[42]

The answer is not very mysterious. John Spanier,[43] a political scientist, has noted that there have always been big questions about what it means to be an American and about what a real American is. We've seen this most recently following the September 11 terrorist attacks. In the wake of the tragedy, people all over the nation sought ways to demonstrate that they are real Americans. They flew the country's flag everywhere they could. President George W. Bush had Muslims and Sikhs to the White House to pose for pictures with him so he could reassure the nation that these, too, are real Americans. Yet Tony Soprano suffers from a more extreme case of identity confusion than most Americans seeking to assert their patriotism.

Many articles have suggested that *The Sopranos* are somehow representative of us. Indeed, *Newsweek* proudly proclaimed that "*The Sopranos* are us," that their anxieties are our anxieties.[44] So it is with the American identity crisis. Tony's identity crisis centers on the notion that he must keep so much of himself hidden from those he loves all the time. At its heart, his problem is one of intimacy. For years, he told his children he was in the waste management business, not that he was a Mafia capo. Part of his great anxiety stems from his fear of being found out.

Keeping parts of one's identity hidden is endemic to American culture. Our heroes do it all the time, both in popular culture and in real life. Superman uses Clark Kent as a useful cover. *The American Monomyth* by Robert Jewett and John Shelton Lawrence claims that the ubiquitous hero in American life is a stranger with no name and no close attachments, who shows up out of nowhere to save innocent and helpless victims from bullying villains. The hero is usually a cowboy, a lone cop on vacation from another city, a private detective, or a secret agent. Sometimes we never find out the hero's real name or identity.[45]

Tony Soprano's identity crisis is, however, profoundly different than the monolithic archetypal American hero. His identity crisis, confusion, and alienation stem from a contradiction so profound that it never leaves him, and it has little to do with his mother. Tony is a thug, someone who, despite all the psychotherapy and Prozac, still runs all manner of illegal businesses, commits murder, and engages in corruption. He also has extramarital relationships almost as a matter of course. The other side of Tony's contradiction is that he views himself as a "good" American: he is a husband, a father, and a Catholic. While on a trip with Meadow to visit New England colleges, Tony sees the following quote from Nathaniel Hawthorne carved into a wall: "No man can wear one face to himself and another to the multitude without finally getting bewildered as to which may be true." Deep down, Tony senses that the things he believes about himself exist in profound conflict.

This contradiction is precisely why Tony has such a profound identity crisis and is constantly on the edge of a panic attack. He lives in constant fear of being found out for the fraud he is. The people who can most easily rip off his mask of respectability are his wife and children, which is precisely why he dares not get too close to them, dares not reveal his secrets to them. Tony's greatest fear is the all-American tragedy: the fear of intimacy.

Real life is loaded with examples of the parts of the self that people keep hidden. Suffice it to say that there is onstage behavior (the image that people project to the public) and backstage behavior (what people are "really like"). This is precisely why supermarket tabloids are so popular. We watch with fascination our favorite movie, television, and recording stars and wonder what are they like in "real life." What we mean by this is what are they like in their private lives, when they don't have their masks on, the ones they present to the public. Then every once in a while they mistreat a cabbie or a concierge, fail to tip a waitress, or sock a photographer in the mouth in public. The great price people pay for being public figures is that their privacy can be invaded at any time by those who seek to learn what the real person behind the public image is like. The great tragedy of our age is that very often those being questioned don't know themselves. They are frequently awash in a sea of confusing values, beliefs, and morals. For along with America's identity crisis goes a crisis of morality and authority.

The Crisis of Morality and Authority

In late 1990, two advertising researchers asked a representative sample of 2,000 American adults 1,800 questions regarding what they really believed about their lives. James Patterson and Peter Kim[46] asked people about a wide range of individual beliefs and behaviors, as well as about leading economic, political, and social problems. The results were so startling that they made headlines in newspapers across the nation. The findings reveal that the majority of Americans suffer a crisis of belief.

Few, if any, stable values exist on which to base decisions about daily life or social issues. Only 13 percent of Americans believe in all of the Ten Commandments. People now choose which rules they will obey. There is no longer a moral consensus in the United States as there was in the 1950s, and "there is very little respect for any rule of law."[47] Many of the results of their survey support this notion:

- The official crime statistics are off by at least 200 percent. Sixty percent of Americans report being crime victims; over half of those report being victimized twice.
- One fourth of Americans say they would abandon their families for $10 million.
- Two thirds believe there is nothing wrong with lying and lie regularly.
- Thirty percent of employees have personally witnessed violations of criminal or ethical codes by their bosses, and 43 percent say they cannot trust their co-workers.
- Eighty percent of Americans want morals and ethics taught in public schools and a majority believe that the leading cause of America's economic decline is "unethical behavior by [business] executives."[48]
- Public confidence in America's institutions is at an all-time low, with 80 percent of Americans saying there are no living heroes. Among the lowest-rated occupations for honesty and integrity are congressional representatives and local politicians, lawyers, TV evangelists, executives in oil, network television employees, labor unions, stockbrokers, and car and insurance salespeople.

Studies in 1987 and 1991 detailed what Americans felt about their political system: they were deeply alienated from the political life of their nation. When the pollster Lou Harris asked a national sample in 1987, toward the end of the Reagan era, if politicians represented their interests, 60 percent said they did not—the highest percentage since Harris first asked the question in 1966. A 1991 Kettering Foundation study found that most Americans believed there is no point to voting and that money has overwhelming influence in political campaigns. This sample of respondents believed that media coverage of campaigns alienates voters, partly because of reliance on "sound bites," politicians' practice of reducing complex public problems to empty slogans.[49] Polls taken in 1992 and 1993, at the end of the first Bush administration, revealed that the average American believed that the federal government wastes forty-eight cents of every dollar, and only 20 percent of the public trusted Washington to do the right thing most of the time (down from 76 percent in 1963).[50]

Pessimism About the Future of the Nation

In the 1991 Patterson and Kim study, toward the end of the twelve-year Reagan-Bush era, Americans felt that their nation had become "colder, greedier, meaner, more selfish and less caring" and they were markedly pessimistic about the future; 77 percent believed the rich will get richer and the poor poorer.

- Seventy-two percent believed that crime rates will have risen and 71 percent believed there will be more violence in the streets.
- Sixty-two percent believed the homeless rate will have risen.
- Sixty percent felt AIDS will have become epidemic, and 60 percent believed that no cure will have been found.
- Fifty-eight percent felt drug and alcohol abuse will have worsened.
- Sixty-two percent saw pollution as worse and 43 percent believed it will be so bad that life will become unbearable.
- A majority believed that such social problems as poverty and racism will outlast their children's lifetimes.

Although most Americans believed that social problems would worsen, they thought their private lives would get better. This means that they had become increasingly alienated from what happens to other people and the nation; yet they believed they were patriotic. People believed they were "little islands, that they don't really belong to any larger unit,"[51/52] something other studies had confirmed.[52] They had withdrawn from public issues. Thus from 1965 to 1990, the percentage of Americans who read a daily newspaper fell from 67 percent to 30 percent, and the percentage of people who watched television news fell from 52 percent to 41 percent. Moreover, today Americans also feel the fear of terrorists attacks, so much so that a majority are willing to give up some of their civil liberties to combat the terrorist threat.

Yet Americans want to do the right thing to resolve the crises of our age. Half say they would volunteer to help prevent child abuse. Forty-one percent say they would volunteer to help others learn to read. Twenty-nine percent say they would volunteer to clean up the environment, and 66 percent say they would pay more taxes to achieve goals such as these.

Much evidence confirms the presence of alienation within the institutions of work, religion, education, and therapy. Tony Soprano's life and environment are replete with alienation. Like most Americans, Tony has trouble trusting the people with whom he works. He suffers job insecurity to a degree unknown by most of us: the fear of being killed or arrested via betrayal. Yet, Tony's insecurities are but an extreme form of uncertainty that characterizes much of the American workforce. The use of part-time workers, even in executive posts, so-called restructurings and layoffs due to mergers and economic downturns now threaten the sense of security of millions of workers.

In Tony Soprano's world, religion, once seen as a source of morals and ethics, has become a scandal-plagued institution. Tony and his Mafia cohorts frequently use their affiliation with the Church as a cover of respectability to hide their criminal acts. For decades, neighborhood institutions, including the Church, protected local Mafiosi from the law. They did this by integrating Mafia members into the web of community life, doing business with Mob-owned front stores and so on. The Church has also found the services of the Mafia of use when it needed aid in a financial crisis.

For the rest of us, the scandals involving religion touch much of American life these days. Televangelists show more concern for dollars than the spiritual well-being of their flock. The Catholic Church is currently having to admit that it has long shielded its pedophile priests from public scrutiny when it should have been protecting its most vulnerable lay members.

Likewise, education, once a source of fascination and citizenship training, has, for the most part, become a gate-keeping mechanism by which the middle and upper classes are guaranteed their place in society, whereas those beneath them are relegated to a relatively powerless existence in an economically unequal society. Tony's upper-middle-class status guarantees that he can find his daughter an exclusive university to attend, and rescue his son from penalties when he makes mischief at school. For those in the working and lower classes, however, their fate is frequently dropping out of school, much like Tony's cohorts. Tony's semester-and-a-half of college makes him a comparative intellectual in his circle.

Inauthenticity and dehumanization pervade the institutions of everyday American life. All of them construct public images designed to convince us they are accomplishing their stated missions. Underlying skepticism and cynicism all too often characterize a bewildered and disillusioned public.

Solutions to the Crises of Tony Soprano's America: The Real Meaning of Tony Soprano

IN ONE OF HIS EARLY SESSIONS with Dr. Melfi, Tony asks the psychiatrist about a painting he observed in her waiting room. He accuses her of planting it there as a psychological test, as he found himself focusing on two features that seemed to him intended to elicit discomfort and fear. He describes the darkened interior of a barn as "scary" and claims that a tree in the foreground appears "rotted out." But Melfi denies any such intention. Instead, Tony has revealed something of his own trepidation about the frightening contents of his own psyche, contents that he needs to confront if he has any hope of a lasting psychological peace.

Tony Soprano represents a piece of our Jungian dark sides that has broken through into the light. It is time we had a look at what he represents metaphorically about us, American culture, and the world in which we find ourselves as we begin the third millennium. What most of us share with Tony is a deep suspicion and cynicism about the present and the future. We no longer know if it is safe to trust our investments and our pension funds. We suspect that a terrorist bomb may await our next trip out in public. We see our national symbols being bombed, but we are never told why these attacks are made on our country. The only explanation given is that the perpetrators are evil people, the new Hitlers who hate America for what we have and what they lack. To so much as ask why the attackers did what they did is to be accused of treason in some circles.[1]

The Sopranos can provide us with a valuable insight into ourselves. We can use these curious cultural phenomena to do some critical soul-searching about our culture and our institutions:

- Why do gangsters fascinate us—to the point of hero worship? Is it because American culture is addicted to violence, sex, and the admiration of those who can take short cuts in achieving success?

- Tony's accumulation of wealth and power reflects the unequal distribution of wealth and power in America and in the global capitalist system and the role these inequalities play in causing social problems.

- Tony is also a symbol of the place of organized crime in the overall crime problem both in America and globally. He is a reminder that crime at all levels is intimately interrelated, and that drug trafficking and terrorism are pieces of these interrelationships.

- Tony's relationships with his mother, wife, and children are symbolic of the familial and sexual dysfunctions plaguing the nation as detailed in this book.

- Tony's interaction in his Mafia family (his workplace), community, church, his children's schools, and with his therapist are reminders of the alienation of present everyday life.

- Finally there is Tony's relationship with Dr. Melfi. Is she really having an ameliorating effect on him or is she merely making him a more productive psychopath? Their entire relationship raises questions about the place of psychotherapy in the social control of deviants in a society that likes to claim that the culture is fine and it is misfits who are the problem.

Tony also lacks a vision of a positive future. He regrets he wasn't around in the heyday of the Mafia. He fears the best of times has passed him by. Like Tony, so it is with our two major political parties. Neither possesses much of a positive vision of the future. Both seem so busy celebrating America, seeing who can wrap themselves in the largest flag, telling us how much they love the family, and posing with big-name celebrities that they fail to offer a positive future vision. One reason for this lack of vision is that many Americans assume that the status quo is as good as it will get. What a contrast from a generation ago when politicians like Bobby Kennedy were writing books like *To Seek a Newer World!* What is needed are unconditional doses of love, healing, and caring in a world that is bleeding from wounds of violence, war, famine, genocide, ignorance, poverty, disease, and ecological trauma.

Meanwhile, the real problems that need addressing, as discussed in this book, go ignored and unresolved. Any work analyzing the great crises of our age that does not provide some vision of solution and hope to readers, I feel, is merely kvetching. This is especially the case in an age as cynical as ours. This chapter offers a vision of what is needed to resolve the crises of our age as presented in this book.

The Real Crises of Our Age

Whenever any author discusses solutions to problems, that person has clearly left the realm of social science and entered the world of policy and ideology. Therefore, let us not pretend that the following discussion is free of values, politics, or bias. Not only is that impossible, it is undesirable and an insult to the reader. Values are an inherent part of the sociological imagination and of being a concerned citizen of a democratic society. The pretense of objectivity that pervades both journalism and the scientific enterprise is both a bore and a danger to liberty itself. The examples of the Nazis using scientific methods to systematically exterminate millions of people they had labeled as scapegoats should be proof enough of the impossibility and undesirability of objectivity in the application of science. Objectivity itself is an ideology and a dangerous one. With that caveat go some assumptions about the nature of our age itself.

On Valentine's Day, 1929, four Chicago gangsters dressed as police officers killed seven members of a rival crime family. The incident, known as the St. Valentine's Day Massacre, sparked outrage all over the nation. A Better Government Association was formed in Chicago, and federal agents, under the direction of Elliot Ness, began an investigation that eventually brought down the leader of one Chicago syndicate, Al Capone, America's first celebrity gangster. Today, in most major American cities, every weekend there is at least one incident similar to the St. Valentine's Day Massacre involving an equal number of murder victims, but there is no corresponding outrage. In fact, an astonishing amount of criminal activity and morally dubious behavior is now tolerated as "normal" in American life.

This mentality of relative indifference now exists on a global scale.

- Tony Soprano symbolizes the end of an era in organized crime, the Italian-American Mafia on the verge of a nervous breakdown. Gone are the days of the old-school godfathers, now replaced by global crime syndicates made up of Russians, Hispanics, and Asians all allied with each other in a global narcotics trade and linked to terrorist groups around the world.
- By 2050 there may be 10 to 15 billion people on the planet, a crisis of uncontrolled population growth.
- Each day some 20,000 people (30 million per year) die of the effects of malnutrition, mostly in Third World nations.
- The average Third World child does not see a doctor before age five.

- 1 billion people (30 percent) in the Third World are unemployed.
- Between 60 and 90 percent of Third World land is owned by 3 to 20 percent of the population.
- Ronald Reagan's administration was characterized by more corruption than any in American history; over 120 of his appointees resigned from office under ethical clouds. The Bush administration that followed was basically a continuation of the "grab it while you can" ethic that began during the Reagan years and continues to this day, especially with the disputed election of the second Bush.
- In 1960, one in every forty white babies and one in five African-American infants were born out of wedlock. By the 1990s, one of every five whites and two of every three African Americans were born out of wedlock.[2]
- In 1987, the American Council on Education took a poll of 200,000 college freshmen. Of those polled, 76 percent said that it was very important to be financially well off. Twenty years earlier, only 44 percent of freshmen held such materialistic views. In 1976, 83 percent of respondents felt it important to develop a philosophy of life. In 1987, only 39 percent of students expressed such a wish.[3]
- A 1990 report by the Carnegie Foundation for the Advancement of Teaching complained of a breakdown of civility on the nation's college campuses. Especially alarming were an epidemic on campuses of cheating, racial attacks, hate crimes, and rapes. Studies at the University of Tennessee and Indiana University found a majority of students at each campus admitted to submitting papers that were written by others or copying large sections of friends' papers.[4]

These examples are symptomatic of socially patterned problems. The overarching problem has many names: "social breakdown,"[5] "social disintegration," the rise of "the morally loose individual,"[6] instrumental and expressive "wilding,"[7] "defining deviancy down."[8] I call it the rise of the antisocial social character.[9] Whatever we call it, the problem is a measurably detrimental aspect of contemporary American life.

The rise of the antisocial social character may be termed a "master trend" of the postmodern society.[10] Here is a social character whose foundation rests on superficial charm, interpersonal manipulation, an unhealthy narcissism, and a disturbing tendency toward what Charles Derber has called "wilding," the commission of immoral or criminal acts without regard to their effects on others.[11] Master trends, or "main drifts," are fundamental mechanisms by which social change takes place. In addition to changes in America's moral climate, other trends promise to bring more unwanted changes, unless something is done to reverse them. These trends include increasing inequalities of wealth and political power, both domestically and globally. These inequalities are the causes of the numerous macro- and micro-level problems, such as unemployment, recession/depression, corporate crimes, and political corruption and related woes. Over 17 percent of Americans are without medical insurance and 25 percent live in poverty. Prison labor is now employed for wages as low as 2 cents an hour to work for corporations such as U.S. Technologies, Victoria's Secret, TWA, Spalding, and AT&T. The lowest fifth of the nation's income earners now receive only 3.7 percent of the nation's income, whereas the highest fifth receive 43 percent (a 27 percent increase over a decade ago).

A hidden violence epidemic pervades America, stretching from child molestation within the Catholic Church to incest and abuse within American families. Domestically, the "main drift" of the postmodern era, the one from which virtually all other patterns flow, has been the unprecedented accumulation of economic and political power in the hands of a small group of elites. The decline of the middle class is a master trend that will spawn other serious social problems. Economist Harold Barnet[12] has argued that the marketing of unsafe products, the polluting of the environment, and violations of

health, safety, and labor laws all increase corporate profits by trans-
ferring various costs to consumers, workers, and the general public.
Moreover, the appalling lack of enforcement of corporate crime laws
and the lenient sentences handed down in such cases serve further
to support the notion that the state functions largely to encourage
capital accumulation, not to discourage elite wrongdoing.

At the elite level, such deviance is part of a "higher immorality."
C. Wright Mills coined that term to refer to an institutionalized set
of values and practices among the nation's corporate and political
elite.[13] Mills believed that America's upper class possesses a moral
insensibility that allows for the commission of various criminal and
deviant acts.[14] The Enron scandal is but the latest in a long line of
such behavior.

Since Mills wrote in 1956 about the higher immorality, the nation
has experienced unprecedented forms of corruption. No longer are
American scandals simply about politicians taking bribes from corporate elites seeking political favors, organized criminal syndicates have
become active players in scandalous situations. Today these practices
run the gamut from material self-enrichment and corrupt acts of
acquiring political power (as in Watergate) to the deception of the
public to manipulate public opinion to misuses of sex to nail down
business deals. What Mills perceived about American political power
in the 1950s was the beginning of what Bill Moyers has termed "the
secret government."[15]

Social character remains the great dependent variable, shaped by
both the political economy and the dominant culture. The master
trend in American social character revolves around identity confusion
and uncertainty about the future of the nation and its values.

Since 1945, social character literature has come full circle.[16] The
social critics of the 1940s and 1950s complained that Americans were
too conformist and insecure and that they were overly receptive to the
opinions of other people. The 1960s and 1970s saw a cultural revolution that encouraged "doing your own thing." Self-help movements
sprang up, stressing consciousness expansion, sexual freedom, and

experimentation. Many members of the middle classes, products of the civil rights, antiwar, and feminist movements of the 1960s, eagerly adopted lifestyles based on self-awareness and self-fulfillment. No sooner had these seemingly independent streaks emerged than the literature of the day began to criticize Americans for their narcissism and neglect of the common good.

By the time the yuppies emerged in the 1980s, social critics had become alarmed over the new lifestyle "enclaves" based solely on material gratification, designer drugs, and greed. Sociologist Robert Bellah and his colleagues noted with alarm the inability of new members of the upper middle class to form emotional bonds of any kind.[17]

Thus in the literature, at least, one notes conflicting trends from one decade to the next. Perhaps the greatest change during the past forty years has been a virtual end of the affluence the generation of the 1950s took as a birthright. Critics like Christopher Lasch noted the rise of a survival mentality among middle-class victims of inflation and unemployment.[18] Additionally, many Americans now possess conflicting values or no values at all regarding faith in their most basic institutions. There is no longer a basic faith in any political ideology or political figure. Business executives are every bit as distrusted as politicians. The main drift of the American character is one of cynicism and alienation.

Much of this alienation stems from the inauthenticity and dehumanization that are the hallmarks of postmodern culture. Americans live in a world where it is increasingly difficult to separate fiction from fantasy, form from substance, and lasting values from fads. The result of these influences on social character is an unprecedented confusion about life's most basic questions, including the question of what to do about resolving our most pressing social problems.

The American Way of Problem Solving

Crime and drugs are somewhat out of vogue as social problems in America at the moment. The history of these problems has been that they are a great deal like icebergs. That is, they periodically rear their ugly heads, only to have a great many resources and media attention thrown at them, whereupon they sink beneath public view for a while, only to reemerge a few years later with a new vengeance.

The official crime rate went down during the Clinton years, but it has already started to climb due to our present economic woes.[19] Moreover, many fear a further upswing as the economy worsens and a new generation of crime-prone youth comes of age.

The real question is always what can be done to prevent crime, or any other social problem, from worsening. More to the point, as sociologist Philip Slater has noted, America tends not to take proactive measures to prevent social problems but only to react to full-blown crises. He calls this approach "the toilet assumption."[20] By this Slater means that Americans leave social problems unattended until there is a crisis, much like a toilet that has backed up because the sewer has clogged. Then they call in some societal plumber to apply a quick fix to the problem. Once the toilet works again (and the problem is flushed out of everyone's mind), Americans go back to their normal routine and the problem is conveniently forgotten about until the next time a crisis emerges.

And so it is with crime and drugs. Over and over again we have declared war on these two problems, and over and over they reemerge in crisis proportions. The great tragedy is that very little will probably be done to break this cycle. This is because the media keeps the entire crime/drug problem steeped in myth, and only rarely does anyone with the facts have a chance to correct the record. For example, President George W. Bush has stated that he feels that capital punishment has a deterrent effect on homicide. There is simply no credible evidence that demonstrates this to be true. In fact, there is emerging evidence that the opposite is true; capital punishment actually seems to increase the homicide rate.

Second, there are many policy initiatives that would probably be effective in combating some of our worst social problems. The problem with them is that they are very threatening to the existing distributions of power and wealth in America. Crime is a prime example. Violent crime is especially rampant in the lower classes and is directly related to poverty, unstable family life, physical and sexual abuse, unemployment, and economic downturns.

Doing something about these problems might require redistributing resources, providing full employment, a Marshall Plan for America's inner cities, and the like. Such proposals are very threatening to those in power and to those who back them with their campaign contributions, because there is no profit to be had here. Likewise, such proposals would dry up a vast pool of cheap labor.

What all of this indicates is that the causes of the great crises of our age are located on four different, albeit interrelated, levels of reality.

First, there is the individual level, characterized by personality traits, biological and social needs, individual rights, and very much influenced by the environments made up of all other environments.

Second, there is the immediate environment of everyday life. Herein are located one's family, neighborhood, workplace, and community of residence. This is the great web of face-to-face interaction in which social life is carried out on a daily basis.

Third, there is the national political economy, the institutions of which determine the big decisions that shape our lives. Will there be war or peace? Will we have prosperity or recession? What sort of media fare will be entertaining us and what new products and services will we be consuming?

Finally, there is a global environment consisting of trading partners, wars, and terrorists acts in places far and near, illegal immigrants, cheap labor, drug traffickers, global crime syndicates, and a host of other influences all of which impact our daily lives in a myriad of ways. Social change does and must take place on all these levels.

Sociotherapy and the Sociological Imagination

The sociological imagination teaches that what often appear as personal troubles are symptoms of widespread harmful conditions, like divorce, drug and child abuse, mental illness, unemployment, and crime. One may try to deny the truth of the environment's impact on daily life, or even escape from it for a time, but such efforts will work only until the realities of our age come crashing through such barriers. Americans confront a host of personal issues. Many experience identity confusion over what values to believe in, what it means to be a man or woman in contemporary life, and how to cultivate a positive sense of self in a society steeped in dehumanization and inauthenticity. The sociological imagination, as a worldview, offers a promise of therapeutic transformation for those in need of meaningful self-help.

America's view of extreme individualism and intense competition for scarce rewards and values (money, recognition, and power) creates a society where relatively few people become great successes. Consequently, many people in America feel they have "failed," and their self-esteem suffers. Having knowledge about America's reward system and the American sense of individualism is a useful form of self-help.

Studying the attitudes and experiences of others can be a liberating experience in a society that encourages self-blame, appearances over realities, and materialism over caring, concern, and emotional intimacy. Studying these dynamics can impart important lessons about what is really important, and lasting in life can aid people in developing a sense of self-worth.

The American social character experiences unmet needs for love, recognition, and identity. These issues are social problems, and the sociological imagination is an ideal paradigm for their analysis. Thus why not combine sociological analysis and self-help in what we may call "sociotherapy," the unity of the sociological and the psychological? Sociotherapy is about the relationship between collective psychic crises and the crises of one's personal life.

Studying the typical psychological problems experienced by members of American culture teaches a great deal about the problems of one's own life. It also teaches some important truths about the contradictions of American culture and society, enabling us to learn to blame ourselves less and focus on the sociological causes of personal problems. This does not mean that we can escape personal responsibility for our actions or violate the norms of society at will. It does mean that we will acquire a greater appreciation for the sociological nature of seemingly personal problems. Just like Tony Soprano, we all must face up to personal as well as social responsibilities if we have any hope for lasting change.

The Local Community and Social Change

Although government at all levels has a role to play in positive social change, its shortcomings since the 1960s have indicated that no government can be made to positively change society on its own. Today, there is a quiet revolution taking place in the United States. Social change intended to ultimately end poverty, hunger, and unemployment is occurring in thousands of voluntary organizations.

In Milwaukee, Esperanza Unida runs businesses through which young people receive job training and jobs. In Ohio, Open Shelter operates a nonprofit auto repair shop that teaches young people how to repair vehicles, rehabilitates houses using carpenter trainees, trains welders, and places trainees into paying positions within the community. Habitat for Humanity, Jimmy Carter's favorite charity, builds houses for the poor using volunteer labor. Other groups feed and shelter the homeless, grow food in their own urban gardens, recycle bottles, cans, and newspapers, help people with HIV, operate neighborhood crime-watch programs, and perform countless other necessary tasks.[21]

A growing body of opinion argues that such groups are much more creative at solving problems, have much more community support, and provide services more efficiently than government bureaucracies. Their supporters argue that government funding for these nongovernmental organizations (NGOs) will not only promote positive solutions to problems but will also allow these nonprofit groups

to provide jobs sorely needed as corporations and government at all
levels continue painful downsizing and restructuring.[22]

The Political Economy

Multinational corporations are a primary barrier to progressive
change. They possess no local or national loyalties and are uncon-
cerned with their role in causing inflation, unemployment, pollution,
and the perpetuation of gross inequalities that inherently corrupt
democracy. One of the best ways to extend much-needed worker
democracy and community control is to have worker representatives
on the boards of directors of large firms. This would not only ensure
worker representation but also would take away the layers of secrecy
from which so much corporate scandal grows. Worker-owned companies are much less likely to experience strikes and the problems
that accompany worker alienation, especially drug abuse, absen-
teeism, and sabotage. These corporations also tend to dominate the
activities and policies of government. They do this by making campaign donations, lobbying, and, on occasion, having business executives run for office.

Thus corporate influence is exactly the problem with government. The system now in place has degenerated into government by
special interests, with reelection campaigns of politicians financed by
such groups. Overcoming these problems is a complex task, but it is
not impossible.

The framers of the U.S. Constitution never dreamed there would
be a class of professional politicians, who made being in office a life's
work. The Constitution says nothing about political parties. Our current pathologies suggest the need for campaign finance reform, federally financed congressional and presidential elections, term limitations for senators and representatives, and an end to corporate
welfare for a savings of $170 billion a year. We also need to encour-
age our closest allies to shoulder their fair share of the global defense

burden while we correspondingly reduce ours. We have played world cop much too long, and those in the defense industries have used up so much of the nation's research and development talent that they have made our economy uncompetitive in some crucial areas, especially manufacturing.[23] To make this sector of the economy competitive again and to promote economic recovery, the government should undertake a policy that is already on the books: that of full employment.

Full Employment

Full employment is the best medicine for our economic woes. There are already several laws that commit the federal government to such a course, including the Humphrey-Hawkins Act. Full employment will solve numerous social problems: it will help reduce violent crime, government deficits and debts, high tax rates, and improve government services (for example, police, fire, libraries, social services, and the like). This policy may require issuing new tax write-offs to employee-owned corporations to expand factories and jobs in the United States. It may also require making government the employer of last resort if not enough corporate-sector jobs are available. There is no question that government is capable of playing such a role, as Franklin Roosevelt's New Deal demonstrated with the Works Progress Administration (WPA), Civilian Conservation Corps (CCC), and similar programs. Granted these programs were undertaken during a time of unique national crisis and involved deficit spending in their creation. However, in our era, such programs could be accomplished by shifting resources from say corporate subsidies, and would not entail deficit spending.

A Program of Social Reconstruction

Rarely has there been such unmet need for social reconstruction: hundreds of billions of dollars worth of streets, roads, railway tracks, and bridges are in disrepair; millions of first-time home buyers cannot afford a home—in California, two thirds of such home buyers cannot afford one. We need better schools and smaller classes, more family doctors and fewer specialists, more nurses and teachers, more computers in education and in homes, more police and fire personnel, more libraries and more drug-treatment facilities. What seems reasonable is a domestic Marshall Plan for America, one similar to the one that rehabilitated the economic stability of European nations after World War II.

The question is, of course, how to pay for these programs. We need to drastically reduce spending on defense weapons systems and to engage in economic conversion to meet these needs. Many corporations can convert their plants to engage in badly needed peacetime activity: manufacturing, mass transit systems, prefabricated housing units, infrastructure development and repair, and development of future technology. These are not altruistic acts we are asking corporations to undertake. They are real needs that the nation has, needs that could be financed by bond issues the way many such needs are now capitalized. Seymour Melman estimates that the cost of building afresh or rebuilding U.S. infrastructure at over $2.1 trillion for such things as schools, replacement of damaged housing, cleaning up radioactive and non-radioactive waste sites, transit investments to 2011, railway electrification, and so on.[24] Imagine the immense number of jobs these projects could provide for years to come. Moreover, whereas economic democracy is a necessity in America, government also suffers from concentrated power within organizations. Secretive organizations can lead the nation into war without a congressional declaration. This is proof enough of democracy's erosion in America. Many proposals exist for extending democracy in America.

Tikkun magazine editor Dr. Michael Lerner has advocated widespread citizen initiatives that would propose new laws or amend existing ones and would appear on ballots after the proper number of petition signatures has been collected. People would then vote the proposals up or down in the next general election.[25]

Lerner also advocates more extensive use of the recall, where a majority of voters can vote a politician out of office. One of Lerner's more provocative notions concerns the use of television to extend democracy. Voters would express their preferences through voting devices attached to their television sets. They would vote after an electronic town hall meeting that debated the issues in question. Representatives would consider the results of the vote.[26]

Public Health

America's most ridiculous war remains the so-called war on drugs. This is the fourth war on drugs we have fought in the past hundred years, and each time the results have brought nothing but disaster and more contradictions, as noted, all the illegal drugs we are trying to save our children from kill some 7,500 people a year, whereas alcohol and tobacco, which we can keep in our homes legally, kill over 600,000. There are very strong relationships between the abuse of tobacco and alcohol and the consumption of the illegal drugs we say we are so concerned with eliminating.

Clearing the contradictions must cease. A national law similar to the one in California that would ban tobacco use in all restaurants, bars, hotel lobbies, and office buildings would be a good beginning, as would a ban on all alcohol advertising. There is clear evidence that the more that alcohol is advertised in a given culture, the higher the per-capita consumption of alcohol. There is also ample evidence that alcohol is sold to underaged children in minority neighborhoods as a matter of course.

If our policy makers aren't informed as to the status of the drug war, why should the public take an interest? Congress has shown almost no imagination and little interest in the public-health approach to drug treatment, as has been successfully utilized in the Netherlands, Great Britain, and other European nations. In the United States, we hear only about the failures, it seems. As a nation, we have never made up our minds whether drug addicts are criminals

or patients in need of treatment. It makes no sense to have this population imprisoned for victimless crime, then coming out of prison
angrier, more resentful, and more in need of treatment than when
they entered. They are a ticking time bomb waiting to explode into
America's next crime epidemic.

Pentagon Capitalism

The United States has political and economic relations and commit-
ments everywhere. The United States has evolved into a military-
industrial complex, with Pentagon programs and property totaling
$1.45 trillion.[27] Between 25,000 and 30,000 corporations are prime
Pentagon contractors, and 2.2 million people are now employed in
firms that have contracts with the Pentagon, as military budgets
have been kept at Cold War levels. Thus there is a vested interest
in keeping the war machine going. Morally, however, America's true
interest and moral principles lie in promoting peace, democracy,
and prosperity/full employment wherever possible.

The resources spent on Pentagon capitalism have meant less
innovation in other sectors of the economy. Much of the manufacturing sector of the American economy has now lost its competitive
edge to other European nations, especially Germany in machine
tools. Millions of manufacturing jobs have been transferred outside
the United States to Third World nations, such as Mexico, nations in
Asia, and so on. Between 1977 and 1996 the number of machine tool
factories in the United States alone declined by 50 percent. At the
same time, the average American corporate executive now earns a
thousand times more than the average American worker, an appalling
disparity greater than in any other modern capitalist democracy.

Why Change Must Come

If we look at the history of progressive social change in America, we
will soon discover a central trend. All the progressive reform of the

nineteenth and twentieth centuries, such as the abolition of slavery, the right to vote for women, the eight-hour work day, the right to collective bargaining, and civil rights and voting rights acts, are the outcome of protracted struggle by collective social movements. Such movements were products of marches and demonstrations by groups of people who aided each other. Despite all the American folklore about the importance of individual heroes, it is collectivities that produce progressive social change, not lone-wolf heroes.

Possessing a sociological imagination involves the realization that positive social change in America has to come about through collective action. These movements involve groups of people who share a genuine concern for each other's well-being and human rights. If we wish to extend democratic life in this society, we must be willing to work for worthy causes, creatively participating in democratic social movements and joining worthwhile groups. The need for people to work for social change has rarely been greater, and the number of groups looking for dedicated volunteers and paid employees is astounding. Part of developing a sociological imagination can mean experience in such organizations.

Working for social change also means staying informed about the issues of the day. One of the assumptions made by many of the framers of the Constitution was that the American citizenry would consist of people who took an active interest in public issues, stayed informed, and engaged in ongoing public debate. Our democracy has degenerated into a place where ten-second sound bites and meaningless political slogans have nearly replaced serious debate about complex issues.

Increasing inequalities of wealth and political power will worsen macro- and micro-level problems such as unemployment, recession/depression, corporate crimes, and political corruption. Partially because of these trends, the social character of our age suffers from a lack of and yearning for stable moral values that will serve as a guide to decision making in daily life. Given constant social changes, stable values seem a long way off at best. Moreover, there is every reason to believe that the current mass disrespect for political and economic elites will continue, perhaps culminating in collective social movements for basic structural reforms necessary to resolve the great social problems of our age. From a sociological imagination perspective, solutions to these problems must take place on the individual, community, and societal levels. Along with a humane transformation in social character, masses of people must be encouraged to engage in collective action that will extend both economic and political democracy. As development expert David C. Korten has argued:

> Over the nearly 600 years since the onset of the Commercial Revolution, we have as a species learned a great deal about the making of money and we have created powerful institutions and technologies dedicated to its accumulation. But in our quest for money, we forgot how to live.
>
> . . . Furthermore, the need to manage the business firm in service to more than purely financial values becomes evident to decision makers who live with the social and environmental consequences of their decisions. [Local residents] are unlikely to sacrifice schools, the environment, product safety, suppliers, employment security, wages, worker health, and other aspects of a healthy community for short-term, shareholder gain when they themselves are the workers, customers, suppliers, and community members as well as the owners.
>
> Political and economic borders define a community of shared interests, identity, and trust—what we call social capital, which makes a community more than a collection of individuals and physical structures. Without borders, social capital dissipates. On the other hand, overly rigid boundaries result in stagnation and a loss of opportunity for the exchange of useful information, knowledge, and culture essential to continuing innovation. As with all living beings, living economies need permeable and managed boundaries. The institutions of money, however, have been using international trade and investment

agreements to remove the political borders essential to maintaining the economic integrity of communities and nations. This process leaves economic resources exposed to predatory extraction, leading to a breakdown of the trust and cooperation essential to any community.[28]

In other words, Dr. Korten favors people in local communities owning the businesses that are located there. He feels local residents have the greatest moral and emotional ties to the local community, and they would manage the businesses they would own in ways that reflect those bonds.

In addition, writes Dr. Korten, "Our existing global economy creates islands of power and privilege in a large sea of poverty. The fortunate hoard and squander resources on frivolous consumption, while others are denied a basic means of living. Furthermore, those who control the creation and allocation of money use this power to generate speculative profits. These profits increase the claims of the speculators to the wealth created through the labor and creative effort of others—while contributing nothing in return to the wealth-creation process."[29]

In our present global economy, corporate-controlled mass media create monocultures of the mind that portray greed and exclusion as the dominant human characteristics. Intellectual property rights are used to preclude the free sharing of information, technology, and culture essential to creative innovation in the community interest. We live in a time when our very survival depends on rapid innovation toward the creation of living economies and societies. Such innovation depends in turn on vigorous community-level experimentation supported by the creative energies of individuals everywhere. Such innovation and experimentation are far more likely to come from diverse self-directed democratic communities that control their economic resources and freely share information and technology than from communities whose material and knowledge resources are controlled by distant corporate bureaucracies intent on appropriating wealth to enrich their shareholders.

A Parting Word

The great lesson of this book is that our nation is rapidly approaching the time when it can no longer continue as Tony Soprano's America, replete with its contradictions and double-dealings surrounding the American Dream. The massive inequalities that confront both the United States and the world are the cause of major social problems both here and abroad. The goods and services that Tony Soprano and others of his ilk provide are themselves a result of these massive inequalities and the great sources of alienation that they spawn.

Tony is on Prozac in no small measure because his way of doing things is rapidly coming to an end, and he realizes this is the case. Today the organized-crime syndicates are global, and they ally themselves with terrorists coming from largely impoverished nations, financed by the global narcotics trade, and aiming their resentment at First World economic and military targets. Tony and his crew teeter on the edge of extinction in a global economy characterized by the successful who possess highly technical skills and the poor and disenfranchised who have problems filling out a job application. Tony is a symbol of this strange new world that is rapidly dividing between the affluent haves and impoverished have-nots.

The one problem so central to understanding the American condition that is almost never confronted on *The Sopranos* is racism. This is the case, perhaps, because it is the one great problem that the nation has never been able to completely resolve in both its legal and economic aspects.

At home, Tony and his family exhibit some of America's most aggravating domestic contradictions. It may well be that Mafia media fare appeals to many males because of the masculine role models depicted. However, the violence exhibited by Tony, his mother, and his sister is symbolic of an epidemic of child and spousal physical and sexual abuse taking place in America on a daily basis. Tony's estrangement from his wife and children represents the familial dysfunctions that exist beneath all the hoopla proclaiming America as the land of Family Values. Moreover, Tony's own alienation from his crew, his Church, and the other institutions in which he spends his daily life symbolizes the decline of local communities wherein people once knew each other and were connected by emotional and moral bonds.

What Tony Soprano symbolizes most, perhaps, is the end of an entire way of life. His depression stems in part from his great uncertainty concerning what will replace what is being lost. America has long been admired by other nations of the world for its optimism, but ever since the 1960s, with its assassinations and wars and the scandals of the subsequent decades, traditional American optimism, the existence of real-life heroes, and faith in the future have waned. Tony's emergence as a hero represents an important opportunity for Americans to take a realistic look at themselves and their world and to ask the great questions that all caring members of civilizations must confront at crucial times:

- In whose American Dream do we wished to believe—the Dream of the Sopranos and the Robber Barons, or the Dream of Martin Luther King Jr., Robert Kennedy, and the others who have appealed to the best in us?
- What kind of political economy do we wish to promote both at home and around the world? Do we want a democracy that is for sale to officeholders and special interests that spend millions to influence elections and legislation thereafter? Or do we want a democracy where equal opportunity to hold office exists regardless of personal wealth and powerful ties?
- What kind of economic democracy do we seek in the future? Why does the wealthiest nation in human history suffer from widespread poverty and resulting high rates of crime? When will having a job and health care become a human right instead of a privilege?
- Do we want an America that continues to fight endless enemies, playing world cop while, at the same time, holding a world arms bazaar, or do we want an America that strives to

end poverty, hunger, illiteracy, and disease here and around the world?

- What kind of cultural values does America wish to promote in the world? Do we want cultural fare and advertising based on gratuitous sex, violence, dependency, and dehumanization? Or do we want an America that says to the world that our highest values center around assuring that all its citizens develop to their greatest potential, and fulfilling the hope that has made this nation a beacon unto the world for its 226-year history?

What history has taught us is that nothing worth achieving in this land has been brought about without collective action. There are progressive groups fighting for all the goals listed above. One reason I decided to write this book is that my academic colleagues and I know we do an excellent job of talking to each other about the problems of our age. They're called conferences, and they're great fun. We do a terrible job, most of the time, of telling our fellow citizens how we feel about the crises of our age. We do an even worse job of letting people know how they can help change things for the better.

It's not terribly hard. Join a local church, synagogue, or mosque that not only wants to feed the hungry but also opposes environmental destruction by global corporations. Look in the back of *The Nation, The Progressive, Mother Jones,* or *The Utne Reader.* Most groups who are fighting for the kinds of goals mentioned above run ads for their cause. Or look on the Web under any of the causes mentioned. It has been said many times that all that is necessary for evil to triumph is for good people to sit and do nothing. Given what's at stake, America needs all of us.

Selected Bibliography

Abadinsky, H. *Drug Abuse*. Chicago: Nelson-Hall, 1989.

———. *Organized Crime*. 3d ed. Chicago: Nelson-Hall, 1990.

Ackerman, Gary. "A Congressional View of Youth Suicide," *American Psychologist*, February 1993, pp. 183–184.

Adams, J. R. *Our Business Civilization*. New York: Holmes and Meier, 1929.

Ade-Ridder, Linda. "Asexuality and Marital Quality in Older Married Couples." In T. H. Brubaker (ed.), *Family Relationships in Later Life*. 2d ed. Newbury Park, CA: Sage, 1990.

Adorno, T. "The Stars Down to Earth." *Telos*, 19 (Spring 1974), pp. 13–91.

Albanese, J. *Organized Crime in America*. 2d ed. Cincinnati: Anderson, 1989.

———. *White Collar Crime in America*. Englewood Cliffs, NJ: Prentice-Hall, 1995.

Albanese, J., and Robert Pursley. *Crime in America: Some Emerging Issues*. Englewood Cliffs, NJ: Prentice-Hall, 1993.

American Council on Education. *Minorities in Higher Education*. Washington, DC: American Council on Education, 1991.

American Psychiatric Association. *Diagnostic and Statistical Manual of Mental Disorders*. 3d. ed., rev. Washington, DC: American Psychiatric Association, 1987.

Amott, T. "Eliminating Poverty." Pp. 166–183 in R. Caplan and J. Feffer (eds.), *State of the Union 1994*. Boulder, CO: Westview Press, 1994.

Anderson, J. "LBJ Sought to Quell Conspiracy Talk," *Washington Post*, April 1, 1985, p. B13.

Anderson, J., and J. Spear. "Witness Tells of CIA Plot to Kill Castro," *Washington Post*, November 1, 1988, p. C19.

Anderson, J., and D. Van Atta. "Death in Dallas: A Plot That Backfired," *Washington Post*, November 2, 1988, p. E15.

Anderson, J., and Daryl Gibson. *Peace, War, and Politics*. New York: Knopf, 1999.

Asimov, Nanette. "U.S. Teachers Pay Ranks Low in Study of Developed Nations," *San Francisco Chronicle,* July 9, 1993, p. A6.

_____. "Alarming Report on U.S. Students Reading Skills," *San Francisco Chronicle,* September 16, 1993, p. A5.

Astroth, Kirk. "Beyond Ephebiphobia: Problem Adults or Problem Youths?" *Phi Delta Kappan,* January 1994, p. 411–413.

Babbie, Earl. *The Sociological Spirit.* Belmont, CA: Wadsworth, 1994.

Bagdikian, B. "Statement to the Federal Trade Commission." P. 388 n A. A. Berger (ed.), *Media U.S.A.,* 2d ed. New York: Longman, 1991.

Baig, E. "Experienced Not Wanted," *U.S. News and World Report,* December 30/January 6, 1992, p. 59.

Baltes, P., and K. Schaie. "The Myth of the Twilight Years," *Psychology Today,* March 1974, pp. 35–40.

Barnet, H. "Corporate Capitalism, Corporate Crime," *Crime and Delinquency,* 27 (January 1981), pp. 4–23.

Barnet, R. J. "The End of Jobs," *Harpers,* October 1993, pp. 47–52.

Bartlett, D. L., and J. Steele. *America: What Went Wrong?* Kansas City, MO: Andrews and McMeel, 1992.

Becker, Howard. "The Career of a Chicago Public School Teacher," *American Journal of Sociology,* 57 (March 1952), pp. 470–477.

Bell, D. "Downfall of the Business Giants," *Dissent,* Summer 1993, pp. 316–323.

Bellah, Robert, et al. *Habits of the Heart.* New York: Harper and Row, 1986.

Benoit, E. "The Case for Legalization," *Financial World,* October 3, 1989, pp. 32–35.

Berger, A. A. (ed.). *Media U.S.A.* 2d ed. New York: Longman, 1991.

Berger, G. *Crack: The New Epidemic.* New York: Franklin Watts, 1987.

Bernard, V. P., et al. "Dehumanization: A Composite Psychological Defense Mechanism in Relation to Modern War." Pp. 16–30 in R. Perrucci and M. Pilisuk (eds.), *The Triple Revolution Emerging: Social Problems in Depth.* Boston: Little, Brown, 1971.

Bernstein, D., and L. Howard. "Reagan Aid Linked to Drug Running Says Former DEA Agent," *San Francisco Weekly,* May 18, 1994, p. 6

Blauner, Robert. *Alienation and Freedom.* Chicago: University of Chicago Press, 1964.

Bluestone, B., and B. Harrison. *The Deindustrialization of America.* New York: Basic Books, 1982.

Bohlen, Celestine. "A Bank Inquiry Retraces a Trail Reaching Lofty Levels in Moscow," *New York Times,* February 18, 2000.

Bonner, Raymond. "Reported Russian Mob Leader Denies Tie to Laundering and Takes Umbrage," *New York Times,* September 11, 1999.

Boroughs, D. "Cost of Crime: $674 Billion" *U.S. News and World Report,* January 17, 1994, pp. 40–44.

Braun, D. *The Rich Get Richer.* Chicago: Nelson-Hall, 1993.

Braverman, Harry. "Work and Unemployment," *Monthly Review,* July 1975, p. 18–31.

Breed, W. *The Self-Guiding Society.* New York: Free Press, 1971.

Britt, Chester. "Crime and Unemployment Among Youths in the United States, 1958–1990," *American Journal Of Economics and Sociology,* 53 (January 1994), pp. 99–109.

Cable News Network (CNN). "Headline News," January 13, 1994.

Calabrese, R. "Adolescence: A Growth Period Conducive to Alienation," *Adolescence,* 88 (Winter 1987), pp. 929–938.

Caldicott, Helen. *Missile Envy.* New York: Morrow, 1984.

Caplan, R., and J. Feffer (eds.). *The State of the Union, 1994.* Boulder, CO: Westview Press, 1994, pp. 63–77.

Castro, Janice. "Disposable Workers," *Time,* March 29, 1993, pp. 43–47.

Cavanagh, J., et al. "Forging a Global New Deal." Pp. 29–45 in Caplan and Feffer (eds.), *The State of the Union, 1994.* Boulder, CO: Westview Press, 1994.

Celis, William. "Study Finds Rising Concentration of Black and Hispanic Students," *New York Times,* December 14, 1993, pp. A1, A11.

Cherlin, Andrew. "A Sense of History: Recent Trends on Aging and the Family." Pp. 5–23 in Maltilda White Riley et al. (eds.), *Aging in Society: Selected Reviews of Recent Research.* Hillsdale, NJ: Erlbaum, 1983.

Chira, S. "Surprising Survey on Kids and Guns–40% Know a Victim," *San Francisco Chronicle,* July 20, 1993, p. A10.

Clinard, Marshall. *Illegal Corporate Behavior.* Washington, DC: U.S. Department of Justice, U.S. Government Printing Office, 1979.

Cohen, S. "The War on Drugs Is Racist." Pp. 76–82 in N. Bernards (ed.), *War on Drugs: Opposing Viewpoints.* San Diego: Greenhaven Press, 1990.

Coleman, James S. "The Asymmetric Society." Pp. 95–106 in M. David Ermann and Richard J. Lundman (eds.), *Corporate and Governmental Deviance,* 4th ed. New York: Oxford University Press, 1992.

Coleman, James S., and Thomas Hoffer. *Public and Private High Schools: The Impact Of Communities.* New York: Basic Books, 1987.

Coleman, James S., et al. *Equality Of Educational Opportunity (The Coleman Report).* Washington, DC: U.S. Department of Health, Education, and Welfare, 1966.

Collins, Brent. "Student Indifference Erodes the Public Schools," *Utne Reader,* September/October 1990, pp. 68–69.

Coontz, Stephnie. *The Way We Never Were: American Families and the Nostalgia Trap.* New York: Basic Books, 1992.

Corn, David. "The Same Old Dirty Tricks," *Nation,* August 27, 1988, p. 158.

Cowley, Geoffrey. "Children in Peril." Pp. 25–27 in Harold Widdison (ed.), *Social Problems 93/94*. Sluice Dock, CT: Dushkin, 1993.

Cox, Harold. *Later Life: The Realities of Aging*. Englewood Cliffs, NJ: Prentice-Hall, 1984.

Curran, Daniel, and Claire Renzetti. *Women, Men, and Society*. Needham Heights, MA: Allyn and Bacon, 1993.

Curran, R. "Too Hot to Handle," *San Francisco Bay Guardian*, March 29–April 4, 1995, pp. 15–17.

Currie, E. "The Market Society," *Dissent*, Spring 1991, pp. 255–258.

D'Amato, P. "An Attack on Civil Liberties." In N. Bernards (ed.), *War on Drugs: Opposing Viewpoints*. San Diego: Greenhaven, 1990.

Davis, J. H. *The Kennedys: Dynasty and Disaster, 1848–1984*. New York: Bantam, 1984.

_____. *Mafia Kingfish*. New York: Signet, 1989.

Davis, N., and C. Stasz. *Social Control of Deviance: A Critical Perspective*. New York: McGraw-Hill, 1990.

Dees, M. "Letter." Montgomery, AL: Southern Poverty Law Center, 1994, pp. 1–5.

Derber, C. *Money, Murder, and the American Dream: Wilding from Wall Street To Main Street*. Boston: Faber and Faber, 1992.

_____. *The Wilding of America*, 2d ed. New York: Worth, 2002.

Desir, Marjorie. "Strategies for Coping with Workplace Depression," *Black Enterprise*, September 1993, pp. 77–79.

Dissent, Special Issue, Irving Howe, (ed.), Spring 1991, pp. 3–33.

Dollars and Sense. "Who Cares for Our Elders?" Pp. 76–77 in H. Widdison (ed.), *Social Problems 93/94*. Sluice Dock, CT: Dushkin, 1993.

Domhoff, G. William. *Who Rules America?* Englewood Cliffs, NJ: Prentice-Hall, 1967.

_____. *The Bohemian Grove and Other Retreats*. New York: Harper and Row, 1974.

_____. *The Power Elite and the State*. New York: Aldine-DeGruyter, 1990.

Dowd, Douglas. *Capitalist Development Since 1776*. Armonk, NY: M. E. Sharpe, 1993.

Durning, A. *How Much Is Enough?* New York: Norton, 1992.

Dye, Thomas. *Who's Running America? The Bush Years*. Englewood Cliffs, NJ: Prentice-Hall, 1990.

Dye, T., and H. Zeigler. *The Irony of Democracy: An Uncommon Introduction to American Politics*. 9th ed. Belmont, CA: Wadsworth, 1993.

Edwards, Richard C., et al. "Alienation and Labor." Pp. 138–140 in R. C. Edwards et al. (eds.), *The Capitalist System*. 3d ed. Englewood Cliffs, NJ: Prentice-Hall, 1986.

Ehrenreich, Barbara. *Fear of Falling*. New York: Pantheon, 1989.

Ehrhart, W. D. "On the Virtues of Dishonesty," *San Francisco Examiner*, March 19, 1993, p. A23.

Elias, Robert. *The Politics of Victimization*. New York: Oxford University Press, 1986.

Erikson, Kai. "On Work Alienation." Pp. 19–35 in Kai Erikson and Peter Vallas (eds.), *The Nature of Work*. New Haven: Yale University Press, 1990.

Eshelman, J., et al. *Sociology: An Introduction*. 4th ed. New York: HarperCollins, 1993.

Ethics, E. Z. "Wreck-reation," *Student Lifelines*, 4 (April 1990), pp. 1, 6.

Etzioni, A. "Is Corporate Crime Worth the Time?" *Business and Society Review*, 36 (Winter 1990), pp. 33–36.

Etzkowitz, H. (ed.). *Is America Possible?* St. Paul: West, 1980.

Farnham, A. "The S & L Felons," *Fortune*, November 5, 1990, pp. 90–108.

Ferrante, J. *Sociology: A Multicultural Perspective*. Belmont, CA: Wadsworth, 1992.

Fisher, David. *Growing Old in America*. New York: Oxford University Press, 1978.

Freitag, Peter. "The Cabinet and Big Business," *Social Problems*, 23 (1975), pp. 137–152.

Friedan, Betty. *The Fountain of Age*. New York: Simon and Schuster, 1993.

Fromm, Erich. *Escape from Freedom*. New York: Holt, Rinehart and Winston, 1941.

———. *The Sane Society*. New York: Holt, Rinehart and Winston, 1955.

Fukuyama, F. *The End of History and the Last Man*. New York: Avon, 1992.

Funiciello, T. *Tyranny of Kindness*. New York: Atlantic Monthly Press, 1993.

Garment, S. *Scandal*. New York: Anchor, 1991.

Garner, Roberta. *Social Movements and Ideologies*. New York: McGraw-Hill, 1995.

Garr, R. *Reinvesting in America*. Reading, MA: Addison-Wesley, 1995.

Garson, Barbara. *The Electronic Sweatshop*. New York: Simon and Schuster, 1988.

Gatto, John Taylor. *The Underground History of American Education*. Oxford, NY: Oxford Village Press, 2000/2001.

Geertz, C. "Ideology As a Culture System." In D. Apter (ed.), *Ideology and Discontent*. New York: Free Press, 1964.

Geis, G. "Upperworld Crime." Pp. 114–137 in A. S. Blumberg (ed.), *Current Perspectives in Criminal Behavior*. New York: Knopf, 1974.

Gerber, Jerg, and Susan Weeks. "Women As Victims of Corporate Crime: A Call for Research on a Neglected Topic," *Deviant Behavior*, 13 (1992), pp. 325–347.

Gerth, H., and C. Wright Mills. *Character and Social Structure*. New York: Harcourt, Brace, and World, 1953.

Gilbert, Dennis, and Joseph Kahl. *The American Class Structure: A New Synthesis*, 4th ed. Belmont, CA: Wadsworth, 1993.

Gintis, Herbert. "Alienation and Capitalism." Pp. 141–149 in R. C. Edwards et al. (eds.), *The Capitalist System*, 3d ed. Englewood Cliffs, NJ: Prentice-Hall, 1986.

Gintis, Herbert, and Samuel Bowles. "Schooling and Inequality." Pp. 235–247 in R. C. Edwards et al. (eds.), *The Capitalist System*, 3d ed. Englewood Cliffs, NJ: Prentice-Hall, 1986.

Gitlin, T. *The Sixties*. New York: Random House, 1988.

Glassman, J. "The Great Bank Robbery: Deconstructing the S & L Crisis," *New Republic,* October 6, 1990, pp. 16–21.

———. "Looking for New S & L Culprits," *Newsweek,* November 26, 1990, pp. 55–56.

Goode, E. (ed.). *Drugs, Society, and Behavior,* 8th ed. Guilford, CT: Dushkin, 1993.

Goodgame, D. "Reigning in the Rich," *Time,* December 19, 1994, pp. 35–37.

Gore, Albert. *From Red Tape to Results: Creating a Government That Works Better and Costs Less.* Washington, DC: U.S. Government Printing Office, 1993.

Gornick, Vivian. "For the Rest of Our Days Things Can Only Get Worse," *Village Voice,* May 24, 1976, pp. 32 ff.

Gozan, June. "Wealth for the Few," *Multinational Monitor,* December 6, 1992.

Graham, M. G. "Controlling Drug Abuse and Crime: A Research Update," *NIJ Reports,* 202 (March/April 1987), pp. 2–7.

Greenberg, D. "Delinquency and the Age Structure of Society." In David Greenberg (ed.), *Crime and Capitalism.* Philadelphia: Temple University Press, 1993.

Greenberg, Edward S. *Capitalism and the American Political Ideal.* New York: M. E. Sharpe, 1985.

Greider, William. *Who Will Tell the People? The Betrayal of American Democracy.* New York: Simon and Schuster, 1992.

Hagan, F., and D. R. Simon. "Crimes of the Bush Era," Presented at the Meeting of the American Society of Criminology, November 1994, Miami.

Hall, S. G. *Christian Anti-Semitism and Paul's Theology.* Minneapolis: Fortress Press, 1993.

Halper, Jan. *Quiet Desperation: The Truth About Successful Men.* New York: Warner, 1988.

Harris, M. *Why Nothing Works.* New York: Simon and Schuster, 1987.

Harris, R. *Drugged America.* New York: Macmillian, 1991.

Harvey, K. D., et al. *Teaching About Native Americans.* Washington, DC: National Council for Social Studies, 1990.

Henderson, J., and D. R. Simon. *Crimes of the Criminal Justice System.* Cincinnati: Anderson, 1994.

Hertsgarrd, M. "Still Ticking. . . ," *Mother Jones,* March/April 1993, pp. 20–23.

Hewitt, J. "Building Media Empires." Pp. 396–403 in A. A. Berger (ed.), *Media U.S.A.* 2d ed. New York: Longman, 1991.

Hilts, Peter. "50,000 Deaths a Year Blamed on Soot in Air," *San Francisco Chronicle,* July 19, 1993, pp. Al, A15.

Hochschild, Arlie. *The Managed Heart.* Berkeley: University of California Press, 1983.

———. "The Second Shift," *Utne Reader,* March 1990, pp. 66–81.

Horney, K. *The Neurotic Personality of Our Time.* New York: W. W. Norton, 1938.

Howe, I. "By Way of a Beginning," *Dissent,* 38 (Spring 1991), pp. 165–169.

Hulbert, Ann. "Home Repairs," *New Republic*, August 16, 1993, pp. 26–32.

Inciardi, J. *The War on Drugs*. Palo Alto, CA: Mayfield, 1986.

Inciardi, J., and T. Rothman. *Sociology*. Houston: Harcourt Brace, 1990.

International Consortium of Investigative Journalists. "Tobacco Companies Linked to Criminal Organizations in Lucrative Cigarette Smuggling," November 29, 2001, pp. 1–6.

Isikoff, Michael. "Teen Alcohol Use Heavy, Survey Finds." Pp. 319–320 in Washington Post Writers Group (ed.), *Society in Crisis: The Washington Post Social Problems Companion*. Needham, MA: Allyn and Bacon, 1993.

Jencks, Christopher, et al. *Inequality: A Reassessment of the Effect of Family and Schooling in America*. New York: Basic Books, 1972.

Jensen, Carl, (ed.), and Project Censored. "The U.S. Is Killing Its Young." Pp. 50–52 in *Censored: The 1994 Project Censored Yearbook*. New York: Four Walls, Eight Windows, 1994.

Jewett, Robert, and John Shelton Lawrence. *The American Monomyth*. New York: Doubleday, 1977.

Kanter, Donald, and Philip Mirvis. *The Cynical Americans*. San Francisco: Jossey-Bass, 1989.

Kantrowitz, Barbara et al. "Striking a Nerve," *Newsweek*, October 21, 1991, pp. 34–40.

_____. "Sexism in the Schoolhouse," *Newsweek*, February 24, 1992, p. 62.

Kanungo, R. A. *Work Alienation: An Integrated Approach*. New York: Praeger, 1982.

Kappeler, Victor, et al. *The Mythology of Crime and Criminal Justice*, third edition. Pp. 159. Prospect Heights, IL: Waveland Press, 2000.

Kassarda, J. and T. Williams. "Drugs and the Dream Deferred," *New Viewpoints*, Summer 1989, pp. 16–26.

Kennedy, P. C. *The Rise and Fall of Great Powers*. New York: Random House, 1987.

Kerbo, Harold. "Upper Class Power." Pp. 223–237 in Marvin E. Olsen and Martin N. Marger, (eds.), *Power in Modern Societies*. Boulder, CO: Westview Press, 1993.

Kobler, J. *Capone: The Life and World of Al Capone*. New York: Fawcett, 1971.

Kohn, Alfie. *No Contest: The Case Against Competition*. Boston: Houghton Mifflin, 1986.

Kohn, M. "Unresolved Issues in the Relationship Betweeen Work and Personality." Pp. 36–68 in Kai Erikson and Peter Vallas (eds.), *The Nature of Work*. New Haven: Yale University Press, 1990.

Korten, David C. "The Post-Corporate," *Yes*, Spring 1999. www.futurenet.org/backissues.html

Kwitney, Jonathan. "Crimes of Patriots." *Mother Jones*, August/September 1987, pp. 15–23.

Larsen, Elizabeth. "The Great Teen Girl Self-Esteem Robbery," *Utne Reader*, January/February 1992, pp. 20–21.

Lasch, C. *The Minimal Self: Psychic Survival in Troubled Times.* New York: W. W. Norton, 1984.

Lazar, D. "The Drug War Is Killing Us," *Village Voice,* January 23, 1990, pp. 22–29.

Lean, Arthur, and William Eaton. *Education or Catastrophe?* Wolfboro, NH: Longwood Academic, 1990.

Lens, S. *The Promise and Pitfalls of Revolution.* Philadelphia: Pilgrim Press, 1977.

Lerner, M. *The New Socialist Revolution.* New York: Delacorte, 1973.

Levine, A. "America's Addiction to Addictions," *U.S. News and World Report,* February 5, 1990, pp. 62–64.

Lindquist, D. "Drugs Said Rampant in Every Industry," *San Diego Times-Union,* March 25, 1988, pp. B1 ff.

Lipset, S. M. *Political Man: The Social Basis of Politics.* Garden City, NY: Doubleday, 1963.

Lipset, S. M., and Earl Raab. *The Politics of Unreason.* Chicago: University of Chicago Press, 1987.

Lord, Walter. *A Night to Remember.* New York: Henry Holt, 1955.

Lupsha, P. "American Values and Organized Crime: Suckers and Wiseguys." Pp. 144–155 in B. Girgus (ed.), *The American Self.* Albuquerque: University of New Mexico Press, 1981.

Lutz, W. *Doublespeak.* New York: HarperCollins, 1989.

Magdoff, H. "Globalization—To What End?" Pp. 44–75 in R. Miliband and L. Panitch (eds.), *The Socialist Register, 1992: New World Order?* London: Merlin Press, 1992.

Magnuson, E. "Did the Mob Kill JFK?" *Time,* November 28, 1988, pp. 42–44.

Malamuth, N. M. "Aggression Against Women: Cultural and Individual Causes," in N. Malamuth and E. Donnerstein (eds.), *Pornography and Sexual Aggression.* New York: Academic Press, 1984.

Marx, Gary T. "Fraudulent Identification, and Biography," Paper delivered at a seminar of the Department of Sociology, San Diego State University, February 1988.

Mattox, William. "America's Family Time Famine." Pp. 16–20 in H. Widdison (ed.), *Social Problems, 1993/1994.* Sluice Dock, CN: Dushkin, 1993.

McCoy, A. "The CIA Connection," *Progressive,* July 1991, pp. 20–26.

_____. "The Afghanistan Drug Lords," *Convergence,* Fall 1991, pp. 11–12, 14.

Mecca, A. M., et al. (eds.). *The Social Importance of Self-Esteem.* Berkeley: University of California Press, 1989.

Melanson, P. *Spy Saga.* Boulder, CO: Westview Press, 1990.

Melman, Seymour. *After Capitalism.* New York: Knopf, 2001.

Messner, J., and S. Rosenfeld. *Crime and the American Dream.* Monterey, CA: Wadsworth, 1994.

_____. *Crime and the American Dream,* 3d ed. Monterey, CA: Wadsworth, 2002.

Miller, N. *Stealing from America.* New York: Paragon House, 1992.

Mills, C. Wright. *White Collar.* New York: Oxford University Press, 1951.

_____. *The Power Elite.* New York: Oxford University Press, 1956.

_____. *The Sociological Imagination.* New York: Oxford University Press, 1959.

_____. *Images of Man: The Classic Tradition in Sociological Theory.* New York: Braziller, 1960.

_____. "Women: The Darling Little Slaves." Pp. 339–346 in I. L. Horowitz (ed.), *Power, Politics, and People: The Collected Essays of C. Wright Mills.* New York: Ballantine, 1963.

Mills, James. *The Underground Empire.* New York: Dell, 1986.

Moberg, David. "All in the Family," *In These Times,* February 22, 1993, pp. 18–21.

Montagu, A., and F. Matson. *The Dehumanization Of Man.* New York: McGraw-Hill, 1985.

Morgenthau, T., and M. Miller. "Tougher Law Enforcement Will Win the War on Drugs." Pp. 207–213 in N. Bernards (ed.), *War on Drugs: Opposing Viewpoints.* San Diego: Greenhaven Press, 1990.

Moyers, Bill. *The Secret Government.* Berkeley: Seven Locks, 1988.

Moynihan, Daniel Patrick. "Defining Deviancy Down," *American Scholar,* Autumn 1993, pp. 1–16.

Mydans, Seth. "11 Friars at California Seminary Molested Students, Inquiry Finds," *New York Times,* December 1, 1993, pp. A1, A12.

Nisbet, R. *The Present Age.* New York: HarperCollins, 1988.

Nixon, W. "Crowded Out," *In These Times,* September 5, 1994, pp. 14–18.

Oakland Tribune. "The Church Confronts Unholy Behavior," December 7, 1993, p. A8.

O'Brien, Timothy, and Raymond Bauer. "A Banker and Husband Tell of Money Laundering Case," *New York Times,* February 17, 2000.

Olsen, Marvin E., and Martin E. Marger (eds.). *Power in Modern Societies.* Boulder, CO: Westview Press, 1993.

Orenstein, Peggy. *School Girls.* New York: Doubleday, 1994.

Orth, Maureen. "Afghanistan's Deadly Habit," *Vanity Fair,* March 2002, pp. 150 ff.

Oswalt, Wendall. *Life Cycles and Lifeways: An Introduction to Cultural Anthropology.* Palo Alto, CA: Mayfield, 1986.

Papson, S. "Bureaucratic Discourse and the Presentation of Self As Spectacle," *Humanity and Society,* August 1985, pp. 223–236.

Parenti, M. *Make Believe Media.* New York: St. Martin's Press, 1991.

_____. *Democracy for the Few,* 6th ed. New York: St. Martin's Press, 1995.

Patterson, J., and Peter Kim. *The Day America Told the Truth.* Englewood Cliffs, NJ: Prentice-Hall, 1991.

Pearce, F. *Crimes of the Powerful.* London: Pluto Press, 1976.

Peele, S. *Love and Addiction.* New York: Bantam, 1978.

————. "A Value Approach to Addiction: Drug Policy That Is Moral Rather Than Moralistic," *Journal of Drug Issues,* Fall 1990, pp. 639–645.

Perdue, William D. *Systemic Crises: Problems in Society, Politics, and World Order.* New York: Harcourt Brace, 1993.

Perot, Ross. *Not for Sale at Any Price: How We Can Save America for Our Children.* New York: Hyperion, 1993.

Phillips, Kevin. *Boiling Point.* New York: Random House, 1993.

Pillemer, Karl. "The Dangers of Dependency: New Findings on Domestic Violence Against the Elderly," *Social Problems,* December 1985, pp. 146–158.

Pillemer, Karl, and David Finkelhor. "The Prevalence of Elder Abuse: A Random Sample Survey," *Gerontologist,* 28 (1988), pp. 51–57.

Pizzo, Steve, and Paul Muolo. "Take the Money and Run," *New York Times Magazine,* May 10, 1993, pp. 56–61.

Pollard, Neal A. *Terrorism and Transnational Organized Crime: Implications of Convergence.* Terrorism Research Center, 2000. trc@terrorism.com

Posner, Gerald. *Warlords of Crime, Chinese Secret Societies: The New Mafia.* New York: Penguin, 1988.

Preston, I. *The Great American Blow-Up: Puffery in Advertising and Selling.* Madison: University of Wisconsin Press, 1975.

Reich, Charles. *The Greening of America.* New York: Random House, 1970.

Reich, Robert. *Tales of a New America.* New York: Vintage, 1987.

Reiman, J. *The Rich Get Richer and the Poor Get Prison.* 3d ed. New York: Macmillan, 1990.

Riesman, David. *The Lonely Crowd.* New Haven: Yale University Press, 1950.

Ritzer, G. *The McDonaldization oF Society.* Thousand Oaks, CA: Pine Forge Press, 1993.

Rosenfeld, Megan. "Broken Children, Broken Homes." Pp. 190–194 in Washington Post Writers Group (ed.), *Society in Crisis: The Washington Post Social Problems Companion.* Needham Heights, MA: Allyn and Bacon, 1993.

Rotfeld, H. J., and I. L. Preston. "The Potential Impact of Research on Advertising Law," *Journal of Advertising Research,* 21 (1981), pp. 9–16.

Rotfeld, H. J., and K. B. Rotzall. "Is Advertising Puffery Believed?" *Journal of Advertising,* 9 (1980), pp. 16–20.

Rouner, S. "Battered Wives: Centuries of Silence." Pp. 195–197 in Washington Post Writers Group (ed.), *Society in Crisis: The Washington Post Social Problems Companion.* Needham Heights, MA: Allyn and Bacon, 1993.

Rubin, L. *Worlds Of Pain.* New York: Basic Books, 1977.

Russell, James W. *Introduction to Macrosociology.* Englewood Cliffs, NJ: Prentice-Hall, 1992.

San Francisco Chronicle, "Classroom Paddling Reported On Rise," September 23, 1993, p. A15.

Saunders, D. "Sex, Video, and the Single 7-Year-Old," *San Francisco Chronicle,* May 12, 1995, p. A25.

Schaef, Ann W. *When Society Becomes an Addict.* New York: HarperCollins, 1988.

Schmoke, Kurt. "Remarks to U.S. Conference of Mayors (1988)" (1990). Office of the Mayor of the City of Baltimore, Maryland.

Schrager, Laura, and James F. Short. "Towards a Sociology of Organizational Crime." *Social Problems,* February 1978, pp. 407–419.

Seeman, M. "On the Meaning of Alienation," *American Sociological Review,* 26 (1961), pp. 753–758.

Select Committee on Assassinations, U.S. House of Representatives. *Investigation of the Assassination of President John F. Kennedy,* vol. 4. Washington, DC: U.S. Government Printing Office, 1979.

Shira, Susan. "Study Confirms Worst Fears on U.S. Children," *New York Times,* April 12, 1994, p. A12.

Shrader, W. *Media Blight and the Dehumanizing of America.* New York: Praeger, 1992.

Simon, David R., "Alienation and Alcohol Abuse," *Journal of Drug Abuse,* 3 (1986), pp. 44–56.

_____. "Dominant Forms of Alienation," Paper presented at the 1990 Meeting of the Society for the Study of Social Problems, August 1990, Washington, DC.

_____. "Watergate and the Nixon Presidency." Pp. 5–22 in Leon Friedman and William Levantrosser (eds.), *Watergate and Afterward: The Legacy of Richard M. Nixon.* Garden City, NY: Greenwood Press, 1992.

_____. "Criminology and the Kennedy Assassination." *Quarterly Journal of Ideology,* Autumn 1993, pp. 33–45.

_____. *Social Problems and the Sociological Imagination.* New York: McGraw-Hill, 1995.

_____. *Elite Deviance,* 7th ed. Boston: Allyn and Bacon, 2002.

_____. *Private Troubles & Public Issues: Social Problems in the Postmodern Era* Ft. Worth, TX: Harcourt Brace, 1997, with Joel Henderson.

Slater, P. *The Pursuit of Loneliness.* Boston: Beacon Press, 1970.

Smelser, N. J. "Self-Esteem and Social Problems: An Introduction," in A. M. Mecca et al., eds. *The Social Importance of Self-Esteem.* Berkeley: University of California Press, 1989.

Streitfeld, David. "Abuse of the Elderly-Often It's the Spouse." Pp. 212–213 in Washington Post Writers Group (ed.), *Society in Crisis: The Washington Post Social Problems Companion.* Needham Heights, MA: Allyn and Bacon, 1993.

Strickland, D. E. et al. "A Content Analysis of Beverage Alcohol Advertising: Magazine Advertising," *Journal of Studies on Alcohol,* 7 (1982), pp. 655–682.

_____."A Content Analysis of Beverage Advertising II: Television Advertising," *Journal of Studies on Alcohol,* 9 (1982), pp. 964–987.

Summers, J. A. *The Secret Life of J. Edgar Hoover.* New York: Putnam, 1995.

Sykes, C. J. *A Nation of Victims.* New York: St. Martin's Press, 1992.

Tagliabue, John. "A Russian Racket Linked to New York Bank," *New York Times,* September 28, 1999, p. A1.

Taylor, Peggy. "The Way We Never Were," *New Age Journal,* September/October 1992, pp. 64–69, 144.

Terkel, Studs. *Working.* New York: Ballantine, 1978.

Thio, Alex. *Deviant Behavior: An Integrated Approach.* 3d ed. New York: Harper and Row, 1988.

Thompson, William, and James Hickey. *Society in Focus: An Introduction to Sociology.* New York: HarperCollins, 1994.

Touhy, John. "There's No Such Thing As Childhood on the Streets," *U.S. Catholic,* March 1993, pp. 18–25.

U.S. House of Representatives, Select Committee on Assassinations. *Investigation of the Assassination of President John F. Kennedy,* vol. 9. Washington, DC: U.S. Government Printing Office, 1979.

U.S. Senate Committee on Aging et al. *Aging America: Trends and Projections.* Washington, DC: U.S. Government Printing Office, 1991.

Vidal, Gore. Speech at University of California, Berkeley, February 14, 1994.

_____. *Perpetual War for Perpetual Peace.* New York: Thunder's Mouth/Nation Books, 2002.

Vobejda, Barbara. "Caring for Three Generations." Pp. 186–189 in Washington Post Writers Group (ed.), *Society in Crisis: The Washington Post Social Problems Companion.* Needham Heights, MA: Allyn and Bacon, 1993.

Voigt, Lydia, et al. *Criminology and Justice.* New York: McGraw-Hill, 1994.

Wald, Kenneth. "Evangelical Politics And Status Issues," *Journal for the Scientific Study of Religion,* 28 (1989), pp. 1–16.

Walker, S. *Sense and Nonsense About Crime and Drugs.* 3d ed. Belmont, CA: Wadsworth, 1994.

Wattleton, Faye. "The Case for National Action," *Nation,* July 24–31, 1989, pp. 138–141.

White House Domestic Policy Council. *Health Security: The President's Report to the American People.* New York: Simon and Schuster, 1993.

Whitman, D. "The Streets Are Filled with Crack," *U.S. News and World Report,* March 5, 1990, pp. 24–26.

Wilcox, Clide. *God's Warriors: The Christian Right in Twentieth-Century America*. Baltimore: Johns Hopkins Univeristy Press, 1992.

Wilkinson, R. *In Search of the American Character*. New York: HarperCollins, 1988.

_____ (ed.). *American Social Character*. New York: HarperCollins, 1992.

Willis, E. "Our Mobsters, Our Selves: Why *The Sopranos* Is Therapeutic," *Nation*, April 2, 2001.

Willwerth, James. "Hello? I'm Home Alone," *Time*, March 1, 1993, pp. 46–47.

Wilson, M. I., et al. "Differential Maltreatment of Girls and Boys," *Victimology*, 6 (1981), pp. 249–261.

Wilson, W. J. "The Ghetto Underclass and the Social Transformation of the Inner City," *Black Scholar*, May/June 1988, pp. 10–17.

Witkin, G. "The Men Who Created Crack," *U.S. News and World Report*, August 19, 1991, pp. 44–53.

World Almanac and Book of Facts. New York: Pharos Books, 1993.

World Almanac of U.S. Politics: 1993–1995 Edition. Mahwah, NJ: Funk and Wagnalls, 1993.

Wyckham, R. "Implied Superiority Claims," *Journal of Advertising Research*, 27 (February/March 1987), pp. 54–63.

Yoachum, S. "The Problem with Gun Control Laws," *San Francisco Chronicle*, July 13, 1993, p. A1.

Zagorin, Adam. "A Dictators' Savings and Loan," *Time*, November 15, 1999.

Notes

Chapter One

1. Jonathan Tolins, *The Twilight of the Golds* (New York: Samuel French, 1995).
2. C. Wright Mills, *The Sociological Imagination* (New York: Oxford University Press, 1959), p 3.
3. Ibid., p. 8.
4. National Center for Educational Statistics, www.nces.ed.gov/
5. Laura Schrager and James F. Short, "Towards a Sociology of Organizational Crime," *Social Problems* 25 (February 1978), pp. 407–419.
6. David R. Simon, "Watergate and the Nixon Presidency," in *Watergate and Afterward: The Legacy of Richard M. Nixon*, Leon Friedman and William Levantrosser (eds.), (Westport, CT: Greenwood, 1992), pp. 5–22; D. R. Simon, *Elite Deviance*, 7th ed. (Boston: Allyn and Bacon, 2002), pp. 3–7.
7. Alex Thio, *Deviant Behavior: An Integrated Approach*, 3d ed. (New York: Harper and Row, 1974); J. Gusfield, "On the Side," in J. Kitsuse and J. W. Schneider (eds.), *Studies in the Sociology of Social Problems* (Norwood, NJ: Ablex, 1984), pp. 31–51.
8. M. Spector and J. Kitsuse, "Social Problems: A Reformulation," *Social Problems* 21 (Fall 1973), pp. 145–159.

Chapter Two

1. Steven Messner and Richard Rosenfeld, *Crime and the American Dream*, 3d ed. (Belmont, CA: Wadsworth, 2002), pp. 79–81.
2. Ibid., p. 6.

3. Elliott Currie, "The Market Society," *Dissent,* Spring 1991, pp. 255–258.

4. See Charles Derber, *Money, Murder, and the American Dream: Wilding from Wall Street to Main Street* (Boston: Faber and Faber, 1992); and his *The Wilding Of America,* 2d ed. (New York: Worth, 2002).

5. James R. Adams, *Our Business Civilization* (New York: Holmes and Meirer, 1929), p. 44.

6. R. K. Merton, "Social Structure and Anomie," *American Sociological Review* 3 (1938), pp. 672–682.

7. Emile Durkheim, *Suicide* (New York: Free Press, 1950).

8. Robert Merton, "Social Structure and Anomie," *Essays in Social Structure* (New York: Free Press, 1994), p. 119.

9. Ibid.

10. See V. Kappeler et al., *The Mythology of Crime and Criminal Justice,* 3d ed. (Prospect Heights, IL: Waveland Press, 2000), pp. 10ff.

11. James Patterson and Peter Kim, *The Day America Told the Truth* (Englewood Cliffs, NJ: Prentice-Hall, 1991).

12. Peter Lupsha, "American Values and Organized Crime: Suckers and Wiseguys," in B. Girgus, (ed.), *The American Self* (Albuquerque: University of New Mexico Press, 1981), pp. 144–155.

13. David R. Simon, *Elite Deviance,* 7th ed. (Boston: Allyn and Bacon, 2002), pp. 15–19.

14. C. Wright Mills, *The Power Elite* (New York: Oxford University Press, 1956), pp. 7–8.

15. C. Wright Mills, *Images of Man: The Classic Tradition in Sociological Theory* (New York: Braziller, 1960), p. 17.

16. Thomas Dye and Harmon Zeigler, *The Irony Of Democracy: An Uncommon Introduction To American Politics,* 9th ed. (Belmont, CA: Wadsworth, 1993), p. 98.

17. See David R. Simon, *Elite Deviance,* p. 16.

18. Ibid., pp. 15ff.

19. Bill Moyers, *The Secret Government* (Berkeley: Seven Locks Press, 1988).

20. Simon, *Elite Deviance,* p. 167.

21. Simon, *Elite Deviance,* p. 162.

22. Dennis Gilbert and Joseph Kahl, *The American Class Structure: A New Synthesis,* 4th ed. (Belmont, CA: Wadsworth, 1993), p. 211.

23. Center for Responsive Politics at opensecrets.org

24. Ibid.

25. Ibid.

26. See Simon, *Elite Deviance,* pp. 5–16 for a review of this research.

27. See on this point David R. Simon and Frank Hagan, *White-Collar Deviance* (Boston: Allyn and Bacon, 1999), Chapters 1 and 2; and the following by G. William Domhoff: *Who Rules America?* (Englewood Cliffs, NJ: Prentice-Hall, 1967); *The Bohemian Grove and Other Retreats* (New York: Harper and Row, 1974); and *The Power Elite and the State* (New York: Aldine-DeGruyter, 1990).

28. Simon, *Elite Deviance,* p. 23.

29. Victor Barnouw, *The Sponsor* (New York: Oxford University Press, 1978).

30. See for example Marvin E. Olsen and Martin E. Marger, eds., *Power in Modern Societies* (Boulder, CO: Westview, 1993) for excerpts from such studies.

31. William Greider, *Who Will Tell the People?* (New York: Simon and Schuster, 1992).

32. Ibid., p. 51.

33. Ross Perot, *Not for Sale At Any Price* (New York: Hyperion, 1993), p. 120.

34. Greider, *Who Will Tell the People?,* p. 48.

35. Ibid., p. 112.

36. Mills, *Images of Man,* p. 17.

Chapter Three

1. C. Wright Mills, *The Power Elite* (New York: Oxford University Press, 1956), pp. 343–361; David R. Simon, *Elite Deviance,* 7th ed. (Boston: Allyn and Bacon, 2002), pp. 47–90.

2. J. Donahue, "The Missing Rapsheet: Government Records of Corporate Abuses," *Multinational Monitor,* December 1992, pp. 17–19.

3. Marshall Clinard, *Illegal Corporate Behavior* (Washington, DC: U.S. Department of Justice, U.S. Government Printing Office, 1979).

4. Amitai Etzioni, "Is Corporate Crime Worth the Time?" *Business and Society Review* 36 (Winter 1990), pp. 33–36.

5. Donahue, "Missing Rapsheet," pp. 17–18.

6. Select Committee on Assassinations of the U.S. House of Representatives, Volume IX (Washington DC: U.S. Government Printing Office, 1979), p. 53.

7. Simon, *Elite Deviance,* pp. 255ff; and P. Shenon, "FBI Papers Show Wide Surveillance of Reagan Critics," *New York Times,* January 28, 1988, pp. A1, A8.

8. David R. Simon, "The Scandalization of America," in Gary Potter (ed.), *Controversies in White-Collar Crime* (Cincinnati: Anderson, 2001), p. 139.

9. Bill Moyers, *The Secret Government* (Berkeley: Seven Locks Press, 1988).

10. Colog.org/humanrights/ElSalvador/?ump.htm

11. Surgeon General of the United States, 2000, sgobesity.niddk.nih.gov

12. Peter Hilts, "50,000 Deaths a Year Blamed on Soot in Air," *San Francisco Chronicle,* July 19, 1993, p. Al.

13. Simon, *Elite Deviance,* pp. 100–102.

14. *Newsweek,* June 24, 2002.

15. Charles Lewis, "The Enron Collapse: A Financial Scandal Rooted in Politics," June 24, 2002, http://publicintegrity.org/dtaweb/home.asp

16. John Nicols, "Enron's Global Crusade," *Nation,* March 4, 2002; and Robert Scheer, "Enron Flew Under the Radar," *Nation,* February 12, 2002.

17. Alex Thio, *Deviant Behavior,* 6th ed. (Boston: Allyn and Bacon), p. 96.

18. June Gozan, "Wealth for the Few," *Multinational Monitor,* December 1992.

19. M. Males, "Infantile Arguments," *In These Times,* August 9, 1993, pp. 18–20.

20. Thio, *Deviant Behavior,* p. 97.

21. Steve Pizzo and Paul Muolo, "Take the Money and Run," *New York Times Magazine,* May 10, 1993, p. 56.

22. Dennis Gilbert and Joseph Kahl, *The American Class Structure: A New Synthesis,* 4th ed. (Belmont, CA: Wadsworth, 1993), p. 2.

23. Walter Lord, *A Night to Remember* (New York: Henry Holt, 1955).

Chapter Four

1. See for example W. D. Perdue, *Systemic Crises: Problems in Society, Politics, and World Order* (New York: Harcourt Brace, 1993); and James W. Russell, *Introduction to Macrosociology* (Englewood Cliffs, NJ: Prentice-Hall, 1992), p. 52.

2. European Union, "The European Union At a Glance," http://europa.eu.int/abc-eu.htm

3. Russell, *Introduction to Macrosociology,* pp. 52ff.

4. David R. Simon, *Elite Deviance,* 7th ed. (Boston: Allyn and Bacon, 2002), p. 188.

5. Oneworld.org/ips2.Jan98/UN.html

6. Perdue, *Systemic Crises.*

7. According to the World Development Forum, the annual service on this debt is $10 billion.

8. Simon, *Elite Deviance,* p. 201.

9. For more, see, e.g., Lucy Komisar, "Russian Cons and New York Banks," *Village Voice,* December 1–7, 1999.

10. Alfred McCoy, "The CIA Connection," *Progressive,* July 1991, pp. 20–26; and "The Afghanistan Drug Lords," *Convergence,* Fall 1991, pp. 11–12, 14.

11. Maureen Orth, "Afghanistan's Deadly Habit," *Vanity Fair,* March 2002, pp. 150ff.

12. Ibid.

13. Ibid., p. 153

14. Neal Pollard of the Terrorism Research Center, www.terrorism.com

15. Global Organized Crime Project at www.csis.org/goc

16. United States Department of State, *Patterns of Global Terrorism, 2000* (Washington, DC: U.S. Government Printing Office, April 2001).

17. Ibid.

Chapter Five

1. "Postmodern" here refers to the historical era that began at the end of World War II. For a discussion of the term, see David R. Simon, *Private Troubles and Public Issues: Social Problems in the Postmodern Era* (Fort Worth: Harcourt Brace, 1997), pp. 31–33.

2. Steven Holden. *The New York Times on the Sopranos.* (New York: I Books, 2000) p. 4.

3. James Patterson and W. Kim, *The Day America Told the Truth* (Englewood Cliffs, NJ: Prentice-Hall, 1991), pp. 45, 49.

4. Ibid., p. 7.

5. Gary T. Marx, "Fraudulent Identification, and Biography," paper delivered at a seminar of the Department of Sociology, San Diego State University (February 1988).

6. Ibid., pp. 1–2.

7. www.idtheftcenter.org

8. William Lutz, *Doublespeak* (New York: HarperCollins, 1989), p. 3.

9. W. D. Ehrhart, "On the Virtues of Dishonesty," *San Francisco Examiner,* March 19, 1993, p. A23.

10. Lutz, *Doublespeak,* p. 5.

11. Department of Advertising, University of Texas. www.utexas.edu/

12. David R. Simon, *Elite Deviance,* 7th ed. (Boston: Allyn & Bacon, 2002), pp. 111ff.

13. See Lutz, *Doublespeak,* pp. 85–94 on this point.

14. Gore Vidal, *Perpetual War for Perpetual Peace* (New York: Thunder's Mouth Press/Nation Books, 2002), Chapter 1.

15. C. Wright Mills, *White Collar* (New York: Oxford University Press, 1951), p. viii.

16. C. Wright Mills, *The Sociological Imagination* (New York: Oxford University Press, 1959), p. 161.

17. Ibid., p. 161.

18. R. Wilkinson (ed.), *Readings in American Social Character* (New York: Harper-Collins, 1992), p. 12.

19. See for example David Riesman, *The Lonely Crowd* (New Haven: Yale University Press, 1950).

20. See on this point Warren Breed, *The Self-Guiding Society* (New York: Free Press, 1971), pp. 203–204; A. M. Mecca et al. (eds.), *The Social Importance of Self-Esteem* (Berkeley: University of California Press, 1989).

21. N. J. Smelser, "Self-Esteem and Social Problems: An Introduction," in Mecca et al. (eds.), *Social Importance of Self-Esteem*, p. 10.

22. Breed, *Self-Guiding Society*, p. 204.

23. Ibid., pp. 197–198.

24. M. Seeman, "On the Meaning of Alienation," *American Sociological Review*, vol. 26 (1961), pp. 753–758.; and J. Israel, *Alienation* (Boston: Allyn and Bacon, 1971), pp. 208–215.

25. V. P. Bernard et al., "Dehumanization: A Composite Psychological Defense Mechanism in Relation to Modern War," in R. Perrucci and M. Pilisuk (eds.), *The Triple Revolution Emerging: Social Problems in Depth* (Boston: Little Brown, 1971), p. 16.

26. J. Hewitt, "Building Media Empires," in A. Asa Berger (ed.), *Media U.S.A.*, 2d ed. (New York: Longman, 1991), pp. 396–403.

27. See www.fair.org/extra/9711/and www.fair.org/extra/best-of-extra/corporateownership.html/

28. Berger, *Media USA*, p. 328.

29. Parenti, *Make-Believe Media*, (New York: St. Martin's Press), p. 10.

30. Ibid.

31. Patterson and Kim, *The Day America Told the Truth*, p. 120.

32. yrbe.edu.on.cal~mkviss/tv/links.htm

33. Jean Kilbourne, *Still Killing Us Softly 3: Advertising's Image of Women*, videorecording (Northampton, MA: Media Education Foundation, 2000).

34. One early study is M. Malamuth, "Aggression Against Women: Cultural and Individual Causes," in N. Malamuth and E. Donnerstein (eds.), *Pornography and Sexual Aggression* (New York: Academic Press, 1984); and see N. Davis. and C. Stasz, *Social Control of Deviance: A Critical Perspective* (New York: McGraw-Hill, 1990), p. 251.

35. See Elizabeth Paolucci, Mark Genuis, and Claudio Violato, "A Metanalysis of the Published Research on the Effects of Pornography, in Mark Geniuis and Claudio Violato (eds.), *The Changing Family and Child Development* (London: Ashgate, 2000), pp. 50–52.

36. D. Saunders, "Sex, Video, and the Single 7-Year-Old," *San Francisco Chronicle*, May 12, 1995, p A25.

37. usfweb.usf.edu/counsellsel fhlp/daterape/.htm

38. See the discussion in C. Wright Mills, *The Power Elite* (New York: Oxford University Press, 1956), pp. 314ff.

39. See the discussion in David R. Simon, *Elite Deviance,* 7th ed. (Boston: Allyn and Bacon, 2002), pp. 340ff.

40. Ibid., pp. 134, 290.

41. Jeffrey Schrank, *Snap, Crackle, and Popular Taste* (New York: Harper, 1977), p. 84.

42. R. Calabrese, "Adolescence: A Growth Period Conducive to Alienation," *Adolescence*, vol. 88 (Winter 1987), p. 935.

43. Mills, *White Collar.*

44. A. Hochschild, *The Managed Heart* (Berkeley: University of California Press, 1983), pp. 234–241.

45. George Ritzer, *The McDonaldization of Society* (Thousand Oaks, CA: Pine Forge Press, 1993), pp. 134–135.

46. S. Papson, "Bureaucratic Discourse and the Presentation of Self As Spectacle," *Humanity AND Society,* 9 (August 1985), pp. 223–236.

47. Christopher Lasch, *The Minimal Self: Psychic Survival in Troubled Times* (New York: W. W. Norton, 1984).

48. R. A. Kanungo, *Work Alienation: An Integrated Approach* (New York: Praeger, 1982), p. 157.

49. Mills, *White Collar,* p. 187.

50. Robert Bellah et al., *Habits of the Heart* (New York: Harper & Row, 1986).

51. Riesman, *The Lonely Crowd,* pp. 3–4.

52. Parenti, *Make-Believe Media,* (New York: St. Martin's Press), p. 14.

53. Ibid., p. 2.

54. Bernard et al., "Dehumanization."

55. Ashley Montagu and F. Matson, *The Dehumanization of Man* (New York: McGraw-Hill, 1985).

56. Karen Horney, *The Neurotic Personality Of Our Time* (New York: W. W. Norton, 1938), p. 284.

Chapter Six

1. NIH.900/news/pr/may98/NIDA–13.htm

2. *New York Times,* July 23, 1990, p. A1; and *New York Times,* May 12, 1991, Section IV, p. 6.

3. *New York Times,* September 29, 1993, p. A1.

4. Jeffrey Reiman, *The Rich Get Richer and the Poor Get Prison,* 3d ed. (New York: Macmillan, 1990), p. 28.

5. See David R. Simon, *Elite Deviance,* 7th ed. (Boston: Allyn and Bacon, 2002), Chapter 3 for a discussion of this issue.

6. See Elliott Currie, *Reckoning: Drugs, the Cities, and the American Future* (New York: Hill and Wang, 1994), pp. 70ff.

7. G. Witkin, "The Men Who Created Crack," *U.S. News & World Report*, August 19, 1991, pp. 44–53.

8. Jay Albanese and Robert Pursley, *Crime in America: Some Emerging Issues* (Englewood Cliffs, NJ: Prentice-Hall, 1993), p. 206.

9. *New York Times*, September 24, 1991, p. A1.

10. Robert Goldstein et al., *Special Report of the New York State Taskforce on Organized Crime* (1990), p. 6, cited in David R. Simon with Joel Henderson, *Private Troubles and Public Issues: Social Problems in the Postmodern Era* (Fort Worth, TX: Harcourt Brace, 1997), Chapter 8.

11. *New York Times,* January 10, 1992, p. A12.

12. Howard Abadinsky, *Organized Crime,* 3d ed. (Chicago: Nelson-Hall, 1990).

13. James Mills, *The Underground Empire* (New York: Dell, 1986), pp. 1130 ff.

14. Abadinsky, *Organized Crime,* p. 231.

15. Ibid., p. 259.

16. Simon, *Elite Deviance,* pp. 35ff.

17. *New York Times,* December 12, 1990, p. A14.

18. Victor Kappeler et al., *The Mythology of Crime and Criminal Justice,* (Prospect Heights, IL: Waveland), p. 85.

19. *New York Times,* March 23, 1991, p. I40.

20. Simon, *Elite Deviance,* p. 52.

21. Ibid., pp. 52–53.

22. Ibid., p. 81.

23. *Toronto Globe and Mail,* February 10, 2000.

24. *New York Times,* August 17, 1990, p. A15.

25. *New York Times,* November 22, 1990, p. A25; and *New York Times,* December 11, 1990, p. B3.

26. FBI.gov/pressrel98/police.htm

27. Ibid.

28. See *New York Times,* July 7, 1994, pp. A1, A4.

29. cnn.com/2002/law/02/28/police.torture.overturn

30. www.criminaljustice.org/public.nsf/freeform/pereztranscripts

31. cnn.com/2001/us/09/07/miami.cops/

32. *Time,* December 15, 1997, p. 78.

33. hrw.org/reports98/police/uspo93.htm

34. hrw.org/reports98/police/uspo94.htm

35. See the discussions in Simon, *Elite Deviance,* pp. 82ff.; Kappeler, *The Mythology of Crime and Criminal Justice,* p. 163.

36. Frank Pearce, *Crimes of the Powerful* (New York: Pluto Press, 1976), p. 150.

37. Christopher Robbins, *Air America* (New York: Putnam, 1979).

38. Gerald Posner, *Warlords of Crime, Chinese Secret Societies: The New Mafia* (New York: Penguin, 1988), pp. 69–70.

39. Ibid., p. 77.

40. S. Wisotsky, "A Society of Suspects: The War on Drugs and Civil Liberties," *USA TODAY*, July 1993, pp. 17–21.

41. P. D'Amato, "An Attack on Civil Liberties," in N. Bernards (ed.), *War on Drugs: Opposing Viewpoints* (San Diego: Greenhaven, 1990), p. 80.

42. nls.org/housing/may/jun00.htm

43. G. Berger, *Crack: The New Epidemic* (New York: Franklin Watts, 1987), pp. 83–84.

44. R. Harris, *Drugged America* (New York: Macmillan, 1991), pp. 167–168.

45. Kappeler, *Mythology of Crime and Criminal Justice*, p. 172.

46. A. Levine, "America's Addiction to Addictions," *U.S. News & World Report*, February 5, 1990, p. 62.

47. Simon, *Private Troubles and Public Issues*, p. 230.

48. James Inciardi, *War on Drugs* (Palo Alto, CA: Mayfield, 1986).

49. Barbara Ehrenreich, *Fear of Falling* (New York: Pantheon, 1989), p. 247.

50. D. E. Strickland et al., "A Content Analysis of Beverage Alcohol Advertising: Magazine Advertising," *Journal of Studies on Alcohol*, 1982, no. 7, pp. 655–682.

51. V. Barnouw, *The Sponsor* (New York: Oxford University Press, 1978).

52. Inciardi, *War On Drugs*, p. 128.

53. Kappeler, *Mythology of Crime and Criminal Justice*, p. 247.

Chapter Seven

1. Norvel Glenn, "What's Happening to American Marriage," *USA TODAY*, May 1993, pp. 26–28.

2. Ann Hulbert, "Home Repairs," in D. Boaz (ed.), *The Crisis in Drug Prohibition* (San Francisco: Laissez Faire Books, 1993), p. 26; and Gannett News Service, November 16, 2001.

3. James Willwerth, "Hello? I'm Home Alone," *Time*, March 1, 1993, p. 46.

4. Faye Wattleton, "The Case for National Action," *Nation*, July 24–31, 1989, pp. 138–141.

5. Barbara Vobejda, "Caring for Three Generations," in Washington Post Writers Group (ed.), *Society in Crisis: The Washington Post Social Problems Companion* (Needham Heights, MA: Allyn and Bacon, 1993), p. 186.

6. S. Rouner, "Battered Wives: Centuries of Silence," in Washington Post Writers Group, (ed.), *Society in Crisis*, p. 195.

7. Susan Shira, "Study Confirms Worst Fears on US Children," *New York Times,* April 12, 1994, p. A12. And 1998 Department of Health and Human Services estimate.

8. www.letswrap.com/divinfor/stats.htm

9. Charles Derber, *The Wilding of America,* 2d ed. (New York: Worth, 2002), p. 99.

10. Peggy Taylor, "The Way We Never Were," *New Age Journal,* September/October 1992, pp. 64–69, 144.

11. Stephanie Coontz, *The Way We Never Were: American Families and the Nostalgia Trap* (New York: Basic, 1992), p. 160.

12. Ann Hulbert, "Home Repairs," *New Republic,* August 16, 1993, pp. 26–32.

13. David Moberg, "All in The Family," *In These Times,* February 22, 1993, p. 20; and *Contrarian,* 5 (August 31, 2001).

14. See C. Wright Mills, "Women: The Darling Little Slaves," in I. L. Horowitz (ed.) *Power, Politics, and People: The Collected Essays of C. Wright Mills,* (New York: Ballantine, 1963), pp. 339–346.

15. Arlie Hochschild, "The Second Shift," *Utne Reader,* March 1990, pp. 66–81.

16. Ibid., p. 68.

17. Thomas Hargrove and Guido Stempel, "Here Comes the Groom," *San Francisco Examiner,* July 29, 1993, pp. C1, C9.

18. Warren Farrell, "Men As Success Objects," *Utne Reader,* May/June 1991, p. 82.

19. Derber, *The Wilding of America,* p. 101.

20. David Fisher, *Growing Old in America* (New York: Oxford University Press, 1978), pp. 82–86.

21. Andrew Cherlin, "A Sense of History: Recent Trends on Aging and the Family," in Maltilda White Riley et al, (eds.), *Aging in Society: Selected Reviews of Recent Research* (Hilsdale, NJ: Erlbaum, 1983), p. 7.

22. J. Eshelman et al., *Sociology: An Introduction,* 4th ed. (New York: HarperCollins, 1993), pp. 275ff.

23. U.S. Senate Committee on Aging et al., *Aging America: Trends and Projections* (Washington, DC: U.S. Government Printing Office, 1991), p. 144.

24. Betty Friedan, *The Fountain of Age* (New York: Simon and Schuster, 1993), p. 62.

25. P. Baltes and K. Schaie, "The Myth of the Twilight Years," *Psychology Today,* March 1974, pp. 35–40.

26. W. Oswalt, *Life Cycles and Lifeways: An Introduction to Cultural Anthropology* (Palo Alto, CA: Mayfield, 1986).

27. Vivian Gornick, "For the Rest of Our Days Things Can Only Get Worse," *Village Voice,* May 24, 1976, pp. 32 ff.

28. Don Colburn, "The Woes of Widows in America," in Washington Post Writers Group (ed.), *Society in Crisis,* p. 207.

29. Friedan, *The Fountain of Age,* p. 201.

30. Linda Ade-Ridder, "Asexuality and Marital Quality in Older Married Couples," in T. H. Brubaker (ed.), *Family Relationships in Later Life*, 2d ed. (Newbury Park, CA: Sage, 1990).

31. Kirk Astroth, "Beyond Ephebiphobia: Problem Adults or Problem Youths?" *Phi Delta Kappan*, January 1994, p. 412.

32. Harold Cox, *Later Life: The Realities of Aging* (Englewood Cliffs, NJ: Prentice-Hall, 1984), p. 291.

33. Ibid., p. 296.

34. William Thompson and James Hickey, *Society in Focus: An Introduction to Sociology* (New York: HarperCollins, 1994), p. 307.

35. Karl Pillemer and David Finkelhor, "The Prevalence of Elder Abuse: A Random Sample Survey," *Gerontologist*, 1988, no. 28, pp. 51–57.

36. David Streitfeld, "Abuse of the Elderly-Often It's The Spouse," in Washington Post Writers Group (ed.), *Society in Crisis*, p. 212.

37. Karl Pillemer, "The Dangers of Dependency: New Findings on Domestic Violence Against the Elderly," *Social Problems*, vol. 33 (December 1985), pp. 146–158.

38. Melinda Beck, "The Flames of a Crusader," *Newsweek*, October 19, 1992, p. 58.

39. www.nursinghomeabuse.com/brig1.html; www.nursinghomeabusecneter.com/; cnn.com/2001/health/30/nursing,home.abuse/?related

40. Neil Postman, *The Disappearance of Childhood* (New York: Vintage, 1994).

41. William Mattox, "America's Family Time Famine," in Harold Widdison (ed.), *Social Problems 93/94* (Sluice Dock, CT: Dushkin, 1993), pp. 19–20.

42. Ibid., p. 19.

43. Steven Messner and Richard Rosenfeld, *Crime and the American Dream* (Belmont, CA: Wadsworth, 1994), pp. 78–81.

44. Geoffrey Cowley, "Children in Peril," in Harold Widdison (ed.), *Social Problems 93/94*, pp. 25–26.

45. M. I. Wilson et al., "Differential Maltreatment of Girls and Boys," *Victimology*, vol. 6 (1981), pp. 249–261.

46. See the Reactive Attachment Disorder Website at http://members.tripod.com/~radclass/ Google.com, 2002.

47. S. Chira, "Surprising Survey on Kids and Guns–40% Know a Victim," *San Francisco Chronicle*, July 20, 1994, p. A10.

48. John Touhy, "There's No Such Thing As Childhood on the Streets," *U.S. Catholic*, March 1993, p. 20.

49. Ibid., p. 22.

50. Ibid.

51. Gary Ackerman, " A Congressional View of Youth Suicide," *American Psychologist*, February 1993, pp. 183–184.

52. "Juvenile Justice," *CQ Researcher,* February 1994, p. 5.

53. Chester Britt, "Crime and Unemployment Among Youths in the United States, 1958–1990," *American Journal of Economics and Sociology,* vol. 53 (January 1994), pp. 99–109.

54. www.feedthechildrenbetter.org/hunger/about/asp; and http//cpmcnet.columbia.edu/dept/nccp/cprb2text.html

55. Michael Isikoff, "Teen Alcohol Use Heavy, Survey Finds," Washington Post Writers Group (ed.), *Society in Crisis,* pp. 319–320.

56. www.health.org/900pubs. See various surveys of the National Clearinghouse for Alcohol and Drug Information.

57. See Substance Abuse and Mental Health Services Administration (SAMHSA), Department of Health and Human Service, Drug Abuse Statistics from Substance Abuse and Mental Health, for 2002, at www.samhsa.gov.

58. www.bls.gov/news.release/youth.nro.htm

Chapter Eight

1. Erich Fromm, *Escape from Freedom* (New York: Holt, Rinehart and Winston, 1941); and *The Sane Society* (New York: Holt, Rinehart and Winston, 1955).

2. Fromm, *Escape from Freedom,* pp. 62–63.

3. E. and M. Josephson (eds.), *Man Alone: Alienation in Modern Society* (New York: Dell, 1962), p. 21.

4. C. Wright Mills, *The Power Elite* (New York: Oxford University Press, 1956), Chapter 13.

5. Fromm, *The Sane Society.*

6. Robert Blauner, *Alienation and Freedom* (Chicago: University of Chicago Press, 1964).

7. Herbert Gintis, "Alienation and Capitalism," in R. C. Edwards et al. (eds.), *The Capitalist System,* 3d ed. (Englewood Cliffs, NJ: Prentice-Hall, 1986), pp. 141–142.

8. Kai Erikson, "On Work Alienation," in Kai Erikson and Peter Vallas, (eds.), *The Nature of Work* (New Haven: Yale University Press, 1990), pp. 19–35.

9. Harry Braverman, "Work and Unemployment," *Monthly Review,* July 1975, p. 25.

10. Richard C. Edwards et al., "Alienation and Labor," in R. C. Edwards et al. (eds.), *The Capitalist System,* 3d ed. (Englewood Cliffs, NJ: Prentice-Hall, 1986), p. 138.

11. M. Kohn, "Unresolved Issues in the Relationship Between Work and Personality," in Erikson and Vallas (eds.), *The Nature Of Work,* p. 41.

12. Ibid., 43.

13. Donald Kanter and Philip Mirvis, *The Cynical Americans* (San Francisco: Jossey-Bass, 1989), p. 34.

14. Janice Castro, "Disposable Workers," *Time*, March 29, 1993, p. 47.

15. Ibid., p. 44.

16. Jan Halper, *Quiet Desperation: The Truth About Successful Men* (New York: Warner, 1988).

17. Castro, "Disposable Workers," p. 43; and www.bls.gov/opub/ils/pdf/opbilsos.pdf

18. See Fromm, *Escape from Freedom.*

19. Clide Wilcox, *God's Warriors: The Christian Right on Twentieth Century America* (Baltimore: Johns Hopkins University Press, 1992); and S. M. Lipset and Earl Raab, *The Politics of Unreason* (Chicago: University of Chicago Press, 1987).

20. "The Church Confronts Unholy Behavior," *Oakland Tribune*, December 7, 1993, p. A8.

21. S. Mydans, "11 Friars at California Seminary Molested Students, Inquiry Finds," *New York Times*, December 1, 1993, pp. A1, A12.

22. Howard Becker, "Whose Side Are We On?" *Social Problems*, 1 (1961), pp. 1–15.

23. J. Inciardi and T. Rothman, *Sociology* (Houston: Harcourt Brace, 1990), p. 411.

24. Alfie Kohn, *No Contest: The Case Against Competition* (Boston: Houghton Mifflin, 1986), pp. 96–131.

25. Ibid.

26. See National Center for Education Statistics, *Annual Report* (Washington, DC: U.S. Government Printing Office, 1990), p. 54.

27. James Coleman and Thomas Hoffer, *Public and Private High Schools: The Impact of Communities* (New York: Basic Books, 1987); James Coleman et al., *Equality of Educational Opportunity (The Coleman Report)* (Washington, DC: U.S. Department of Health, Education, and Welfare, 1966).

28. Herbert Gintis and Samuel Bowles, "Schooling and Inequality," in R. C. Edwards et al. (eds.), *The Capitalist System*, 3d ed. (Englewood Cliffs, NJ: Prentice-Hall, 1986), p. 235.

29. Ibid., p. 236.

30. See, for example, Howard Becker, "The Career of a Chicago Public School Teacher," *American Journal of Sociology* 57 (March 1952), pp. 470–477.

31. William Celis, "Study Finds Rising Concentration of Black and Hispanic Students," *New York Times*, December 14, 1993, pp. A1, A11.

32. Brent Collins, "Student Indifference Erodes the Public Schools," *Utne Reader*, September/October 1990, pp. 68–69.

33. Arthur Lean and William Eaton, *Education or Catastrophe?* (Wolfboro, NH: Longwood Academic, 1990), p. 41.

34. Ibid., 29.

35. Nanette Asimov, "Alarming Report on U.S. Students Reading Skills," *San Francisco Chronicle*, September 16, 1993, p. A5.

36. John Taylor Gatto, *The Underground History of American Education* (Oxford, NY: Oxford Village Press, 2000/2001).

37. Nanette Asimov, "U.S. Teachers Pay Ranks Low in Study of Developed Nations," *San Francisco Chronicle,* July 9, 1993, p. A6.

38. Lean and Eaton, *Education or Catastrophe?* p. 55.

39. E. Willis, "Our Mobsters, Our Selves: Why *The Sopranos* Is Therapeutic," *Nation,* April 2, 2001.

40. *New York Times,* December 29, 2001, p. A13.

41. *New Yorker,* April 2, 2001, pp. 38–44.

42. *San Francisco Chronicle,* February 15, 2002, p. A1.

43. John Spanier, *American Foreign Policy Since World War II,* 4th ed. (New York: Praeger, 1990).

44. *Newsweek,* April 2, 2001, p. 51.

45. Robert Jewett and John Shelton Lawrence, *The American Monomyth* (New York: Doubleday, 1977).

46. James Patterson and Peter Kim, *The Day America Told the Truth* (Englewood Cliffs, NJ: Prentice-Hall, 1991).

47. Ibid., p. 6.

48. Ibid., p. 237.

49. *Seattle Post Intelligencer,* June 11, 1991, p. A3.

50. Al Gore, *From Red Tape to Results: Creating a Government That Works Better and Costs Less* (Washington, DC: U.S. Government Printing Office, 1993), p. 1.

51. Patterson and Kim, *The Day America Told the Truth,* p. 217.

52. Robert Bellah et al., *Habits of the Heart* (New York: Harper and Row, 1986).

Chapter Nine

1. See Gore Vidal, *Perpetual War for Perpetual Peace* (New York: Thunder's Mouth/Nation Books, 2002).

2. Daniel Patrick Moynihan, "Defining Deviancy Down," *American Scholar,* Autumn 1993, p. 17.

3. L. Shames, *The Hunger for More* (New York: Times Books, 1989), p. 43.

4. Charles Derber, *Money, Murder, and the American Dream: Wilding from Main Street to Wall Street* (New York: St. Martin's Press, 1992), pp. 101ff.

5. See Special Issue, Irving Howe, ed., *Dissent,* Spring 1991, pp. 3–33.

6. R. Nisbet, *The Present Age* (New York: HarperCollins, 1988).

7. Charles Derber, *The Wilding of America,* 2d ed. (New York: Worth, 2002).

8. Moynihan, "Defining Deviancy Down."

9. David R. Simon, with Joel Henderson, *Private Troubles and Public Issues: Social Problems in the Postmodern Era* (Fort Worth, TX: Harcourt Brace, 1997), pp. 33–34.

10. C. Wright Mills, *The Sociological Imagination* (New York: Oxford University Press, 1959).

11. Derber, *The Wilding of America.*

12. Harold Barnet, "Corporate Capitalism, Corporate Crime," *Crime and Delinquency,* 27 (January 1981), pp. 4–23.

13. C. Wright Mills, *The Power Elite* (New York: Oxford University Press, 1956), Chapter 13.

14. David R. Simon, *Elite Deviance,* 7th ed. (Boston: Allyn and Bacon, 2002), Chapter 2.

15. Bill Moyers, *The Secret Government* (Berkeley: Seven Locks Press, 1988).

16. R. Wilkinson, *In Search of the American Character* (New York: HarperCollins, 1988); R. Wilkinson, (ed.), *American Social Character* (New York: HarperCollins, 1992).

17. Robert Bellah et al., *Habit of the Heart* (New York: Harper and Row, 1986).

18. Christopher Lasch, *The Minimal Self: Psychic Survival In Troubled Times* (New York: W. W. Norton, 1984).

19. See Samuel Walker, *Sense and Nonsense About Crime and Drugs,* 5th ed. (Belmont, CA: Wadsworth, 2001), pp. 3–5.

20. Philip Slater, *The Pursuit of Loneliness* (Boston: Beacon Press, 1970).

21. R. Garr, *Reinvesting in America* (Reading, MA: Addison-Wesley, 1995).

22. D. Osborne, Foreword in ibid.

23. See on this point Seymour Melman, *After Capitalism* (New York: Knopf, 2001).

24. Ibid., p. 149.

25. Michael Lerner, *The New Socialist Revolution* (New York: Delacorte, 1973).

26. Ibid.

27. Seymour Melman, *After Capitalism,* p. 25.

28. David C. Korten, "The Post-Corporate," *Yes,* (Spring 1999), http://www.futurenet.org/backissues.html

29. Ibid.

Index

AARP. *See* American Association of Retired Persons

Abu Sayyaf Group (ASG), 73

Accounting standards, 54

Achievement
and the American Dream, 17

Acting
and service economy, 99–100

Adams, James, 19

Adaptation mode, 90–91

Addiction
and material culture, 140

Addictive personalities, 140

Administrative sideliners, 183

Advertising, 140
and inauthenticity, 97–99
and substance abuse, 222
and tobacco abuse, 141

Advertising laws
violations of, 37

Afghanistan
drug trafficking in, 68, 73–74, 74
and U.S. national security, 75

African American Guerrilla Family, 122

African Americans
and crime syndicate, 121–122

Ageism, 152–163

Agent Orange, 45–46

Aging, fear of, 155. *See also* Ageism

Agnew, Spiro, 40

Alcoa, 29

Alcohol abuse, 112, 222
and advertising, 97–98, 140
and individualism, 107
and youth, 170–171, 175

Alienation, 87, 205, 214, 227–228
and blue-collar workers, 181–182
and child abuse, 167–168
and deviant behavior, 178
and education, 192–196
and inauthenticity, 100, 102
and marriage, 150–152
and the media, 92–93
and micro-social problems, 102–105
nature of, 88–92
and part-time workers, 184, 187
and religion, 187–192
and unemployed workers, 187
at universities, 197–198
and white-collar workers, 182–184,
185–186
and workplace, 180–187
See also Dehumanization; Inauthenticity

Allende, Salvador, 41

Allstate, 30

American Association of Retired Persons
(AARP), 153

American Dream
and crime, 14–17
definition of, 16–17
elements of, 17–23

American Enterprise Institute, 32

American family
  myth of, 147–150
  See also Family
American hero, 200
American Legion, 26
American Mafia, 119
  and drug trafficking, 119
The American Monomyth (Jewett and
  Lawrence), 200
American Psychiatric Association, 199
Americas, the, 61
Amnesty International
  and El Salvador, 65
Amylin Pharmaceuticals, 30
Andersen, Arthur, 54
Anomie, 20. *See also* Normlessness
Antisocial social character, rise of, 211–212.
  See also Social character
Antitrust laws
  violations of, 37
AOL-TimeWarner, 93
Apathy
  and students, 195
Arbenz, Jacobo, 64
Arbusto, 28
Archer Daniels Midland, 29
Armey, Dick, 50
Army Chemical Corps, 41
Arthur Andersen, 49–50, 53
Aryan Brotherhood, 122
Asea Brown Boveri, 30
ASG. *See* Abu Sayyaf Group
Ashcroft, John, 51, 52
Asian crime syndicates, 199
Asian Pacific bloc, 61
AT&T, 32, 212
Attachment disorder, 165–166
Authoritarianism
  and Fundamentalism, 190
Authority
  crisis of, 202–204
Azerbaijan, 72

Baker, James A., III, 52
Banker's Trust, 31–32
Bank of New York (BONY), 31–32, 66–67
Banks
  and drug trafficking, 123–125
  and organized crime, 66–67
Bay of Pigs, 40, 122
A Beautiful Mind, 200

Becker, Howard, 192
BECS, 66
Bekaa Valley
  drug trafficking in, 71
Belief, crisis of, 202–204
Bellah, Robert, 214
Benex, 66
Bennett, William, 138
Berlin, Peter, 66
Bertelsmann, 93
A Better Government Association, 210
Bin Laden, Osama, 71, 86
Biotech foods, 29
Blow, 112
Blue-collar workers
  and alienation, 181–182
Bohemian Grove, 28
Boland Amendment, 42
Bolivia, 69
BONY. *See* Bank of New York
Bowles, Samuel, 194
Bracco, Lorraine, 199
Brown, Nicole, 131
Bureaucracies, 179–180
  and inauthenticity, 101, 102
  and lying, 192
Bureaucratese, 83
Burma, 136
Bush, George H. W., 42, 43, 44, 85
Bush, George W., 28–29, 32, 200, 211
  and capital punishment, 215
  and Enron scandal, 50, 51
Bush (George H. W.) administration, 56, 64
  corruption in, 211
  and El Salvador, 43
Bush (George W.) administration, 138,
  204
  and Enron scandal, 48–54
  and national energy policy, 49,
    52–53
Business, 24
  and government, 15–16
  locally owned, 225, 226
  regulation of, 14–15

Calgene Inc., 29
Calvin, John, 189
Calvinist theology, 189
Campaign contributions
  and Enron, 50–52, 53
  and power elite, 29

Capitalism, 179–180
and education, 193
Capital punishment
and Bush, George W., 215
Capone, Al, 6, 210
Careerism
and family values, 164–165
Cargill, 29
Carter, Jimmy, 218
Casey, William, 41
Castro, Fidel, 38, 40
Catholic Church
child molestation scandal in, 178,
190–192, 205–206
and Mafia, 188
See also Religion; Religious institutions
CCC. *See* Civilian Conservation Corps
Central Intelligence Agency. *See* CIA
Chase Manhattan Bank, 25, 31–32
Chemical Bank, 67
Cheney, Dick, 28, 49, 52–53
Chiang Kai-shek, 136
Chicago Tribune, 30
Child abuse, 147, 166
Child molestation scandal
in Catholic Church, 178, 190–192,
205–206
and the Vatican, 191–192
Child neglect, 166
Child rearing, 15
Children
victimization of, 165–167
Children's television, 95
Chile
human rights violations in, 65
China
and drug trafficking, 136
Cholon Triad, 136
Christopher, Warren, 43
Christopher Commission, 131
CIA, 26, 41, 42, 43, 44, 45, 77, 122
and Afghanistan, 68
and Chile, 65
and drug trafficking, 135–136
and Guatemala, 64
Citibank, 25, 31–32, 67
Citizen initiatives, 222
Civic associations
and power elite, 31
Civilian Conservation Corps (CCC),
220

Civil liberties
and terrorism, combating, 205
Civil rights abuses
and drug laws, 137–139
Class structure
and victimization, acts of, 57–58
Clayton Antitrust Act of 1914, 25
Clinical depression
in workplace, 187
Clinton, Bill, 52
and Agent Orange, 46
and impeachment, 84, 85–86
Clinton administration, 43
crime rate during, 215
and family and medical leave bill, 15
Cold War
and power elite, 24
Coleman, James, 194
Collective social movements, 224–225, 229
Collins, Brent, 195
Colombia
drug trafficking in, 69–70, 74
and U.S. national security, 75
Colombian drug cartel, 120
Command cynics, 183
Commodity Futures Modernization Act, 53
Community
and family values, 146
and social change, 218–219
Community colleges, 197
Competition, 106–107, 179, 217
and crime, 140
and education, 193
and self-esteem, 193
Conformity, 107
Consumerism
and advertising, 98
Control
and workplace, 185
Cooperation
and self-esteem, 193
Coors, Joseph, 32
Corporate crime, 37, 212–213
Corporate crime laws, enforcement of, 213
Corporate scandals, 19
Corporate sector
and power elite, 24–25
Corporations
and drug trafficking, 123–125
and government and organized crime,
65–67, 123

and mass media, control of, 226
and social change, 219–220
Corruption, 9
    police, 125–135
    in Reagan/Bush administrations,
        211
Costello, Frank, 128
Council on Foreign Relations, 31
Crédit Mobilier scandal, 37–38
Crime, 109–113
    and the American Dream, 14–17
    causes of, 139–141
    as common phenomenon, 20–21
    and competition, 140
    and drug abuse, 142–143
    and globalization, 77
    identity, 80–81
    and individualism, 107
    prevention of, 215–216
    and victimization, acts of, and runaways,
        167–170
    youth, 169
    See also Corporate crime; Crime
        syndicates; Organized crime; Street
        crime
Crimeogenic role models, 21
Crime rate
    during Clinton administration, 215
Crimes, sex
    and the media, 96–97
Crime syndicates, 119–122
    globalization of, 227
    and mental health, 199–202
    See also individual syndicates; Mafia;
        organized crime
Criminal justice system
    and drug trafficking, 125–127
Cronkite, Walter, 38
Cuba, 69, 122
Cuban Mafia, 122
Cuomo, Mario, 129
Curtis, Tony, 80
Cynicism
    and workplace, 183–184

Dahl, John, 95
Daily life, crises of, 178
d'Aubuisson, Roberto, 43
Davis, Len, 135
Deep acting, 100
The Deer Hunter, 94

Defense contracts, 26, 27
Defense industry, 26–27, 220
Defense Intelligence Agency, 26
Defense spending, 221, 223
Defining deviancy down, 212
Dehumanization, 101, 108, 178–179, 214
    and marriage, 150
    and the media, 104–105
    See also Alienation; Inauthenticity
DeLay, Tom, 50
Delinquency, 169
Demara, Waldo, 80
Democrats, 24
Department of Defense, 26
Department of Justice, 50
Depression, clinical
    in workplace, 187
Depression era, 13
Derber, Charles, 212
Deviant behavior, 21–23
    and alienation, 178
    and the workplace, 181
Diploma Scam (DIPSCAM), 80
DIPSCAM. *See* Diploma Scam
Disney, 93
Disordered children, 166–167
Divorce, 9, 146, 148–149, 150, 152
DKB, 66
Doublespeak, 85–86
    and advertising, 99
    types of, 82–84
    See also Lying
Doublethink, 84
Dowd, Michael, 130
Drug abuse, 222
    causes of, 139–141
    and crime, 142–143
    and individualism, 107
    and youth, 171–173, 174–175
Drug laws
    and civil rights abuses, 137–139
Drug policy, U.S., 142
Drugs, legal
    and advertising, 98, 140
    and illegal, connection between, 141
Drug testing, 138, 139
Drug trafficking
    and banks and corporations, 123–125
    and crime, 110–113
    and criminal justice system, 125–127
    and intelligence agencies, 135–136

international, 69–74
and organized crime, 67–78, 117–122
solution to, 74–76
and street crime, 113–115
and street gangs, 115–117
and terrorism, 67–78
and white-collar crime, 122–123
Drug treatment, 141–143
public-health approach to, 222–223

Eastman Kodak, 29
Eastwood, Clint, 94
Economic pressure
and family values, 164
Education, 9, 24, 206
and alienation, 192–196
and labor force, 186
and money, 15
and social class, 193–195
Education, home-based, 196
Edwards, Lucy, 66
Ehrlichman, John, 41
Eisenhower, Dwight D., 24, 44
Eisenhower administration, 64
Elder abuse, 147–148, 152–162
Elderly, 190
criminal victimization of, 159–160
and inadequate housing, 160
and nursing homes, 161–162
stereotypes, 155–158
Elite
and deviant behavior, 21, 23
and power, 22–23
See also Power elite
Ellsberg, Daniel, 40
ELN (National Liberation Army), 70
El Rukins, 121–122
El Salvador
atrocities in, 43
human rights violations in, 65
Emotional needs, 88–89
Employment
and government, 220
and social change, 220
and youth, 174
Enron scandal, 48–54
Enterprise, the, 42
Entitlement, sense of, 20
Environmental Protection Agency (EPA), 47
EPA. *See* Environmental Protection Agency
Escape from Freedom (Fromm), 178

Esperanza Unida, 218
Estrangement, 89. *See also* Self-estrangement
EU. *See* European Union
Euphemism, 82
Europe, 223
drug treatment in, 223
European currency, 60–61
European Union (EU), 60–61
Extreme individualism, 106. *See also* Individualism
Exxon, 25, 32

Fadlallah, Sayyed, 41
Failure, fear of, 17
Familial abuse, 147
Familial stability, 152
Family, 9, 145–147
and money, 14–15
See also Family values
Family and medical leave bill, 15
Family leave, 15
Family vacation policy, 15
Family values, 174–175, 227
and youth, 162–173
See also Family; Values
FARC (Revolutionary Armed Forces of Colombia), 69–70
FBI, 41, 44, 48, 77
Uniform Crime Reports statistics, 68
Fear
of aging, 155
and individualism, 106, 107–108
FEC
and Enron scandal, 50
Federal Age Discrimination Act, 154
Financial harm, 10, 47–54
Fiorentino, Linda, 95
First World, 60–61
Flamingo Bank, 66
Food and Trade, 29
Food industry
and physical harm, 46–47
Ford, Gerald, 29
Ford Motor Company, 25
and Pinto scandal, 36, 37
Ford Pinto scandal, 36, 37
Fort, Jeff, 121
Fortune 500 companies
and corporate crime, 37
and part-time workers, 187
Fortune magazine, 29

Foundations
    and power elite, 31
Frank, Antoinette, 135
Fraud, 80–81
    and financial harm, 48
    and Fundamentalism, 190
Freedom, 107, 178–179
French connection, 135
Fried, Frank, Harris, Shriver, and Jacobson,
    54
Fromm, Erich, 178–179, 180, 188
Fuhrman, Mark, 131
Fundamentalism
    and ageism, 154
    See also Religion; Religious institutions

G. D. Searle, 29
Gangsters, 13
    fascination with, 208, 227
GAO. *See* General Accounting Office
Gatto, John Taylor, 196
General Accounting Office (GAO), 53
General Dynamics, 30
General Electric, 25, 32, 93
General Instrument, 29–30
General Motors, 25, 32
Genetically engineered food, 29
Geoghan, John J., 191
Germany, 223
Gibson, Mel, 94
Gilead Sciences, 30
Gintis, Herbert, 194
Globalization
    and crime, 77
    and crime syndicates, 227
Goal orientation
    and higher immorality, 35–36
Gobbledygook, 83
The Godfather, 13, 110, 187–188
The Godfather Part II, 188
The Godfather Part III, 188
Golden Triangle, 136
GoodFellas, 110
Good Housekeeping, 100
Goodman, Ron, 131
Gossens, Salvador Allende, 65
Gotti, John, 117
Government
    and business, 15–16
    and corporations and organized crime,
        65–67, 123
    and employment, 220
    and social change, 219–220
Government regulation
    and corporate sector, 25
Government scandals, 37–45, 48–54
    and lying, 84–86
    See also individual scandals
Gramm, Phil, 50
Great Britain
    drug treatment in, 223
The Great Impostor, 80
Greider, William, 32, 33
Groves, Kim, 135
Guatemala
    human rights violations in, 64–65
Gulfstream Aerospace, 30
Guys and Dolls, 13

Habitat for Humanity, 218
Haldeman, H. R., 41
Halliburton, 28, 49
Halper, Jan, 185
Happiness
    and money, 14
Harken Energy, 28
Harris, Lou, 203–204
Harrison Act of 1914, 138
Harvard School of Public Health, 47
Hawthorne, Nathaniel, 201
Hekmatyar, General, 68
Helsinki Agreement of 1975, 63
Heritage Foundation, 32
Hezbolah, 71
Higher immorality, 35–37, 213. *See also*
    Morality
HIV infection, 112
Hoffa, James, 39
Home-based education, 196
Homicide rate
    and capital punishment, 215
Homosexual priests
    and the Vatican, 191–192
Hoover, J. Edgar, 128
Horney, Karen, 106
House Energy and Commerce Committee, 50
House of Representatives
    and power elite, 32
House Special Committee on Assassinations
    (HSCA), 39
Housework, 151
Housing, inadequate, and the elderly, 160–161

Housman, Angie, 169
HSCA. *See* House Special Committee on
    Assassinations
Human needs, 88–89
Human rights violations, 63–65
Humphrey-Hawkins Act, 220
Hyde, Henry, 86

IBM, 25
Identity, 89, 178–179, 213
Identity crime, 80–81
Identity crisis, 200–202
Idolatry, 188–189
Impeachment, Clinton, 84, 85–86
Impression management, 100–101
IMU. *See* Islamic Movement of Uzbekistan
Inauthenticity, 99–102, 108, 178, 214
    and advertising, 97–99
    and marriage, 150
    See also Alienation; Dehumanization
Incest, 166
India
    drug trafficking in, 73
Indifference, 210
Individualism, 102, 103, 105–108, 178–179,
    217
    and the American Dream, 18
Industrialization
    and ageism, 153–154
Industrial pollution
    and physical harm, 47
Inequalities
    and social problems, 227
    See also Wealth and income, inequalities
        of; Wealth and power, inequalities of
Insurance companies, 25
Intelligence agencies
    and drug trafficking, 135–136
    and gangsters, 13
    See also individual agencies
Interlocking directorate, 25
International narcotics trafficking, 69–74. *See
    also* Drug trafficking
International Paper, 29
International Policy Council on Agriculture,
    29
Intimate relations, 106
Iran-Contra affair, 19, 36–37, 41–43, 44
Irangate, 40
Iraq, 28

Islamic Movement of Uzbekistan (IMU),
    71–72
Italian-American Mafia, 119
Italo-Sicilian Mafia, 119

Japan, 74
    crime syndicate in, 120–121
Jargon, 82–83
Jewett, Robert, 200
JFK, 22
Johnson, Lyndon B., 38, 84–85
Johnson administration, 39
Judge, Father Michael, 191–192
Junior colleges. *See* Community
    colleges

Kazakhstan, 71
Kellogg, 30
Kelly, Thomas, 112
Kennedy, John F.
    assassination of, cover-up/investigation of,
        38–39
    and poverty, 11
Kennedy, Robert, 39, 209, 228
Kim, Peter, 202
King, Martin Luther, Jr., 228
King, Rodney, 131
KLA. *See* Kosovo Liberation Army
Klaas, Polly, 169
Knapp Commission, 129
Knickerbocker Club, 28
Kohn, Alfie, 193
Korten, David C., 225–226
Kosovo
    drug trafficking in, 71
Kosovo Liberation Army (KLA), 71
Kraft, 29
Kurdistan Workers Party (PKK), 71
Kyrgyzstan
    drug trafficking in, 71, 72

Labor, 24
    and capitalism, 179–180
    prison, 212
Labor force
    changes in, 186
    See also Blue-collar workers; Part-time
        workers; White-collar workers;
        Workplace
Lansky, Meyer, 128
La Nuestra Familia, 122

Laos, 136
Lasch, Christopher, 214
The Last Seduction, 95
Latchkey kids, 146
Law, Cardinal Bernard, 191
Lawrence, John Shelton, 200
Lay, Kenneth, 49, 50, 51, 52,
    53–54
Lay, Linda, 51
Layoffs, 186
Lead poisoning, 165–166
Lebanon
    drug trafficking in, 70
Lerner, Michael, 221–222
Liberation Tigers of Tamil Eelam (LTTE),
    72–73
Lindsey, Lawrence, 49
Lobbyists
    and Enron, 52–54
    and power elite, 32
Loland, 66
Loneliness, 91, 106
Long, John, 112
Los Angeles
    police corruption in, 131–132
Los Angeles Times, 30
Louima, Abner, 131
Love, 88
Lowlands, 66
LTTE. *See* Liberation Tigers of Tamil
    Eelam
Lucent Technologies, 29
Lumumba, Patrice, 41
Lupsha, Peter, 21–22
Luther, Martin, 189
Lutheran theology, 189
Lutz, William, 82
Lying, 79–81, 81–84
    and alienation, 92
    and attachment disorder, 166
    and bureaucracies, 192
    and government scandals, 84–86
    and societal institutions, 87–88
    See also Doublespeak

Machine tool factories, 223
Macro-micro link, 87–88
Mafia
    and Catholic Church, 188
    fascination with, 208, 227
    and Kennedy, John F., 38–39
        and mental health, 199–200
        See also Crime syndicates; Organized crime
Mafia pop culture
    and family, 145–146
Magazines, men's, 96. *See also* Mass media;
    Media
Main drifts, 212
The Majestic, 200
Manufacturing sector, 223
Mao Zedong, 136
Marijuana Tax Act of 1937, 138
Marriage, 9
    and alienation, 150–152
    stereotypes, 151, 152
Maryknoll Sisters, 41
Mass media, 93–97
    corporate-controlled, 226
    and stereotypes, 104–105
    See also Media
Mass socialization, 87. *See also* Socialization
Master trends, 212
Material culture
    and addiction, 140
MDM, 66
Meaninglessness, 90
Media
    and alienation, 92–93
    and crime/drug problem, 215
    and dehumanization, 104–105
    and monopolies, 92–93
    and power elite, 31–32
    and sex crimes, 96–97
    See also Mass media
Menchu, Rigoberta, 64
Men's magazines, 96. *See also* Mass media;
    Media
Mental health
    and crime syndicates, 199–202
    and Mafia, 199–200
    See also Therapy
Mental illness, 9–10
Mexican Mafia, 122
Mexico
    drug trafficking in, 70
Miami
    police corruption in, 132–133
Micro-social problems, 92
    and alienation, 102–105
    and individualism, 105
    See also Social problems
Military-industrial complex, 24, 26, 223

Military sector
  and power elite, 26–27
Mills, C. Wright, 44
  and higher immorality, 213
  and inauthenticity, 99
  and mass media, 93
  and "network of rackets," 24–25, 33
  and personal troubles, 8
  and power, distribution of, 23–24
  and power elite, 24
  and sociological imagination, 7, 86
Mitchell, John, 41
Moler, Elizabeth, 52
Mollen, Milton, 128
Mollen Commission, 129–131
Money
  and the American Dream, 14–15, 17–18
Money laundering, 66–67
  and drug trafficking, 123
Monopolies
  and the media, 92–93
Monsanto, 29
Moore, Mary Tyler, 100–101
Moral climate, changes in, 212
Moral harm, 10, 54–58
Morality
  crisis of, 202–204
  See also Higher immorality
Morally loose individual, rise of, 211–212
Morgan Guaranty, 25, 31–32
Mother Jones, 229
Mothers, working, 149–150, 163
Motorcycle gangs, 122
Motorola, 30
Movies, 96. *See also* Mass media; Media
Mujahedin, 68
Murder, 147
  of youth, 168–169
Myanmar, 73, 74

The Nation, 229
National Commission on Product Safety, 46
National energy policy, 49
  and Enron, 52–53
National Energy Policy Development Group, 52–53
National health care, 15
National Law Journal, 112
National Liberation Army. *See* ELN
National security, U.S., 68–69, 75
National Security Act of 1947, 44

National Security Council, 26
Nepal
  drug trafficking in, 72
Ness, Elliot, 210
Nestlé, 29
Netherlands, the
  drug treatment in, 141, 143, 223
"Network of rackets," 24–25, 33
New Deal, 220
New Orleans
  police corruption in, 134–135
News Corporation, 93
News media, 68. *See also* Media; Mass media
Newspeak, 84
New York
  identity crime in, 81
  police corruption in, 129–131
New York Times, 40, 79
Ngo Dinh Diem, 41
NGOs. *See* Nongovernmental organizations
1984 (Orwell), 82, 84
Nixon, Richard, 39–41, 51, 85
  and Watergate scandal, 10
Nongovernmental organizations
  (NGOs)
  and social change, 218–219
Normlessness, 90–91. *See also* Anomie
North, Oliver, 42
North American Free Trade Agreement, 61
Northern Alliance, 74
North Korea
  drug trafficking in, 74
Nursing homes, 161–163

Objectivity, 209–210
Olin Foundation, 32
O'Neill, Paul, 29
OPEC. *See* Organization of Petroleum
  Exporting Countries
Open Shelter, 218
Optimism, 228
Oregon
  identity crime in
Organization of Petroleum Exporting
  Countries (OPEC), 62
Organized crime, 14
  and corporations and government, 65–67,
  123
  definition of, 118
  and drug trafficking, 67–78, 117–122
  and terrorism, 67–78

See also Crime syndicates; Mafia
Orwell, George, 82, 84
Oswald, Lee Harvey, 38
Other-directedness, 102
Our Business Civilization (Adams), 19
Ovando, Javier, 131–132

Pacific Union, 28
Pacino, Al, 129
Pai, Lou L., 51
Part-time workers
    and alienation, 184, 187
Patterson, James, 202
Pennington, Richard, 135
Pentagon, 27
Pentagon defense programs, 223
Pentagon Papers, 40
Pepper, Claude, 80
Perez, Rafael, 131–132
Permanent-war forces, 38
Perot, H. Ross, 16
Personal gain, quest for, 18
Personality traits, 86–87, 87–88
Personal problems
    and social problems, 7–11
Peru, 69
Pessimism, 204–206
    about the future, 204–206
PFLP-GC (Popular Front for the Liberation of
    Palestine-General Command), 70
Phao Srivananda, General, 136
Pharmacia, 29
Philadelphia
    police corruption in, 133–134
Philippines
    drug trafficking in, 73
Physical harm, 10, 45–47
Pinochet, Augusto, 65
Pitt, Harvey, 54
Pizza Connection case,
    124–125
PKK. *See* Kurdistan Workers Party
Police corruption, 125–135
    in Los Angeles, 131–132
    in Miami, 132–133
    in New Orleans, 134–135
    in New York, 129–131
    in Philadelphia, 133–134
Political economy
    and power elite, 23–27
Political propaganda, 97, 108

Political system
    trust in, 203–204
Politics
    and vision, 209
Pollution laws
    violations of, 37
Pop culture, mafia
    and family, 145–146
Popular Front for the Liberation of Palestine-
    General Command. *See* PFLP-GC
Pornography, 96
Poverty, 11
    and deviant behavior, 22
Power
    and elite, 22–23
    See also Power elite
Power, distribution of, 23–24. *See also* Power
    elite
Power and wealth, distribution of
    and crime, 215–216
Power elite, 23–27, 212–213, 226
    and financial harm, 47–54
    and higher immorality, 35–37
    and lying, 82
    members of, 27–33
    and moral harm, 54–58
    and physical harm, 45–47
    See also Elite
Powerlessness, 90
    and the workplace, 180
Prabhakaran, Velupillai, 72
Prescription drug industry, 48
Price-fixing, 47–48
Price gouging, 48
Prime-Time Live, 96
Prison labor, 212
Procter and Gamble, 33
Profits, 14–15
The Progressive, 229
Prostitution
    and runaways, 167
Public-health approach
    to drug treatment, 222–223
Puffery, 83
Pushouts, 167

Qaddafi, Muammar al-, 121
Quayle, Dan, 83
Quiet Desperation (Halper), 185
Quinn, Jack, 52

Racicot, Marc, 49, 52
Racism, 227
Rand Corporation, 27
Rape
and runaways, 168
Reagan, Ronald, 42, 43, 85, 139
Reagan administration, 36–37, 41–43, 44, 56, 64, 65, 211
Reagan-Bush era
and wealth, accumulation of, 18
Recall, 222
Reed, Ralph
and Enron, 52
Regulation, government, 25
Religion
and alienation, 187–192
See also Catholic Church;
Fundamentalism; Religious institutions
Religious extremism, 189. *See also* Fundamentalism
Religious institutions
scandals in, 178, 190–192, 205–206
See also Catholic Church;
Fundamentalism; Religion
Repair fraud, 48
Republicans, 24
Research and policy-formulating sector
and power elite, 27
Resentment
and the workplace, 181–182
Rizner, Boris, 66
Rizzo, Frank, 134
Roark, Mike "Mad Dog," 128
Roberts, Oral, 190
Rockefeller, Nelson, 129
Rodino Committee, 85
Role models, crimeogenic, 21
Romantic love, 106–107
Romero, Oscar, 43
Roosevelt, Franklin, 220
Rove, Karl, 49
Ruby, Jack, 38
Rumsfeld, Donald, 29–30
Runaways
and crime and victimization, acts of, 167–170
Runyon, Damon, 13
Russian organized crime, 66, 122, 199
and drug trafficking, 69–70

The Sane Society (Fromm), 178
Savings and Loan scandal, 44, 48, 56
and media, 31–32
Scandals, 213
in Catholic Church, 178, 190–192, 205–206
characteristics of, 44
and government, 37–45, 48–54, 84–86
See also individual scandals
Schwarzennegger, Arnold, 94
Seagram, 93
Sears, 30
SEC. *See* Securities and Exchange Commission
Second World, 61–62
Secrecy
and goal orientation, 36
Secret government, 26
Securities and Exchange Commission (SEC), 50
and accounting standards, 54
Self, 103
Self-alienation, 105. *See also* Alienation
Self-directed dehumanization. *See also* Dehumanization
Self-esteem, 89, 106–107
and competition, 193
and cooperation, 193
and the workplace, 181–182
Self-estrangement, 91
and white-collar workers, 185
See also Estrangement
Self-help movement, 213–214
Senter, Cassidy, 169
September 11 terrorist attack, 67–78, 146, 191, 200. *See also* Terrorism
Serial monogamy, 175
Serpico, 129
Serpico, Frank, 129
Service economy
and inauthenticity, 99–100
Sex
and violence, 95–96
Sex and the City, 95, 101
Sex crimes, 96–97
and the media, 96–97
Sexual behavior, 95–96
Shining Path, 69
Sicilian Mafia, 119
Sicilian Zips, 119
Simpson, O. J., 86, 131

Skilling, Jeffrey, 51, 54
Sobinbank, 66
Social breakdown, 211–212
Social change, 223–226
    and community, 218–219
    and corporations, 219–220
    and employment, 220
    and government, 219–220
    and nongovernmental organizations,
        218–219
Social character, 102–105, 107, 212–214,
        217, 225
    and alienation, 102
    antisocial, rise of, 211–212
Social class
    and deviant behavior, 22
    and education, 193–195
    and standard achievement tests, 194
Social disintegration, 211–212
Social harm, 10–11
    and Fundamentalism, 189–192
Socialization, 87
    and education, 192–193
Social problems, 211–212
    and the American Dream, 17–23
    definition of, 11
    and inauthenticity, 101
    and individualism, 107
    and inequalities, 227
    and personal problems, 7–11
    and social harm, 10–11
    solutions to, 227–229
    and wealth and income, inequalities of,
        55–56
    and wealth and political power, inequalities
        of, 140, 212, 224–225
    See also Micro-social problems
Social reconstruction, 220–222
Social Register, 27–28
Social Security Act of 1935, 154
Social security numbers (SSNs), 80–81
Social security pension
    and ageism, 154
Social structure, 89
Societal institutions
    and lying, 87–88
Sociological imagination, 6–7, 8, 11, 86, 178,
        216–217, 224
Sociotherapy, 217
Sony, 93
Soprano, Tony

    as hero, 228
    as symbol, 208, 210, 228
The Sopranos
    description of characters in,
        1–6
    as ourselves, 208–209
    story line, 2
South America, 69
Southern Christian Leadership Conference,
        41
Spalding, 212
Spectrum 7, 28
Spitzer, Eliot, 81
Spousal abuse, 9, 147
Squeezed cynics, 183
Sri Lanka
    drug trafficking in, 72–73
SSNs. See Social security numbers
St. Valentine's Day massacre, 210
Stallone, Sylvester, 94
Standard achievement tests
    and social class, 194
Stanford Research Institute, 27
Stereotypes
    among teachers, 195
    and the elderly, 155–158
    and marriage, 151, 152
    and mass media, 104–105
Stone, Oliver, 22
Street crime, 9
    and drug trafficking, 113–115
    and poverty, 22
    See also Crime
Street gangs
    and drug trafficking, 115–117
Students
    and apathy, 195
Substance abuse
    and advertising, 222
    See also Alcohol abuse; Drug abuse;
        Tobacco abuse
Success
    and money, 14–15
"Suckers," 22
Suicide
    and runaways, 168
Summers, Anthony, 128
Superficial acting, 100
Sutton, Joseph, 51
Swaggert, Jimmy, 190

Tajikistan
  drug trafficking in, 71–72
Taliban, 73, 74
TCI Cable, 93
Teachers
  stereotypes among, 195
Teapot Dome scandal, 38
Teen pregnancy, 146
Teleculture, 93–97
Televangelists, 205
Television, 96. *See also* Mass media; Media
Television, children's, 95
Temporary employees. *See* Part-time workers
Terrorism, 32, 69, 227
  combating, and civil liberties, 205
  and drug trafficking and organized crime,
    67–78
  See also September 11 terrorist attack
Testing
  and education, 192
Texas Syndicate, 122
Thailand, 136
Therapy, 177–178, 198–202. *See also* Mental
    health
Think tanks, 27
  and power elite, 32–33
Third World, 62–63, 223
Tikkun, 221
Titanic, 57
Tobacco abuse, 112, 222
  and advertising, 97–98, 141
  and youth, 172–173
Tolins, Jonathan, 7
Tolson, Clyde, 128
Tonkin Gulf incident, 84–85
To Seek a Newer World! (Kennedy, R.),
    209
Tracking system, 195, 197
Traffic, 112
Transnational organized crime, 69–74. *See also*
    Organized crime
Travelgate, 40
Trujillo, Rafael, 41
Trust
  in political system, 203–204
  and workplace, 185–186, 186–187
Turkey
  drug trafficking in, 71
Turkmenistan, 71
TWA, 212
Twilight of the Golds (Tolins), 7

Unemployed workers
  and alienation, 187
Unemployment, 8
United Auto Workers, 41
United Fruit Company, 64
United Nations Commission on the Truth, 43
United Nations Declaration of Human Rights
    of 1948, 63
Universalism
  and the American Dream, 17
Universities, 27
  alienation at, 197–198
  and power elite, 31
Upper class
  and power elite, 27–28, 30–31
U.S. Postal Service, 181
U.S. Technologies, 212
The Utne Reader, 229
Uzbekistan, 71

Value relativists, 79
Values, 209
  and the American Dream, 19–20
  and social character, 103–104
  See also Family values
Vatican
  and church sex scandal, 191–192
Veneman, Ann, 28–29
Veterans Administration, 26
Veterans of Foreign Wars, 26
Viacom, 93
Victimization, acts of
  and children, 165–167
  and class structure, 57–58
  and the elderly, 159–160
  and runaways and crime, 167–170
Victoria's Secret, 212
Vidal, Gore, 86
Vietnam War, 19, 39, 40
  drug trafficking during, 136
  and physical harm, 45–46
Vinson and Elkins, 29
Violence
  hidden, 212
  and the media, 94–96
Violence, against women,
    147
  and the media, 96
Violent street crime, 9
  and poverty, 22
  See also Street crime

Vision
    and politics, 209
Voting, 222

Walsh, Lawrence, 43
War on drugs, 110–113, 138–139, 222
War on Poverty, 11
Warren, Earl, 38
Warren Report, 38
Watergate scandal, 10, 19, 39–41, 44, 85
Wealth, accumulation of, 14, 17–18, 22
Wealth and income, inequalities of
    and social problems, 55–56
Wealth and power, inequalities of, 212
    and crime, 140
    and social problems, 224–225
Wealthy elite, 179. *See also* Power elite
Weapons of mass destruction, proliferation of,
    69
Weasel words, 83–84
Weinberger, Caspar, 43
White-collar crime
    and drug trafficking, 122–123
White-collar workers
    and alienation, 182–184, 185–186
    and inauthenticity, 99–102
Wilding, 212
"Wiseguys," 22
Women, violence against, 147
    and the media, 96
Workaholism, 164

Workforce. *See* Blue-collar workers; Labor
    force; Part-time workers; White-collar
    workers; Workplace
Working mothers, 149–150, 163
Workplace
    and alienation, 180–187
    and capitalism, 179–180
    and clinical depression, 187
    and control, 185
    and trust, 185–186, 186–187
Works Progress Administration
    (WPA), 220
World War II
    and power elite, 24
WPA. *See* Works Progress Administration

Yakuza, 120–121
Youth
    and alcohol abuse, 170–171, 175
    and drug abuse, 171–173, 174–175
    and employment, 175
    and family values, 163–173
    and runaways, 167–170
    and tobacco abuse, 173–174
Youth crime, 169
Yuppies, 214
    and family values, 162–164

Zippergate, 40